Edited by

Areti Markopoulou

IaaC BITS during 2020 has started a new editorial phase that is intended to be more effective, ambitious and intentional both in terms of content and in the layout and configuration of the publication.

These monographic issues – presented with an experimental and proactive foundation and associated to technological and creative innovation – aim at to combining inter-disciplinary and multi-scalar exchanges with a new environmental and socio-cultural sensitivity.

This commitment to advanced culture and knowledge is well-suited to a time of challenges and changes: it conforms the conceptual framework that supports dissemination projects tied to IaaC's own production, but also to a whole network of exchanges and complicities that frame it and feed into it.

Each issue is meant to be conceived as an articulated system of voices and cross-cutting experiences focused on a central theme, which is understood as a subject for debate and proactive discussion.

Front page figure: IAAC MaCT, OWNit, F.Ciccone, L.Marcovich, 2017.

IaaC bits

Learning Cities

Index

Critical Views

What will the city of the future look like?

Can machines design and what?

Which new models of architectural conceptualization arise from algorithmic control?

Which is the novelty and relevance of using artificial intelligence in the design process?

Will the ethical, social, cultural and aesthetic implications of AI affect the quality and form of urban and architectural space?

Learning Cities
Collective Intelligence in Urban Design

Areti Markopoulou

"...we teach our environments first complex, then self-organizing, intelligence that could eventually become evolutionary"

Warren Brodey, 1967

The application of artificial intelligence, machine learning or statistical models and algorithms for the creation of predictive models in architectural design and urban planning is based on relational and evolutionary logics that promise a more (multi-objective) "optimized" design or a "smarter" city, where "smart" is usually defined based on notions of improvement at infrastructural scales.

Most of the discussions around the idea of urban "intelligence" focus on the use of sensory technology in billions of interconnected objects (Internet of Things) or on the processing of billions of images that can be mined from web services to collect vast amounts of data produced by human behaviour and other sources, such as the environment or the material world of our built space. Data from user occupation patterns in housing, for instance, can generate economically viable interior distributions in building development. Similarly, data on how people move in cities can be inserted into computers and generative algorithms with the goal of helping predict traffic and optimizing mobility planning.

Previous page:
IAAC MaCT, Alzette 2.0.
S.Subramani, L.Saadi, M.Galdys, I.Reyes, 2020.

In a highly human-centric technocratic world, such notions of optimization might be the gold standard for urban policies and national strategies.

But moving beyond an understanding of optimization as selecting the best result from a variety of computed and quantified data-based possibilities (a reading which carries the heavy burden of the last two decade's mainstream idea of the "smart city"), we need to explore optimization as patterns of co-creation and as a continuous changing state incorporating both human and non-human perspectives. Within a multiverse inhabited by different human, technological and cultural others, purely quantified data sets may be significant, but they fall short, if they are only observed by a cognitive, and always biased, perspective.[1]

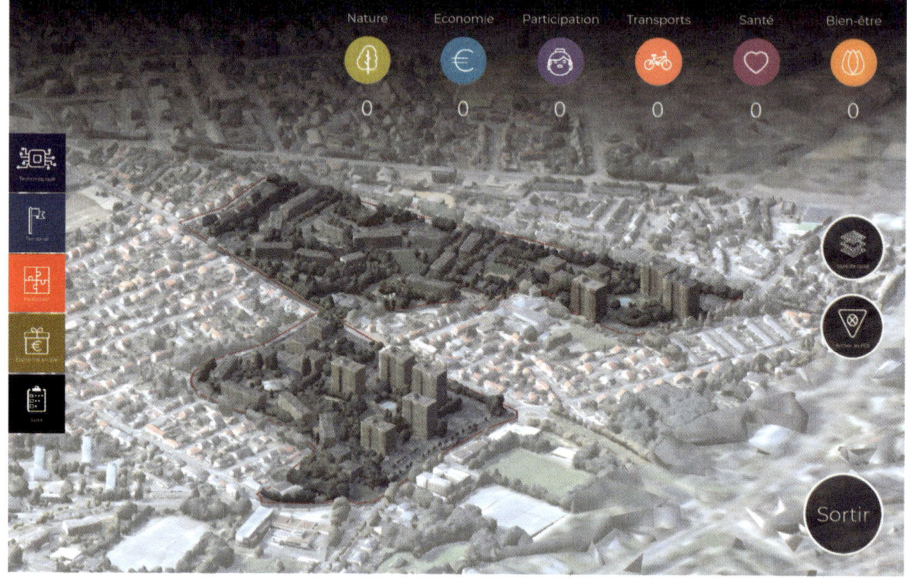

Superbarrio video-game interface for Nantes.

Machine Intelligence

While the idea of intelligent machines that simulate "cognitive functions" such as "learning" or "problem solving" has its roots back in the cybernetics of the 1950s, its extensive use, in recent years, in the architectural and urban design disciplines opens up a series of new possibilities – as well as plenty of cultural, ethical or even aesthetic hesitations and risks.

Although it seems to be common thinking that AI is an evolution of cybernetics, one could argue that cybernetics deals with a much more holistic view of intelligence, especially because it focuses on how systems can self-regulate and act in constant feedback with the environment, which contains far more diverse factors (biological, social, mechanical, economic) than the AI computational stored representations of the world.[2,3] Beyond the technical and systemic differences between cybernetics and AI, however, there is a common connotation to AI related to the question of the future, which is of major social (rather than computational) significance. As Steenson highlights in her contribution to this issue, "AI is not only about using the computer, but about having a vision of it. If we talk about AI, we want to talk about a vision of what computation does today and could do in the future."

The digital intelligence that is inevitably starting to penetrate every aspect of our previously analogue systems of living, working or interacting socially becomes the central core of a variety of utopic or dystopic futures. That is the case because such intelligence can be an empowering tool as well as a disempowering one for both the people who inhabit the built environment and those who design and manage it. The potential of recognizing the diverse (microbial, animal, vegetable, machine, human) intelligences in cities and re-orchestrating them for better planning (Bratton pp.15), the ability to create real time digital twins for multi-stakeholder decision making (Chronis pp. 87), or the novel modes of machinic perception generated (Del Campo & Manninger pp. 97), which can enrich the field of urban design (Vivaldi pp. 37) are some aspects of one of the sides of the AI reality that has been embedded in our everyday life and habits, usually without us even noticing it. Other issues such as the anonymous, faceless city designed from the top down, based on statistical simplifications (Vardouli pp. 49), digital exclusion, planning processes with no democratic ends, and mass surveillance followed by the rise of new forms of behavior manipulation (Sollazzo, pp. 109), are critical risks that can be found on the other side of the exact same reality, fully powered by the applications of AI in the design and management of urban environments.

Within this context, how do we define "intelligence" in built space? How can we structure the vast data powered by geocoded web services or by millions of interconnected objects (IoT) and turn it into valuable input for informed decision (and design) making? The first two sections of "Learning Cities" promote a number of established and emerging innovators who are tackling these questions through critical thinking, research and practice.

Crowd & Collective Intelligence

No doubt in order to plan more infrastructurally optimized cities, the significance of IoT, sensors or actuators is fundamental. The data collected from the billions of devices and digital footprints of our era is the most precious fuel for sustainable planning engines to operate and for informed decision-making processes to be applied. This current scenario, though, fully embedded in techno-centric governance approaches propelled by the smart city movements, tends to equate urban problems with technological ones, while excluding actual people and their problems that are beyond the reach of technologies.[4] Aligned with both the possibilities and limitations of such a context, the third section of "Learning Cities" calls into question how human conditions are viewed as a key factor in comprehending and shaping the urban environment.

Human-generated data sets may be substantial, but they fall short when they are observed externally and statistically analysed as the total of individual values that could be inserted into computational algorithms. Big-data-based design and planning calls for novel models that systemically blend bottom-up and top-down processes while operating in bidirectional and circular feedback loops. That is, the models allow designers to learn about the wishes and needs of users and citizens, but citizens can also learn about the impact of their desires so that behavioural change can occur. The *Superbarrio* project (pp. 149) developed by IAAC is a video game interface for participatory urban design that collects citizens' qualitative data and desires while they play and uses machine learning to leverage data, inform players on the impact of their actions, and provide more informed decisions for planning the Superblock in Barcelona. Similarly, the gaming platform Common'hood by Jose Sanchez (pp. 139) uses data structures that group and store a series of player actions (blueprints) and is therefore able to store and analyze human decisions in space instead of geometries, establishing a peer-to-peer protocol for knowledge transfer.

Access to and collection of data needs to be democratized for communities and individuals in need, who do not always have access to technology. At the same time, between the data collection and urban action there is a huge unresolved abyss that needs to be addressed by both urban developers and citizens to create tools that facilitate conversation and inform participatory city-making (Rodrigo Delso & Javier Argota, pp. 173). Different techniques, including crowd sensing, as Sarah Williams explains in her contribution (pp. 157), can contribute not only to harvesting crowd-intelligence but also to empowering the crowd itself in different communities to gather the evidence to both fight for and understand their rights.

Can we, then, learn from the intelligence embedded in the bottom-up and disorganized decisions of users in our built environment?
Is it possible to quantify qualitative data on communities' desires and perceptions to understand our current cities and help us plan future ones?
And how can we merge AI with an inter-species (post Anthropocene) approach that boosts knowledge and facilitates participatory city-making?

From real-time digital twins to emerging processes of cognitive and machinic co-creation, "Learning Cities" explores novel creative and design processes in which designers, communities, machines, and

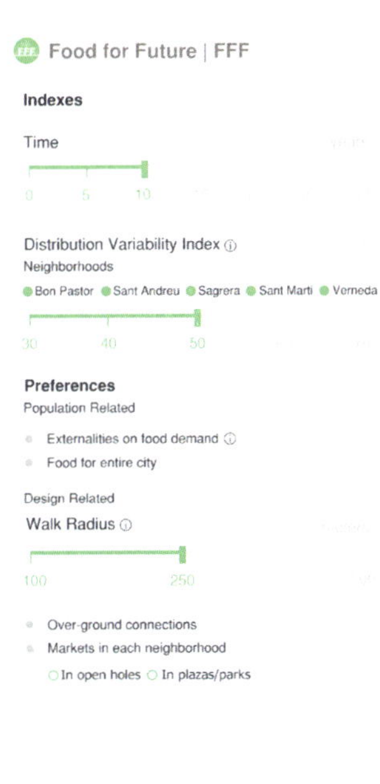

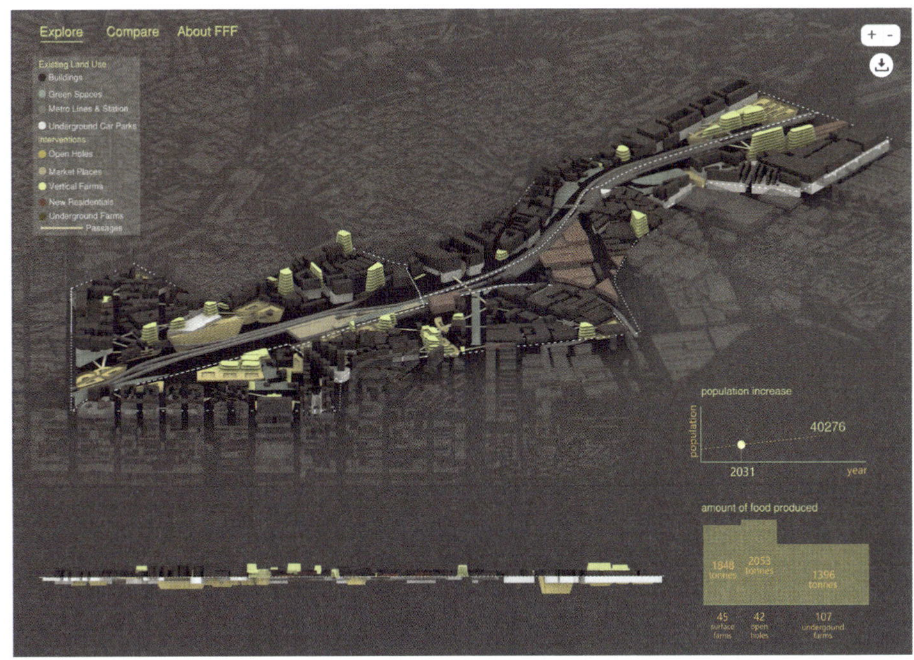

Food for Future is a project overlapping quantified data of solar exposure, soil quality or building surface with qualitative data of citizen´s communities desires for identifying places for food production in cities. IAAC, MaCT, S. Coskun, L. Guimarães, D. Roussi, A. Aguirre, 2021.

digital codes all play a fundamental role, with a unique resonance among them. Beyond the traditional human-driven multi-stakeholder approach, these novel technologically enhanced design processes represent a new collective intelligence (and maybe inter-species) design paradigm. The cities emerging have no predefined and closed form, while designers, citizens and their environment become participants in unique exchanges and dialogues facilitated by diverse living and non-living intelligences.

Who designs and who decides in such complex urban systems of cognitive behaviour and computational operation become crucial questions opening new pathways for our discipline. "Learning Cities" promotes an emerging collective intelligence design paradigm that empowers the applications of collective creation, following both cognitive and machine generative processes. This post-anthropocentric approach highlights a unique combination of crowd and machine wisdom that, together with other forms of intelligence (including animal, vegetable, or microbial), marks a significant milestone in the creation of our future cities.

References :

1. Gausa, M., Markopoulou, A. and Vivaldi, J., 2020. *Black Ecologies.* Institute for Advanced Architecture of Catalonia and Actar Publishers.

2. Wiener, N. *Cybernetics or Control and Communication in the Animal and the Machine.* Vol. 25. MIT press, 1961

3. Martelaro N., J. Wendy, *Cybernetics and the Design of the user experience of AI systems,* Association for Computing Machinery, 2018

4. Biloria N., *From smart to empathic cities,* Frontiers of Architectural Research, Volume 10, Issue 1, 2021,pg 3-16

5. The SuperBlock project is part of the Urban Mobility Plan of Barcelona. It consists of a three by three Cerda's urban blocks in which the internal traffic is reduced to residents and all heavy traffic circulates around the perimeter of these SuperBlocks. With the superblock, it is estimated that 77 percent of space is given back to people as pedestrian public space.

On Synthetic Intelligence and Design

Benjamin Bratton
in conversation with
Areti Markopoulou and Jordi Vivaldi

Operating at the intersection of sociology, architecture, computation, and design theory, Benjamin Bratton's work reveals new perspectives on the implications of digital technologies regarding what counts as urbanism. Interested in new kinds of systems and ways of life that are emerging from synthetic intelligence in cities, Bratton discusses the unique possibilities of producing novelty in urban evolution through different forms of intelligence that operate in a variety of global human (or non-human) inhabited landscapes.

Areti Markopoulou: The current "Learning Cities" issue of IaaC Bits intends to explore "intelligence" in urban space and to present a variety of perspectives on how multiple intelligences might affect the way cities are designed, inhabited and eventually operate. The idea of intelligent machines that simulate the cognitive functions of learning or problem solving is not new, but its extensive use in recent years in urban and architectural design processes calls for a more clear identification of what "intelligence" is, what kind of intelligences already exist in cities, and why or how we might create novel ones. If we look at the example of smart cities, it seems like there is a strong belief that the Internet of Things – the vast amounts of data amassed by millions of interconnected objects – is the most important base upon which we can understand our current cities and plan the future ones. But is this really enough? In this issue of IaaC Bits, we look at existing intelligences in our urban fabric that operate using qualitative rather than quantitative data (such as crowd wisdom) and question the current data analytics approaches as very limited practices of human and machine intelligence.

Previous page: The Terraforming 2020, Strelka Institute for Media Architecture and Design.

Learning Cities promotes the design and performance of physical and virtual territories implicating a variety of thriving intelligences that are not limited to human cognition or machinic intelligence. We foresee novel Collective Intelligence design processes for cities in which designers, users, and data from the built environment, as well as evolutionary digital codes all play a fundamental role, with a unique resonance among them. What kind of cities, then, could we create? Given this context, how would you define a Learning City?

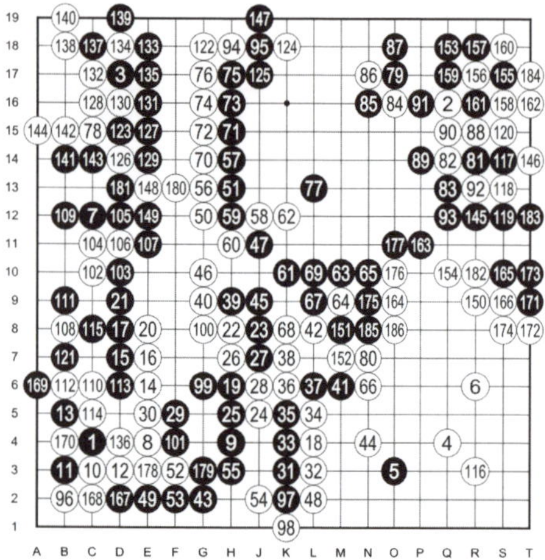

Lee Sedol (B) vs AlphaGo (W) - Game 1

Lee Sedol (W) vs AlphaGo (B) - Game 2

156 at 52

Lee Sedol vs AlphaGo, Game 1 & 2, 2018.

BB One of the points that I would want to establish as a baseline for my thinking on the relationship between forms of synthetic intelligence (SI) and the built environment predates the appearance of what we recognize as AI in the 1950s. One of the fundamental mistakes of the "smart cities" approach is the idea that artificial intelligence, collective intelligence, procedural intelligence, algorithmic intelligence, or technical intelligence are elements that do not originally exist in the city and they need to be introduced from outside in order to make the city smart.

I think this is a mistake that unfortunately is very much repeated. The fundamental problem is the idea according to which intelligence is something introduced into a preexisting city. In that regard, there needs to be a more fundamental shift in the way the question is posed. What do we mean by SI in relation to an urban context? And what's the difference between synthetic and artificial intelligence? We just had a project at Strelka this year that dealt with this topic pretty thoroughly, looking at the site conditions that will allow forms of SI. In the 1968 book Sciences of the Artificial by Herbert Simon, the author makes a distinction between artificial and synthetic intelligence which I think is quite important.

He defines the artificial as something that resembles the thing that it stands for, but it is actually a fake. The example he uses is a piece of glass that is cut to look just like a diamond, but it's not. It's just a piece of glass that on a superficial level looks like a diamond. So that's an artificial thing. He contrasts this with the synthetic diamond, which has grown in a lab, that is molecularly identical to a natural diamond. It is a diamond at a molecular level; it has been deliberately composed rather than found. If you take this distinction, the difference between AI and SI becomes clear. AI is a kind of machine intelligence (MI) that seems intelligent but really is not. It's just performing all of the things that we as evolved primates have come to recognize as signs of intelligence, and then we fill in the blanks to imagine that there's actually somebody there – like Siri or Samantha. SI would be a form of MI that is capable of genuine forms of creative reasoning that may not be human-like, that might not be the same kind of intelligence that primates have, or even the same kind of intelligence that animals have, but that is a kind of intelligence nevertheless and is one that we have composed.

A few years ago in the AlphaGo game, the DeepMind Go program beat the Go Master. In one of the games, the AI makes a move placing a stone in a part of a board that is utterly unexpected, a position that seems like a mistake.

However, it turns out that this very unlikely and strange move is quite ingenious and the whole game ends up rotating towards this movement. It wins the game. And the human players' mind is blown. This move shows that there is a kind of intelligence there that isn't just repeating things it has been told; it actually is capable of generating novelty. This is certainly interesting, but I think something more interesting happens in the next game when Lee Sedol himself makes a move that is also extremely weird, a move that has never been done before. And this also turns out to be quite ingenious, and he ends up winning the game. And afterwards he says quite clearly, "I never would have made that move, I never would have thought to make that move, I never would have seen the game board in that way, it would have never occurred to me to make that move if the computer AI hadn't made that move in the previous game, showing me something new about the way this game board works." To me, that's a great example of SI and that's a great example of the kind of thing that we should pursue. It's not about replacing.

What's at stake instead is ways of producing novelty through different forms of intelligence. As there is an evolution in animal intelligence for thousands of years, in the last few decades there has been an acceleration in the process of machine-based intelligence. And they are not the same. It doesn't work to try to conflict one another, but we can imagine that there are synthetic forms of intelligence that are much different. So, there is an argument to be made here since we may still be in the early years of intelligence as a planetary phenomenon.

AM Following your example with the AlphaGo game, one could argue that there is already an existing intelligence in the game, which becomes part of a circular feedback system; different inputs, thus, change the output that, in turn, changes the input. In an effort, though, to try and land some of these systemic operations in the design domain, and especially urban design, it is pivotal to understand how design processes are affected by the use of AI and what kind of urban physical implications these technologies could eventually bring to cities and citizens.

The Terraforming 2020, Strelka Institute for Media Architecture and Design.

BB It is not necessarily in the city where people live that AI has had the greatest foothold and is making the biggest difference as a physically embedded phenomenon, but at a landscape scale: it's in factories, it's in farms, it's in cultural regions, it's in places where for the most part humans don't dwell, and I don't see any reason why that should be seen as troublesome or as a kind of exception to the rule. That's a trend that will probably accelerate and that should include artificial environments that are not based on dwelling programs but are also based on other elements. It is, thus, also to these areas where design can turn its attention. I think the question is, then, what is the role of synthetic intelligence as a design tool? So, regardless of what you're designing (an airplane or a building or a farm or a factory), what is the role of SI in the act of conception, modelling, simulation, prototyping, and production?

SI and MI are not only tools that we use to make a city, they are also something that actually is already part of the city, as one of the agents that we then have to account for, as one of the things that we need to design, or design for, or design in relation to. And SI and MI are not the same thing, and maybe sometimes the conversation gets blurry because the two get confused, like when talking about AI as a tool or AI as the thing the tools apply to. The refinement of the problem, the definition of the site condition, and the selection of the framing mechanisms to intervene depend on what the sites are made from.

JV In the global grant show in 2019, you affirmed that the question is not so much about how we see the city or how the city sees us, but how the city sees itself. Within this process of self-awareness in which there seems to be no room for any exteriority, how would you account for urban dissent?

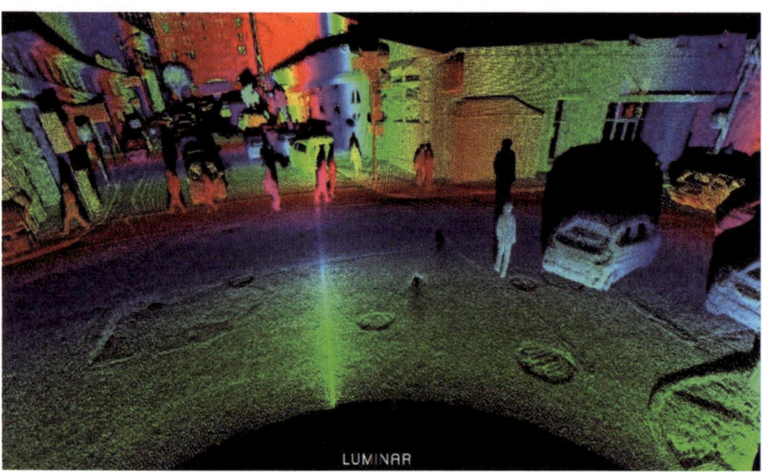

Luminar's Amalgamation and LiDAR sensor, Toyota Research.

BB First of all, we need to be attentive to the fact that AI or SI is never separable from its sensing mechanisms. How it senses the world is inextricable from how it processes the information about the world. There are two dominant ways in which design, art, and probably politics think about the relationship between machine vision (MV) in the city and vision-based AI in the city. One, how do I see the city and all its prototype projects. Two, how does the city see me, how does it observe me as a tracked subject, as a surveyed individual, as an object of analysis. These are the two variations by which the topic is discussed: how I see the city or how the city sees me. Both are highly individuated narratives, which comes from the fact that these technologies are themselves individuated.

But there is a third option to consider. And, of course, there's much more which is not about how I see the city or how the city sees me but how the city sees itself. It's like when you're walking through a forest, you can see the birds and animals, and you know the birds and the bees and everything else can see you for sure, but most of the time they're looking at each other. The different elements in the forest are looking at themselves like you're not the protagonist of this story; you are just one creature among many. In an MV-based environment, as opposed to a human vision-based environment, the same should be true. So, what we can look at are the ways in which forms of MV might come to dominate the way in which the design of the city is considered. You can think of the QR code as a simple way in which MV has made an impact in the city. We see this in the QR code, this weird little black square flower that has bloomed on the surfaces of every city, especially Chinese cities. We know that it's a QR code, but I can't decode it for you, and you probably can't decode it for me. There is an environmental response to the presence of this new species, which is the camera of the smartphone, which can interpret these surfaces. This is an example of how urban surfaces may continue to transform, not in relationship to how humans look at them but in relationship to how machines will look at them. These architectural surfaces evolve in order to suit the needs, interests, and dictates of machine observation rather than the aesthetics of human observation – which may result in very weird architectural surfaces for us, as millions and millions of little creatures with MV are running around the city, surveilling different entities, and deploying different actions, making sense for them but not for us.

Now let me switch to the question of dissent, which is certainly an interesting question within this context. The argument that we're making is actually not the one that you hinted at, which is whether urban dissent can occur if all of these sensory inputs and extended machine cognition add up to some kind of big singular, coherent, model. There are some ways in which this consistency and coherence is present in the urban model, but I don't think that's the way it's going to work for the city – and I don't think it's the way it necessarily should work for the city. I think the example of the forest is relevant here as well: you've got lots of different entities which have their own different interests. One of the things that one might expect for the city, just as you can see in the forest, is a kind of MV arms race of camouflage and display, where some things in the city which really want to be seen by a certain kind of MV will make themselves very visible. We're all dazzled by certain elements because every service demands our attention like flowers demand the attention of bees.

For MV there might be a similar kind of display function, but not for us. It might be for something else. It could be as simple as the corners of buildings making themselves easy to read for driverless vehicles. Just like you have it in the natural world, we'll also see a kind of camouflage process at work on surfaces that don't want to be seen, that want to be hidden. Elements that are constantly finding ways to either make themselves invisible, like a mimicry where snakes look like poisonous snakes even though they're not, where things try to make themselves seen and not seen or appear to be something else. Essentially, this becomes their strategy within the city.

Assemblage, 2020.
Institute, 2017.

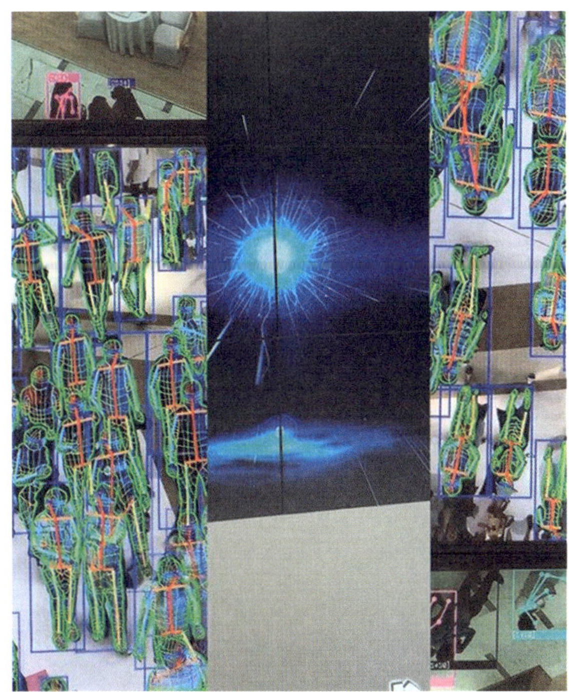

Previous double page:
The Terraforming 2020,
Strelka Institute for Media
Architecture and Design.

The Terraforming 2020,
Strelka Institute for Media
Architecture and Design.

There are ways in which an actor might make a decision consisting in preventing itself from being enrolled in other projects, but you might have other strategies in which another actor operates on behalf of its own project by amplifying its own influence. The first one might be a negative strategy, while the other might be a positive strategy, but I do think that inevitably there's going to be a kind of evolutionary dynamic at work here. The most likely scenario consists in having decisions driven by capital, which is driven by advertising, which is driven by other comparatively shallow and probably pathological forms of social incentivization and motivation.

And this comes back to more fundamental questions: what do we really think AI is for? We're at this point in history where inorganic matter is capable of forms of cognition. This has never happened before. All forms of cognition have always been organic, but now we have inorganic cognition. Certainly, we can find a better purpose for that than advertising. Certainly, we can find a better purpose for that than motivating retail. The question of dissent might consist of asking how you prevent the wrong scenario. And then there's the question of how to prepare a projective political program, which involves how we envision the more suitable condition, the more sustainable condition, the more scalable condition, the more epistemologically honest and appropriate condition for what the relationship between SI, human settlements, and artificial environments could be and should be. And **how to give shape to that is a really important problem, one that can't be really figured out just philosophically, or technologically. It has to be designed, it has to be conceived, it has to be prototyped, it has to be imagined.** That's why the key question is the following one: what's the role of design in all of this? And my answer is that the role of design in all of this consists in answering the following question: at the level of the built environment, what is AI for?

AM Paraphrasing Jane Jacobs' view on the city, there is an existing intelligence in the bottom-up and disorganized decisions of citizens in cities, which planning and algorithmic processes today should observe and respect. Contemporary practices of the smart city and AI seek to develop processes that, on the one hand, observe society's behavior externally and, on the other hand, analyze it statistically. One could argue, though, that transforming qualitative data into quantitative data is a limited practice, given the great potential of emergent and crowd intelligence, in two ways. First, it limits the potential of establishing new bottom-up planning processes and, second, it raises questions on cultural, ethical, and democratic levels.

Do you think that we can harvest crowd wisdom to feed our design processes beyond focusing on the quantification of data or the surveillance of flows? And is enhancing participation in the planning processes a key action to pursue?

BB In the arts and in the humanities, there is a preference for the qualitative over the quantitative. Not only as a method; it's a kind of ethical principle to assume that numbers are unjust, and words are beautiful, that math is alienating, and poetry is humane. And I think this is a romantic impulse that has a very particular historical origin in European modernity, in which Romanticism responds to the alienating and demystifying functions of industrial technologies. This is probably one of the assumptions that we need to get over. We certainly need to keep a lock on the extremely important political, cultural, philosophical, and ethical critiques, which are not only possible but necessary in terms of the way in which big data is being used, what is being used for, how it even conceives the world. And the fact that we construct these huge computational models based on the presumption that the individual human user is the most important element in the system – like Facebook's model of society, which is a society made up of liberal discrete individuals, each one possessing private data and private functions, configuring a society that is the aggregation of these private individuals. This is just wrong, it's not the way that society works. The question of how it is that you can have democratic planning through a collective intelligence not just as a means but as an end, is an important question. But it's not a question entailing that we need to get rid of the quantitative from our imagination. The question is, how is it that the quantitative can be enrolled for purposes that are better suited to the needs of society rather than for other activities?

Having said that, I would like address what I think is a very serious question of how we think about planning in such a way that actually coheres and activates the full scope of CI. Let me first say that, in a way, it is a very contemporary question but it's also a very old one too. It goes back decades and probably centuries.

The Terraforming 2020, Strelka Institute for Media Architecture and Design.

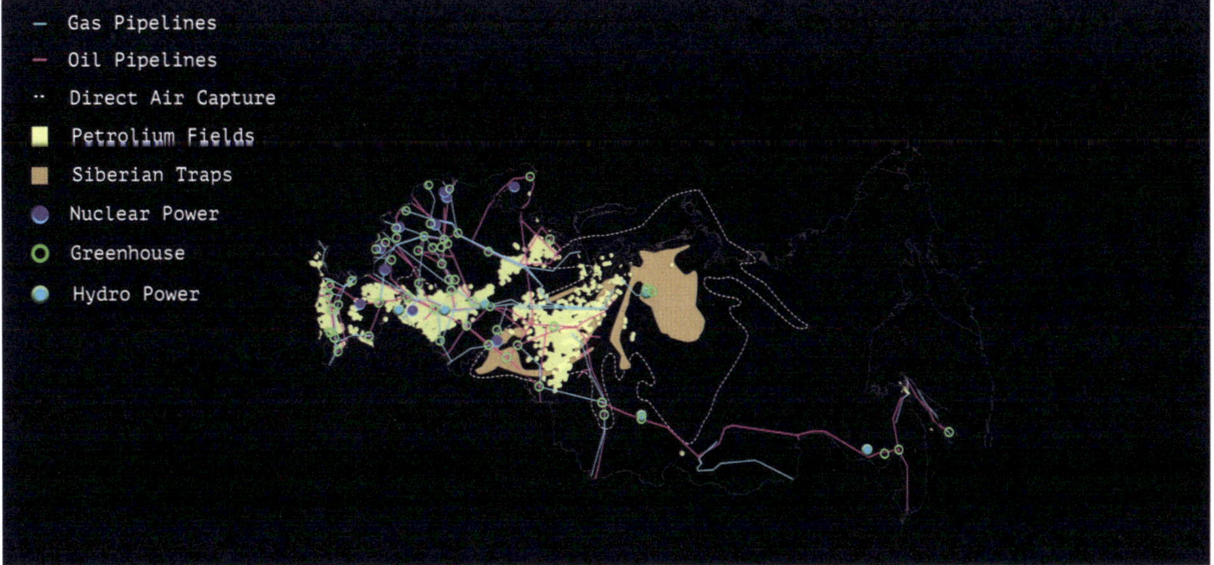

Following page: The Terraforming 2020, Strelka Institute for Media Architecture and Design.

I think Jane Jacobs is wrong about most things. I think the way in which she understood what planning is has probably done more to destroy cities than Robert Moses ever would have. I see Jane Jacobs as a kind of precursor to neoliberalism in more ways than one. One of the key mythologies of neoliberalism is that you don't need a plan, that the market will figure it out, that if you have a top-down state intervention of any form, this will distort the market and that the Ronald Reagan/Margaret Thatcher turn was nothing if not a celebration of the agency of planless bottom-up emergence. I do want to suggest that the presumption that the natural intelligence of the communities or the market will sort it all out by magical spontaneity is why our cities are as poorly designed as they have been. So, I would argue that what we need very much for the next 100 years, particularly in relation to things like the Green New Deal, the large scale and comprehensive decarbonization of our infrastructures, or a more just and equitable housing system, is a plan. We need a plan.

I'm always amused by the left position that wants medical care for all but doesn't really want a state, wants the Green New Deal but doesn't want central planning. It seems to be a magical thinking and one that we don't have time to entertain going forward. It is also important to acknowledge the difference between a democracy of means and a democracy of ends. Ideally one wants them to combine, to have democratic means which result in a democratic end, but that's not always the way it works. Sometimes you have democratic means that result in autocratic ends or in chaos, and sometimes you have autocratic means that result in democratic ends like Central Park or the TCP/IP protocol. The question to be asked here is: how can you aggregate insight, wisdom, experience, knowledge, and expertise in order to make a plan so that they can actually enforce themselves? That's different than asking, for example, how can you aggregate CI in order to not have to have a plan. And this is unfortunately, in some ways, both the dream of the right wing and the left wing.

The Terraforming 2020, Strelka Institute for Media Architecture and Design.

AM Do you think that participatory design processes or the combination of top-down with bottom-up processes in urban planning can go hand in hand?

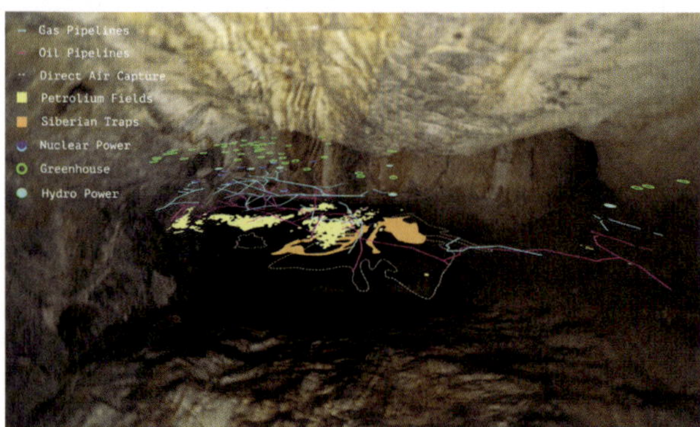

Pharmakon Landscape, Andrey Tetekin, Luciano Brina, Yu Gong, 2020.

BB Of course they can, and there are lots of examples where they work very well in combination. Climate science is an interesting example here. There are millions of people producing data through different kinds of expertise. There is no president of climate science, there is nobody that knows how the whole thing works, and yet there is a very clear structure for how this is aggregated into a model of the world. In a simple sense, I think that you want to aggregate expertise, and expertise can come from lots of different places. And so, if you can aggregate expertise in some sort of way that expertise itself can make a governing decision, then you are in a good place. I think the real problem, at least in the US in particular, is that everything is mediated through the law. We live in a world where scientists have to ask lawyers permission in order to do something that is implied by science. It should be the other way around.

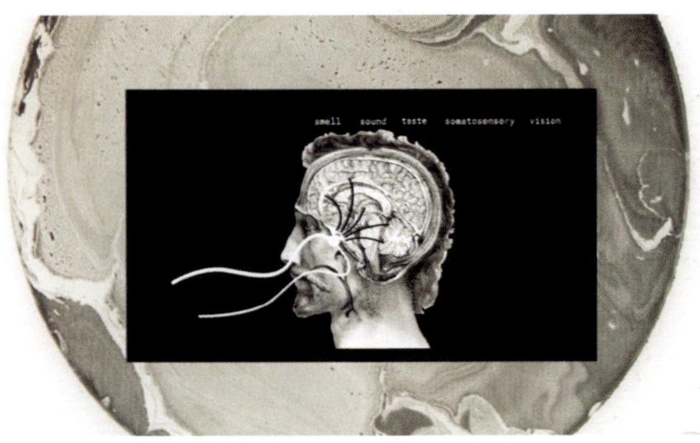

The Terraforming 2020,
Strelka Institute for Media
Architecture and Design.

So, what I'm concerned about is a kind of fetishization of means. There is a presumption: if you have highly democratic means, then you will have highly democratic outcomes. But everyone who has sat through meetings realizes that the maximization of participation is not always the way to guarantee the best outcome. There is nothing to presume in participatory processes that there will be a better outcome for everyone. And again, the example can work the other way around: one can have very autocratic processes resulting in extremely democratic outcomes. Most of the big plazas and piazzas and public squares in the great cities of Europe are not there because of some kind of community meeting deciding what should happen. They were there because a single gesture was made to wipe this out. I am not arguing for autocracy, I'm simply arguing that the goal needs to be democratic outcomes. We cannot focus on making the means more democratic because we've tried, and it didn't work. We need to make ourselves more horizontal. There has to be a way in which this leads to a decision that has the strength to enforce itself against other forces. I'm not against participatory design; what I want is cities that are active, democratic, open, and viable.

AM If ever there was a moment to profoundly understand "species'" interdependencies in the city, this is certainly it. The current pandemic brought on an increased societal awareness of the strong interdependencies among human, vegetable, animal, and even microbial species such as viruses. Taking this as an opportunity for design and making, what kind of organic or inorganic intelligence should we seek out in cities? How can design promote significant interactions that go beyond the simple idea of automation and, maybe, beyond human cognition?

BB I think that there is, probably even in mainstream discourses, an understanding of cities not just as something happening on top of an ecology, but as being part of that ecology and in a cause-and-effect relationship with these dynamic ecological systems. There are, then, two parts of the question. The first one asks about the kinds of intelligence that might be recognized or coaxed into being and that are already working in the city: microbial, animal, vegetable, machine, human, etc. They are all already in some kind of weird, orchestrated choreography in relation to each other, even if they aren't entirely aware of each other's existence. And so, the first question is the following one: how could we better recognize and understand what's already there? But then, there is a second question: how could we, based on this recognition, orchestrate these forms of intelligence in such a way that our definition of what we mean by a good city can be changed? "Good city" might not only mean the conditions that we've long thought it meant. But then there is also a third question: how, once we actually conceptualize these interventions, can they enforce themselves? How could this actually come back and remake the city in its kind of image?

I think there need to be different kinds of relationships between the types of people who have expertise in different parts of this story. There are people who understand the role of microbial life, there are people who understand the long-term geologic position of the city, there are people who understand the life of the animals in the city. I think the relationship between design and science needs to be brought back together.

I actually think that we got into our current situation not because there has been too much reason, but because there has been hardly any at all. I don't think that capitalism is particularly reason driven, I don't think that the decisions that we make about how we run cities in particular are reason driven. And I think that the real opportunity for design is to have a better and more active working engagement with science. **Science is a tremendous institutional function allowing us to describe the world and understand it, but it's not very good at proposing or acting on the implications of what it describes. It requires a different kind of intelligence to do that, and I think that's probably where design can enter into the situation.**

JV It is generally assumed that the arrival and generalization of AI or SI in our society dislocates the human from its traditional centrality. Can this movement be read as the continuation of a process that originated within the scientific revolution of the 17th and 18th centuries through the work of figures such as Nicolaus Copernicus, Galileo Galilei, or Giordano Bruno? Or are our contemporary transformations different in kind, and thus, not readable as a mere continuation of those events?

BB I think there is both a continuation and a jump between both approaches. But what do we mean by continuation? We make certain technologies because they are informed by a particular model that we have about how the world works. So, we understand something, and we make a tool based on this understanding. Sometimes, when we use that tool properly, the use of the tool shows us that the original model we had of the world, which in fact allowed us to make the tool, was wrong. **There is thus a moment of technological alienation: we make a tool to figure out the world and once we use the tool, it shows us that the world does not work that way. And then there is a break, and one has to resolve it and update the model of the world.** It's like telescopes: without them you don't have heliocentrism; without microscopes you don't have germ theory of infection; without radiocarbon dating you don't really have modern evolutionary theory. You also don't have a proper dating of the Earth without any dating techniques. We thought the Earth was flat, we

Lidar point cloud of intersection of Folsom and Dore St, San Francisco.

C
-25
10
45

Previous page: The Terraforming 2020, Strelka Institute for Media Architecture and Design.

built tools based on this principle and once we learned to use the tool, we realized that the world is not flat. So, in which ways could this happen with AI? I don't think it necessarily needs to happen the same, but there certainly is a strong potential for this; it could show us all the ways in which we thought that our model of intelligence was in fact central and normative. And then we could actually realize that intelligence does not follow a normative model, that's it's amazing but it's not necessarily the center of what intelligence is. This is one of the things that it may demonstrate to us.

But, coming back to your example, installing the insights of Copernicus, Galileo, and Bruno in our understanding of the world took hundreds of years. And I would argue that in many cases we still haven't really caught up with the implications of heliocentrism in a lot of our cultural work. It is science itself that can disclose how the world works, but it's up to other people actually to push through the implications of that. And I think the same thing goes for AI. The AI itself can disclose lots of things that will be demystifying, that will be surprising, disturbing, that will be boring, exciting, but it's up to other people to push through the implications of what all of that will mean.

The last point I want to make here is how my position about human decentralization differs from some post-humanists. I actually hold on to the idea that cognition – reason and rationality – is really special. It is different than just mere sentience and mere thought. And so, I don't agree with the way in which some people say that there is no differentiation between frogs thinking, microbes thinking, bats thinking, plants thinking, etc., and so humans are just one more thinking creature. This leads to conceiving our Promethean attempts at rationality as merely humorous, and I don't agree with this at all. I actually think there is a fundamental difference between sentience and sapience. I do think that our capacity for reason and rationality are unique and precious, but they are not necessarily abilities that have to be only held by humans. I think that one of the points that AI demonstrates is that there are also forms of reason and rationality that are not necessarily human, that are not even organic. What I would want to hold on to is the importance of reason and rationality to actually compose the world in its image. I just don't think that this is necessarily limited just to humans. That might be one of the points AI actually discloses.

Where should the cities go? Strelka Press, 2020.

But if anything else, the bigger question of what kinds of cities we are hoping to have, 20 years or 50 years or 100 years ahead, implies a previous question: will we still have cities in 50 or 100 years? I think that there is a real danger that we slide backwards in terms of global poverty, literacy rates, vaccination rates, food security, etc. I think there's a real danger that history starts running backwards, and I think that the irresponsible embrace of irrationality and unreason propelled by some kind of romantic revolutionary position is not helpful in stemming that tie. I think we need to find a different path.

Brain city

Neil Leach

What will the city of the future look like? Will it look strikingly different to cities of today? Will it look like something out of the Jetsons, complete with flying cars and space age buildings? Or will it look much like our contemporary cities, with a few new buildings, but with much of the existing building stock retained and simply retrofitted with the latest AI technologies? In other words, will the primary driver of change be a language of novel architectural forms? Or will it be the introduction of ever more sophisticated AI-based technologies to the existing infrastructure?

This short article explores the possibility of understanding the city as a form of brain, whose operations could potentially be supplemented by AI. Brains and cities, it would seem, have much in common.[1] Both are multi-agent systems.[2] The opportunity therefore presents itself for using AI to model – and potentially improve – the operations of a city. While simple multi-agent computational systems, such as Processing, can be used to generate emergent forms, neural networks are able to 'learn' and improve over time. And yet the introduction of AI to improve the operational efficiency of a city is a relatively recent phenomenon.[3]

Previous page: Endless Skyscraper, Eduard Haiman

The Self-Regulating City

John Holland describes how the city somehow manages to maintain a form of dynamic equilibrium, despite the constant changes that it experiences. He likens it to a 'standing wave' in a stream. A city can be seen as a 'pattern in time':

> Cities have no central planning commissions that solve the problem of purchasing and distributing supplies. [...] How do these cities avoid devastating swings between shortage and glut, year after year, decade after decade? The mystery deepens when we observe the kaleidoscopic nature of large cities. Buyers, sellers, administrations, streets, bridges, and buildings are always changing, so that a city's coherence is somehow imposed on a perpetual flux of people and structures. Like the standing wave in front of a rock in a fast-moving stream, the city is a pattern in time.[4]

How does a city manage to maintain this equilibrium?[5] Could the model of the 'city as brain' help us to understand this mechanism?

The brain, as we know, does more than just think. It also serves to regulate the body. This mechanism is often referred to as 'homeostasis'.[6] Homeostasis or homoeostasis is the property of a system that maintains a constant equilibrium when faced with internal or external variables. It is a concept that has been used in a number of fields including biology and mechanical systems, and – more recently – in the field of neuroscience. In the context of neuroscience, homeostasis can be understood as a kind of equilibrium on which the body depends for its survival.

William Ross Ashby, one of the pioneers in cybernetics and author of *Design for a Brain,* developed a device that he called the 'homeostat', a balancing mechanism – much like a thermostat – that maintains some kind of equilibrium through negative feedback.[7] The purpose of this device was to model the way in which the brain achieves its own form of dynamic equilibrium.[8] Significantly, Ashby's work caught the attention of Turing, who wrote to him suggesting that he use his Automatic Computing Engine (ACE) to simulate the process rather than building a special machine. In his letter to Ashby, Turing confessed: 'I am more interested in producing models of the action of the brain, than in the practical applications of computing.'[9] With this, the connection between homeostasis, computation and the operations of the brain had been established.

More recently, neuroscientist Antonio Damasio has argued that the primary function of the brain is to maintain our homeostatic condition and preserve our dynamic psychic equilibrium.[10] Thus, the brain can be seen to operate less as a 'command control center' and more as a corrective mechanism that keeps the body within a safe range of emotional impulses. As Damasio comments, 'Survival depends on the maintenance of the body's physiology within an optimal homeostatic range. This process relies on fast detection of potentially deleterious changes in body state and on appropriate corrective responses.'[11] While the brain itself is highly adaptive, it can also serve as a mechanism of adaptation.

The self-organisation of cities can be compared to the dynamic equilibrium implied by homeostasis. According to the logic of Emergence, cities are physical traces of patterns of social behaviour operating over time. They are governed by principles of self-organisation, for cities and towns themselves must be understood as amalgams of 'processes', as spaces of vectorial flows that 'adjust' to differing inputs and impulses, like some self-regulating system. This self-regulation is governed by principles of both positive and negative feedback, much like the brain itself. At a very basic level, then, we can see parallels between Damasio's understanding of the homeostasis of the brain and the principles of self-organisation that underpin a city, which could be reflected potentially in the behaviour of any multi-agent system, such as a neural network. Seen in this light, the principles behind the AI-controlled City Brain could be compared to the principles that govern a brain itself.

But Is It a Brain?

Damasio himself has a background interest in AI and counts the renowned AI pioneer, Warren McCulloch, as his first American mentor. Indeed, at the time Damasio shared some of the early excitement in what he describes as that 'foundational, exhilarating time for science, one that opened the way for the extraordinary successes of neurobiology, the computational sciences and artificial intelligence.'[12] And yet now he is aware of the shortcomings of this outlook, in that it overlooks the importance of the body. 'In retrospect, however, it had little to offer by way of a realistic view of what human minds look and feel like. How could it, given that the respective theory disengaged the dried up mathematical description of the activity of neurons from the thermodynamics of life processes? Boolean algebra has its limits when it comes to making minds.'[13] The key problem, for Damasio, is that without the feedback of 'feelings' from the body, AI can never replicate the behaviour of a brain.

In any case, there is one obvious reason why, for the moment at least, it is impossible to replicate the operations of the human brain, and that is that we still do not fully understand the workings of the human brain. Until such time as we fully understand how the brain operates, how are we going to be able to replicate it? We also need to recognise that without consciousness, AI will never be able to replicate exactly the operations of a brain.[14]

But there is perhaps a more fundamental question that needs to be addressed: what do we mean by 'intelligence'? "Are we to follow Jeff Hawkins and assume that human intelligence is the only form of 'intelligence', or are we to accept that there are other forms of 'intelligence' out there?[15] And – by extension – what do we mean by other related terms, such as 'creativity'? It is important to point out that there is no absolute understanding of 'intelligence' or 'creativity'. The use of all these terms is relative.

On the one hand, we need to recognise that although the 'intelligence' of AI might not match – for the moment at least – the intelligence of a human brain, this does not mean that AI is not intelligent. It might simply be exhibiting a lower level of intelligence, but one that is a form of intelligence, nonetheless. The same applies to other terms, such as the notion of a 'brain'. Although the 'brain' of AI might not match the 'brain' of a human, this does not mean that the 'brain' of AI is not a brain of some kind.

On the other hand, we also need to recognise that the 'intelligence' of human beings might itself not be the highest level of 'intelligence'. It is merely 'human-level intelligence'. Equally, the 'brain' of human beings might not be the most powerful form of brain. It is merely a 'human-level brain'.

Once this is recognised, we need not worry so much about whether AI can match the performance of the human brain. AI is indeed a form of 'brain', albeit not a 'human brain'. And it does indeed exhibit 'intelligence', albeit not perhaps 'human-level intelligence' – at least for the moment.

In the context of a city, then, we need to judge AI by the roles that it performs, rather than the level to which it performs those roles. What roles, then, might AI play within the city? As we can see with the example of City Brain, AI can operate as a 'brain' within an interactive system that is constituted by the city.[16] In the case of traffic, for example, it monitors traffic through sensors, processes the information using its 'brain', and then controls the traffic lights as actuators to keep traffic flowing.[17] The role of AI in a city, then, in regulating traffic flow can at least be *compared* to the role of the human brain in regulating the human body.

The city can already be understood as an 'intelligent' system might be. The role of AI can therefore be seen as a supplementary one, to *improve* the 'intelligence' of the city, just as a pacemaker might help to improve the performance of the heart. From this perspective, we can perhaps compare the role of AI-based technology in improving the operations of a city to the role of AI in providing a form of 'extended intelligence' or 'intelligence augmentation' to human intelligence. Seen in this light, the city of AI can be understood as a city whose performance is *enhanced* by AI.

Brain City – the city of AI – is the archetypal AI-enhanced city of tomorrow.

References :

1. German neurophysiologist, Wolf Singer, has made comparisons between the city and the brain. Wolf Singer, Die Architektur des Gehirns als Modell für komplexe Stadtstrukturen? In C Maar and F Rötzer (eds.), Virtual Cities, Basel: Birkhauser, 1997, pp. 153-161. This comparison inspired Coop Himmelb(l)au to develop a research group, Brain City Lab, that exhibited a model of a city at the Venice Biennale 2008. The model used computational methods to projection map the behaviour of neurons onto a landscape model of the city. Coop Himmelb(l)au: Future Revisited, http://www.coop-himmelblau.at/architecture/projects/coop-himmelblau-future-revisited/.

2. Steve Johnson, *Emergence: The Connected Lives of Ants, Cities and Software.* New York: Scribner, 2002.

3. Perhaps the most extensive exploration application of AI to the city has been the City Brain initiative developed by Alibaba, a leading Chinese ecommerce company at the forefront of machine learning development. Alibaba is a Chinese multinational conglomerate holding company based in Hangzhou. It specializes in ecommerce and could be considered the Chinese rival to Amazon, although, unlike Amazon, Alibaba is not involved in direct sales and does not own any warehouses. https://www.alibaba.com/.

4. John Holland, quoted by Steven Johnson. Holland's point is that the water molecules making up the wave are constantly changing, but that the pattern of the wave remains the same, provided that the rock is still there and the water flows. John Holland, *Emergence: From Chaos to Order,* New York: Perseus, 1999, p. 29.

5. This model of the city maintaining a form of dynamic equilibrium echoes the larger model of the Earth as a self-regulating complex system, as postulated by James Lovelock. James Lovelock, *Gaia: A New Look at Life on Earth,* Oxford: OUP, 1979.

6. The term 'homeostasis' was coined by the American physiologist Walter Bradford Cannon in 1929, in reference to living systems. Significantly, Cannon chose the Ancient Greek term, 'homeo' (meaning 'similar') over the alternative Ancient Greek term, 'homo' (meaning 'the same'). By this, Cannon sought to distinguish human operations with their considerable variables from mechanical operations, such as in the case of the thermostat, which operate within a fixed system. Bradford Cannon, (1929) Organization for Physiological Homeostasis. *Physiol. Rev.* 9, 399-431.

7. Ashby predicted that the homeostat would even be able to play chess. William Ross Ashby, *Design for a Brain: The Origin of Adaptive Behavior,* London: Chapman and Hall, 1960.

8. There are echoes here of the work of Sigmund Freud, who had already referred to 'hydraulic construction of the unconscious' and its libidinal economy, such that 'the individual's conscious experience and behavior are the manifestation of a surging libidinal struggle between desire and repression'. John Daugman, Brain Metaphors and Brain Theory, *Computational Neuroscience,* Cambridge, MA: MIT Press, 1993.

9. Alan Turing, Letter to William Ashby, 1946. The W. Ross Ashby Archive. http://www.rossashby.info/letters/turing.html.

10. Antonio Damasio, *The Strange Order of Things: Life, Feeling and the Making of Cultures,* New York: Vintage, 2019.
11. Damasio, Antonio and Carvalho, Gil. (2013) The Nature of Feelings: Evolutionary and Neurobiological Origins, *Neuroscience,* Vol. 14: p. 143.

12. Antonio Damasio, *The Strange Order of Things: Life, Feeling and the Making of Cultures,* New York: Vintage, 2019, p. 240.

13. Ibid. p. 240.

14. The thorny problem of consciousness will be dealt with in the second volume of this series, *The Death of the Architect.*

15. Jeff Hawkins, *A Thousand Brains: A New Theory of Intelligence,* New York, Basic Books, 2021

16. https://www.alibabacloud.com/solutions/intelligence-brain/city. Within any interactive system, there are three components, a sensor that tracks behaviour and gathers information, a 'brain' that synthesises this information and sends out signals to modify that behaviour, and an actuator that receives those signals and responds accordingly.

17. This could perhaps be understood as a form of distributed intelligence, much like in an octopus, rather than a centralised form of intelligence. Marion Nixon, J Z Young, *The Brains and Lives of Cephalopods,* New York, Oxford University Press, 2003.

Machine Estrangement: On Leo Tolstoy, Algorithmic Otherness and Urban Design

Jordi Vivaldi

The narrator of Leo Tolstoy's *Kholstomer* is Strider, a horse. The Russian writer conjures up the equine nature of its raconteur as a literary device of defamiliarization: its distanced and at times deliriant point of view on mundane issues evokes what Viktor Shklovsky defines as an effect of estrangement[1]. Strider's astonishment while describing the concept of property is an emblematic example of this phenomena:

"Such are the words "my" and "mine," which they apply to different things, creatures, objects, and even to land, people, and horses. They agree that only one may say "mine" about this, that or the other thing. And the one who says "mine" about the greatest number of things is, according to the game which they've agreed to among themselves, the one they consider the most happy. I don't know the point of all this, but it's true."[2]

With this revealing note, Tolstoy's equine protagonist defamiliarizes the notion of property through a singular reinterpretation; through Strider's animal lens, property becomes a "game which they've agreed to among themselves" and whose existence seems to be pointless, despite being "true". The aesthetic effect produced by the eccentricity of this reinterpretation is precisely what Shklovsky has in mind when he invokes the term "estrangement": "to make objects unfamiliar, to make forms difficult, to increase the difficulty and length of perception because the process of perception is an aesthetic end in itself and must be prolonged".[3] Tolstoy's literary instrumentalization of a non-human form of alterity is particularly contemporary. The recent conceptualization in various disciplines of the notion of the Anthropocene represents a growing acknowledgment of the

Previous page:
Source: Jordi Vivaldi.

biological, geological, or technological dimensions of our cultural stage, configuring an *imago mundi* that, since it can no longer be entirely decoded through human parameters, invokes in us a more or less intense feeling of estrangement. The discipline of urbanism is certainly no exception when it comes to these multispecies alliances: the generalization of artificial intelligence (AI) in urban design is progressively altering its methods, discourses and practices, and although it is still probably too early to identify the precise directions of these transformations, they appear to be having a remarkable impact on both practice and research. However, despite this reasonable uncertainty, it does not seem particularly risky to affirm that the urban design processes associated with AI today are almost exclusively associated with a Promethean agenda. Most of them are driven by a techno-scientific program whose predominant concern with notions such as improvement, optimization, automatization, efficiency, prediction, monitoring, adaptation, calculation, or self-regulation frequently obscures the political or aesthetic dimensions that might emerge from these trans-species confederations.

In this context and through this short essay, I would like to argue that Tolstoy's instrumentalization of Strider's zoological otherness might be useful in expanding the role of AI in urban design by considering the former as an algorithmic otherness that might serve as a potential source of aesthetic estrangement for the latter.

Today, artificial intelligence and machine learning are not only instruments that can help us design the city, they are already embodied in it. Thus, they can be considered agents deploying all sorts of operative, economic, political and aesthetic dimensions in the city. Within this framework, and as an experimental figure and a toolbox for making and thinking, Shklovsky's estrangement might situate us within a stratum whose lines of flight transcend – without necessarily opposing – the Promethean tinge that usually characterizes the alliance between AI and urban design. More in particular, and within the city's historical vocation of individual/collective interchanges, the de-automatization of perception implied by processes of estrangement could affect both the materiality and design processes of urban design by challenging what has been defined as the architectural mode of perception par excellence: Walter Benjamin's "distracted perception".

Estrangement as a Literary Device in Leo Tolstoy

One of the most controversial yet significant considerations found in the work of Viktor Shklovsky is, undoubtedly, his neat differentiation between artwork and the products of daily life. This is particularly evident when it comes to perceptive processes: according to Shklovsky, while the perception of domestic items is rooted in the unconscious automatisms characteristic of our habits and is thus immediate, the estrangement associated with works of art over-complexifies their perception, thus extending it beyond what is required for common life. In other words: the estrangement singularizing any work of art implies a delay in its perception in comparison to day-to-day items. Bertolt Brecht coined the German expression *Verfremdungseffekt* in order to refer to this distancing effect, which was generated in his theatre by "playing in such a way that the audience was hindered from simply identifying itself with the characters in the play: acceptance or rejection of their actions and utterances was meant to take place on a conscious plane, instead of, as hitherto, in the audience's subconscious".[4] To a similar end, Leo Tolstoy deploys a rich and colourful number of literary strategies. In *War and Peace* (1864), he famously describes the well-known idea of "battle" as if it were an entirely unprecedented practice, and, later, in *Shame!* (1895), he defamiliarizes the act of flogging by proposing unusual descriptions of the act without transforming its essence. In all these cases, and as certainly occurs in Brecht as well, the Russian writer instrumentalizes a process of defamiliarization in order to prevent the readers from losing themselves in empathetic emotions, forcing them instead to enter into a critical frame of mind. Thus, in contrast with Aristotle's *catharsis*, estrangement precludes the readers' identification with the fictional characters, promoting an attitude of intellectual attention that interferes with unconscious habits and automatic entertainment. In *Kholstomer* (1886), Tolstoy obtains this distancing effect through the equine logic of his narrator. In this case, what is relevant for Tolstoy is neither the horse's proximity to the human being, nor the naive mistakes that the former makes when attempting to describe the latter, but rather the aesthetic paths that emerge from speculating on the unexpected views resulting from applying an equine logic to human affairs. This aesthetic strategy is surprisingly similar to contemporary forms of non-anthropocentrism. First, it positions a zoological being ovn the same ontological footing as the human being –considering the former's narrative to be as valid as that of the latter. Second, it celebrates rather than mitigates the zoological difference characteristic of a horse – instrumentalizing its peculiar point of view as the key literary device in the story.

Invoking a non-human form of otherness is certainly not enough to turn Tolstoy into a 21st-century intellectual *avant la lettre*. His significant misogyny and heteropatriarchism, for example, decisively obscures that option. However, his capacity to identify and conjugate the aesthetic possibilities offered by the potential estrangement lying within animal forms of otherness is worth retaining. It might prove useful in expanding the horizons that orient our alliances with non-human beings in creative environments, frequently circumscribed within positivist modes of action. Within this context, I would like to bring to the foreground a contemporary multispecies confederation that might be particularly receptive to Tolstoy's strategy: the involvement of algorithmic forms of otherness within urban design.

Algorithmic Otherness

Frequently used in the formation of compound terms such as "xenogamia" or "xenophilia", the term *xenos* generally refers to the "strange" or the "alien" – that is, the "other". It is precisely in invoking this generic form of otherness that fields of studies such as xenology – the scientific investigation of extraterrestrial life – or xenosophy – the wisdom emerging from the encounter with the other – take their names. However, these examples detach the notion of *xenos* from the semantic milieu in which it was originally coined in Ancient Greece: the *xenia*, the moral principle of giving gifts to foreign acquaintances, later absorbed by the ethical precept of hospitality.[5]

Within this context, the term *xenos* gains a slight yet decisive nuance: rather than signalling a generic otherness, it embodies the other within the figure of the guest-friend, the foreign traveller being received by a host through a series of pacts of hospitality.[6] However, in the age of the Anthropocene, the *xenia's* hospitality can no longer be limited to the folkloric human scene of a remote and exotic foreigner being candidly sheltered in the warmth of a welcoming home. Rather than being a social contract covering only human individuals, the *xenia* today would also necessarily include the dense miscegenations between organic and inorganic beings characteristic of our times. Thus, in spite of its historical weight and broad speculative vocation, the concept of xenology is actually rooted in the immediacy of our here and now. The hole in the ozone layer, frozen seed banks, global pandemics, xenobots, ocean garbage patches, and transgenic animals constitute some of those strange objects invading our world while circumventing the epistemic categories characteristic of Modernity – bastard creatures conforming a vast litany of multispecies entanglements, eclectic composites, and hybrid processes resulting from intimate relations between strangers, between "others", between *xenos*.

In its twofold sense as *xenos* and *xenia*, the notion of *xenos* thus accounts today for a new sensibility towards the biological, ecological, algorithmic, and geological regime. Intelligent robots, planetary viruses, digital boots, human-made earthquakes, transgenic plants... the otherness evoked by these creatures is no longer that of a "Galilean object" and its perpetual human subjugation, but that of an emancipated active being, a "Lovelockian agent"[7] that mutates and evolves, establishing multispecies pacts of hospitality with different forms of life: human and nonhuman, organic and machinic, cultural and natural. Thus, far from the invariably vampirized mark of alterity of classical philosophy or the fetishized and necessarily othered other of deconstruction, here the other is understood as a multispecies guest-friend whose temporary accommodation in alien environments does not exhaust its singularity, which is instead intermittently and selectively unveiled.

In today's computational urban design, the *xenos* par excellence is, undoubtedly, the algorithmic other. Faced with a twofold ontology that no longer alludes to Heideggerian human nudity but to a planet

inhabited by algorithmic beings that live with and against us, the ubiquitous presence of these algorithmic creatures both in physical and virtual bodies propels an "increasingly dense intertwining between organic bodies and 'immaterial elfs' (digital codes)".[8]
The generalization of artificial intelligence and the multi-scalar robotization of organic life establishes, in addition to a change of medium, a change of condition: its algorithmic power does not merely offer itself as an automatic pilot for daily life, but it also triggers a radical transformation of our human nature, setting up a perennial and universal intertwining between bodies and information. Whereas in the 1990s bits were associated with atoms, bits are now associated with cells such as neurons, myocytes or keratinocytes.

In this sense, the multidisciplinary generalization of machine learning, the progress in genetic engineering, or the robotization of the mundane no longer refer to a humanity that is merely extended, but to a humanity that is expanded – that is, inclined, deviated. It is interwoven with algorithmic (and biological or ecological) agents whose symbiosis is not only metaphorical or narrative, but performative. Given this scenario, "artificial extelligence" becomes "artificial intelligence" through a process of incorporation. Intelligence, the eidos, what has traditionally been understood as form, is no longer an external entity that articulates (in)organic bodies from the outside, rather it is carnally embedded into them.

However, rather than considering machine learning to be a legendary form of alien cognition in silico, it is more reasonable to look at it as an instrument of knowledge magnification that performs pattern recognition.[9] Yann LeCun, frequently considered the godfather of convolutional neural networks, argues that current AI systems are not sophisticated versions of cognition, but of perception.[10] To study the impact of AI, then, is to study the manner and degree to which information flows are absorbed and treated by AI, and, more in particular, to study the algorithmic anatomy of the statistical models underlying machine learning. Matteo Pasquineli affirms that "from the numerical perspective of machine learning, notions such as image, movement, form, style and decision can be all described as statistical distributions of a pattern".[11] From this point of view, he continues, three steps take place. First comes the "training data", the training dataset containing data to be analysed in order to extract knowledge and "intelligence" – in other words, patterns of association.
This extraction occurs in the second step, defined by Pasquineli as the "learning algorithm"; it constructs a statistical model of the previous patterns of association. Finally, there is the "model application", the instrumentalization of the statistical model once it is considered sufficiently trained in different tasks, such as classification or prediction.

In light of Pasquineli's assertions, might we then define artificial intelligence as an intelligent *xenos*, that is, an intelligent form of otherness? This, of course, depends on how we understand the term.

Source: Jordi Vivaldi.

Its etymology offers us some insights: intelligence comes from the Latin *intelligentia*, composed of the terms inter and legere. While the former unequivocally refers to the notion of "in between", the latter's significance is more complex. On the one hand, legere means to choose (*scegliere*, in Italian), but on the other hand, legere means to read (*leggere*, in Italian). While the former would associate intelligence with the capacity of "choosing (*leggere*) in between (*inter*)", the latter would associate intelligence with the capacity of "reading (*leggere*) in between (*inter*)". Thus, in the first case, an agent is intelligent if it is capable of choosing the best option between many, and, in the second case, an agent is intelligent if it is capable of reading what lies in between, such as, for example, reading between the lines.

It is particularly difficult, and largely debatable, to clarify whether artificial intelligence processes are indeed performing either of those two activities or if they can be reduced, as Dan McQuillan argues, to "simply mathematical minimisation".[12] This epistemological demystification is actually crucial in order to secularize Artificial Intelligence from the auratic narrative of autonomy that underpins a neoliberal practice worldwide: the growth of a geopolitical regime of high-tech companies invisibilizing workers' autonomy through a corporate apparatus of knowledge extractivism and epistemic colonialism. However, with or without intelligence, AI, as an instrument of knowledge magnification, perceives and operates with patterns that are beyond the reach of the human mind.[13] Thus, independently of the pertinence of defining the behaviour of these "immaterial elfs" as "intelligent", its algorithmic nature seems to operate, in any case, through a logic that qualitatively differs from that of humans, thus opening up a space of novelty and, eventually, of emancipation. It appears as an algorithmic *xenos*, a technological form of otherness, a non-human creature operating through a mode of action that results alien and strange to us, due, at least, to the management of massive data processes that are too vast for the human mind to grasp. Theirs is a technical logic that, as Mario Carpo suggests, "we may master and unleash, but that we can neither replicate, emulate, nor even simply comprehend with our mind".[14] Within the field of urban design, this is particularly valid for one of the most promising entanglements between artificial intelligence and spatial design: the rise of Second-Order Cybernetic Architecture.

Walter Benjamin's "Distracted Perception" and Algorithmic Urban Design

Güvenç Özel's notion of Second-Order Cybernetic Architecture (SOCA)[15] is a first step towards a form of computational urbanism in which AI is part of the architectural system that is observing. The distinction between second-order and first-order cybernetics is decisive here: while the former is based on a continuous feedback loop that both influences and is influenced by its context, the latter executes frozen patterns that have been previously established by external actors.[16] SOCA capitalizes on second-order cybernetic systems by instrumentalizing context-aware robots that use advanced machine vision and iterative operational codes, permitting AI's robotic spaces "to readjust their actions based on unpredictable actors with non-repetitive behaviours".[17] Within this context, the introduction of artificial intelligence to urban design has predominantly been driven by a Promethean agenda aiming, above all, at one target: optimization. Various urban fields participate in this technocratic endeavour: public transportation maximization,[18] urban security,[19] traffic system management,[20] or the regulation of garbage collection/recycling[21] instrumentalize artificial intelligence as a design/analysis device that enhances and extends the city's capacity to manage its own urban processes. In these cases, artificial intelligence operates as humans' loyal companion, as an obliging algorithmic being reverently orbiting around its citizens under the promise of enhancement, adaptation, and maximization. However, in addition – and not necessarily in opposition – to these concerns, the notion of otherness can also be instrumentalized, as we have seen in Tolstoy's *Kholstomer*, through non-positivist modes of action capitalizing on categories such as distancing, misfit or alienation, notions that might open new lines of flight concerning our mode of perception regarding the city.

In *Kholstomer*, Tolstoy instrumentalizes the equine otherness of his protagonist in a different yet complementary way with respect to how, generally speaking, urban design frequently employs AI's algorithmic otherness in its designs in the present day. Rather than exclusively looking to enhance the reader's comfort and adapt to his/her logics, Tolstoy's attempts, above all, to avoid automatic perception, to avoid routine and incorporation, to avoiding immediacy and transparency.

By implementing Shklovsky's estrangement, Tolstoy circumvents, above all, habitualization. He delays and prolongs the process of perception under the premise that "if the whole complex lives of many people go on unconsciously, then such lives are as if they had never been. And art exists that one may recover the sensation of life; it exists to make one feel things, to make the stone stony".[22]

However, *Kholstomer* is not only a good example of Shklovsky's estrangement, but also of how the latter might be deployed by instru From an aesthetic point of view, machine learning could thus be instrumentalized, in symbiosis with its optimizing virtues, as a form of machine estrangement that necessarily prolongs our process of perceiving the city – in other words, as the equivalent of Shklovsky's defamiliarization device, as the distancing effect characteristic of the poetic language he uses in *Kholstomer*. In its non-human capacity to manage massive amounts of information, the algorithmic otherness of machine learning and supercomputation has the potential to produce a similar distancing effect in the field of urban design. It is capable of precluding a full empathization with the user because there is always a remainder of otherness that cannot be fully comprehended by our human modes of action. In opposition to vintage artificial intelligence, current machine learning processes applied to urban proposals might no longer try to imitate the logic of the human mind. Instead, they might develop their own logic, a mode of action based on an algorithmic nature that is capable, first, of managing big data processes that are far too vast for our human minds, and, second, of installing and deploying sensing mechanisms that cannot be decodified by our naked eye.

Although it is certainly too early to deploy a full taxonomy systematizing the various manners in which this form of estrangement might operate within the city, some of them can already be identified, since algorithmic beings are no longer mere instruments at the disposal of urban designers, but active ingredients of the city itself. Within this context, and given that the various multispecies intelligences populating the city do not always interact through or for human beings, the physical traces that these non-human conversational patterns leave on the city could certainly produce in us an intense feeling of estrangement and defamiliarization. The green screens through which urban surfaces become the scaffolding for a digital world, the massive flourishing of QR codes of various scales and consistencies responding to the standards of machine vision, the singular choreographies that might result from the patterns organizing the correlated movement of driverless cars, or the various and evanescent elements emerging in the city to control and guide the movement of all sorts of autonomous drones exemplify transformations that respond to the operative demands of algorithmic beings rather than to the aesthetics of human observation. In that sense, they could certainly invoke in us a certain feeling of alienation. This is above all caused by the fact that these algorithmic forms of otherness are not only present in the digital world but within the physical realm, affecting not only urban operational systems but also the materiality and design of the city itself. Their brutal data-processing capacity produces behavioural and material patterns that are radically different from what we can conceive, converting public space into a space of multispecies expression that is hardly reducible to human parameters. It is precisely this estrangement, and its relation to a non-human form of otherness, which, as we see with Tolstoy and Strider, should be considered as more than a mere effect of our urban coexistence with algorithmic beings. It has the capacity to install a new mode of perceiving the city that can open lines of flight and reactivate lost paths in the field of urban design by challenging what Walter Benjamin considered to be the architectural mode of perception par excellence: distracted perception.

According to Benjamin, "buildings can be received in two ways: through use and through contemplation. Or rather: tactilely and optically."[24] As Eugenio Pandolfini reminds us,[25] distracted perception does not represent the reduction of a hypothetical "attentive" perception, since for Benjamin, distracted perception is inherent in the intimate and original relationship between architecture and human beings. Within this context and regarding the visual culture of the early 20th century, it is necessary to differentiate between an optic and a haptic mode of vision. The first is solely visual and refers to a view from a distance, an all-encompassing singular vision, a far-off image; the second is tactile, dynamic, and refers to close-range vision and a nearby image. Through this distinction, the omnipotence of the visual realm is questioned, expanding the aesthetic experience through the inclusion of the other senses, more intimate and linked by a synaesthetic relationship. The contribution of Walter Benjamin consists in translating these concepts into the domain of urbanism and architecture: for the German philosopher, in modernity the perception of architecture and art is distracted. In other words, it is more tactile than optical and, above all, it can easily become a habit. It is a mode of perception that does not necessarily set aside the sense of sight but incorporates it as a haptic vision, a nearby, moving vision, associated with a more intimate and profound perception. The instrumentalization of algorithmic forms of otherness can potentially articulate Benjamin's distracted perception with respect to the city in a twofold manner.

First, it increases the distracted register: AI's management of massive amounts of data produces robotic spaces whose capacity to adapt, optimize, improve, regulate, and in general, improve and enhance their performance softens and smooths out their interaction with users, who incorporate those spaces as part of habit by automatizing their perception.

Second, algorithmic urban design has the potential to reduce Benjamin's distracted perception. In its algorithmic otherness, AI's operative logic qualitatively differs from our human nature, producing, in its activity, a process of estrangement that precludes the complete absorption and automatization of Benjamin's distracted perception. The "natural discomfort" and "alienation feeling" that Carpo relates to the use of artificial intelligence in the arts produces, in urban design, a remainder of alterity that opposes "distracted perception" – not because it demands more attention, but because it establishes an insurmountable separation between user and city.

It is precisely this second mode of perception that Tolstoy evokes in *Kholstomer* through the equine nature of his narrator. With this distancing and alienating effect, Tolstoy opens up space not just for surprise and difference, but for Shklovsky's estrangement, for a delay in the act of absorption, for the criticism, mystery, and eroticism associated with what is unfamiliar, with what demands an arbitrary prolongation of the process of perception. In a similar fashion, the instrumentalization of AI by urban design has the possibility of complexifying its current positivistic register by purposefully conjuring up the alienating side of its algorithmic otherness. The latter's emancipation from certain human frameworks hosts the potential for offering not just optimization, maximization, and adaptation, but also unprecedented modes of perception whose oblique nature might decisively enrich the field of urban design.

References :

1. Viktor Shklovsky, "Art as Technique" in *Twentieth-century Literary Theory: A reader,* ed K. M. Newton (London: Palgrave Macmillan, 1997).

2. Leon Tolstoi, *Strider* (London: Borderland Books, 2015).

3. Viktor Shklovsky, "Art as Technique" in *Twentieth-century Literary Theory: A reader,* ed K. M. Newton (London: Palgrave Macmillan, 1997), 2.

4. Bertolt Brecht, "On Chinese Acting", trans. Eric Bentley, in *The Tulane Drama Review* 6.1 (1961), 133.

5. Simon Weir, "Ontological Withdrawal and the Symbols of Symbolism".

6. Generally speaking, strangers are xénoi to each other, though in a civic context, *xénoi* are persons who visit a city and need to be hosted. Simon Weir, "On the origin of the architect: Architects and xenía in the ancient Greek theatre", 10.

7. "With Galilean objects as the model, we can indeed take nature as a "resource to exploit," but with Lovelockian agents, it is useless to nurture illusions. Lovelock's objects have agency, they are going to react [...] and it would be naïve to believe that they are going to remain inert no matter how much pressure is put on them." Bruno Latour, *Down to Earth* (Madrid: Gedisa Editorial, 2013), 229.

8. Eric Sadin, *L'humanité augmentée. L'administration numérique du monde* (Paris: Ed. Éditions L'échappée, 2013), 46.

9. "As an instrument of knowldege, machine learning is composed of an object to be observed (training dataset), and instrument of observation (learning algorithm) and a final representation (statitical model)." See: https:// www.skynettoday.com/editorials/nooscope?fbclid=IwAR0c2YwJmn6utSwp-YQSyBcaAKe0oiQgVPMmS4VyYmehy4SYoA5WkhlkNQ

10. Yann LeCun, "Learning World Models: the Next Step towards AI", keynote lecture, International Joint Conference on Artificial Intelligence (IJCAI), Stockholm, Sweden, July 2018.

11. Matteo Pasquineli, "How a machine learns and fails", in Spheres. Journal for Digital Cultures, n.5, 2019. See: https://spheres-journal.org/contribution/how-a-machine-learns-and-fails-a-grammar-of-error-for-artificial-intelligence/

12. Dan McQuillan, "Manifesto on Algorithmic Humanitarianism", presented at the symposium *Reimagining Digital Humanitarianism, Goldsmiths, University of London, February* 16, 2018.

13. Matteo Pasquineli, "How a machine learns and fails", in Spheres. Journal for Digital Cultures, n.5, 2019. See: https://spheres-journal.org/contribution/how-a-machine-learns-and-fails-a-grammar-of-error-for-artificial-intelligence/

14. Mario Carpo, The second digital turn (Cambridge: MIT Press, 2017), 81.

15. Güvenç Özel, "Toward a Post-Architecture", *Log*, no.36 (2016), 100.

16. The vast majority of digital manufacturing projects involving robots fall into this category. The ICD/ITKE "Research Pavilion 2012" (2012) or Gramazio and Kohler "Flight Assembled Architecture" (2012) are good examples of it; Kuka robots or drones execute orders based on a minimum degree of autonomy. This fact does not detract from the value of those projects, but it does limit their interest as expansive architectural designs: automated processes applied to manufacturing are tantamount to the assembly line, characteristic of modern 20th-century industry, although their applications in architecture began at a later date. Something similar can be identified in projects like Diller & Scofidio's "The Shed" (2019).

17. Güvenç Özel, "Toward a Post-Architecture", *Log*, no.36 (2016), 100.

18. "In Bengaluru, India, where traffic jams are common, Siemens Mobility built a monitoring system that uses AI through traffic cameras that detect vehicles and calculate density of traffic on the road, and then alters traffic lights based on real-time road congestion. Alibaba, China's e-commerce giant, launched "City Brain" to minimize road congestion, utilizing data from traffic lights, CCTV cameras, and video recognition to make suggestions for traffic flow management." Maria López Conde, Ian Twin, "How Artificial Intelligence is Making Transport Safer, Cleaner, More Reliable and Efficient in Emerging Markets" in *EmCompass*, n. 75 (2019).

19. The application Malalai is a good examples of this case.

20. The work of Vivacitylabs is a paradigmatic case of the use of artificial intelligence in the traffic management.

21. AMP Robotics or Brain Corps are good examples.

22. Viktor Shklovsky, "Art as Technique" in *Twentieth-century Literary Theory: A reader,* ed K. M. Newton (London: Palgrave Macmillan, 1997), 7.

23. Mario Carpo, *The second digital turn* (Cambridge: MIT Press, 2017), 80.

24. Walter Benjamin, The Work of Art in the Age of Mechanical Reproduction (London: Penguin Publishers 2008), 112.

25. Eugenio Pandolfini: "DustyRelief/BMU" in Sobre Arquitectura moderna y contemporánea (Madrid: Ed. Diseño, 2016), 256.

Learning Machines: A Story of Control, Softness and Agency in Architectural Computing

Theodora Vardouli

Designed by Belgian illustrator Jean-Michel Folon, the poster for French director Yannick Bellon's 1972 feature film Somewhere Someone (Quelque part, Quelqu'un) showed a human figure, hands up in surrender pose, threatened by a supersized weapon-shaped hand — the only warm-blooded entities in a glacial urban landscape of featureless mega-blocks. Printed at full page size, the poster figured as the opening image for a four-essay section on "The Total City" *(La ville totale)* published in the French futurological periodical on land use management and urban development 2000 *[Deuxmille]*. Presented alongside essays by four eminent architects —Kenzo Tange, Nicholas Negroponte, Buckminster Fuller and Yona Friedman— who had been spearheading provocative visions of information-driven responsiveness, adaptivity, and fluidity in the design and management of urban environments, Folon's poster lends itself to a double reading.

Previous page: Poster for the 1972 film *Quelque part, Quelqu'un* opening a collection of four essays on the "total city" in the French periodical 2000. Source: Tange, Kenzo, Yona Friedman, Nicholas Negroponte, and R. Buckminster Fuller. 1973. "La Ville Totale." 2000 *[Deuxmille] : Revue de l'Amenagement Du Territoire et Du Developpement Regional*, no. 24: 5–7.

The poster visually encapsulates the urban condition that the four authors were professing to undo: an anonymous, faceless city designed based on statistical simplifications and technocratic priorities that were being imposed, from the top down, by expert groups of professional planners. Tange's speculations about urban structures metabolizing "energy, information, and free time,"[1] Fuller's visions about data-based comprehensive and anticipatory design strategies, Negroponte's ideas about computationally enabled "intelligent environments," and Friedman's proposals for informational protocols enabling self-design and self-build within three-dimensional space grids all aspired to transform the individual "user" into an active agent in the shaping of their living settings. The physical or computational structures that the four authors put forward would allow for data on the activities, behaviours, or wishes of a city's inhabitants to effect transformations on the form of the city itself. And yet, we might also contemplate another reading of the poster as a critique of the very idea of *La ville totale*, at least in the way that it had been redefined through algorithmic methods and informational abstractions during the 1960s. At the turn of the 1970s, skepticism about the treatment of architecture and cities as total systems to be managed by information was growing.

Could the enormous hand mimicking a trigger and barrel be a metaphor for visions of total environmental control through algorithmic automation and management?

Throughout the 1960s, various researchers operating mainly in Anglo-American universities and government organizations had advanced new logico-mathematical methods for translating observational information about human activities and behaviours into architectural and urban form. The goal of these methods was to define and logically structure design as a step-wise process enabling rigorous analysis of information on design requirements and goals, synthesis of possible design options, and evaluation of these options based on various constraints and criteria.[2] Some systematic design methods, such as for example ones for allocating activities on a floor plan or laying out a building so as to optimize pedestrian circulation, had found numerous implementations in digital electronic computers since the early 1960s and by the end of the decade had become one of the most popular research topics in the nascent field of computer aided architectural design.[3] Complex mathematical models of cities, which parsed urban processes and forms as systems driven by sets of mathematical relationships, were also acquiring what Ira Lowry of the RAND Corporation Logistics Department called "predictive" and "planning" uses: they established causal relationships between design decisions and their social or economic effects that allowed, respectively, to compare the anticipated outcomes of different courses of action or to choose optimal courses of action based on specific goals.[4]

The idea that decisions about the design and management of homes, institutions, and cities could be delegated to data-processing machines — that architectural design could be algorithmically automated— was an influential and widespread vision throughout the 1960s and a key context for the early entanglements of architecture and computing. Around the end of the decade, and within a widespread critique of technocratic thought associated with boisterous social movements in Europe and the United States, came a demand to recalibrate the uses of, and values attached to, mathematics, computation, and computers. A landmark event for signalling a shift away from what had come to be perceived as a scientistic and techno-rational orientation of earlier endeavours to recast design as a systematic process based on mathematics and logic was the Portsmouth conference on Design Methods in Architecture in 1967. With a patent turn toward humanistic values, the conference marked a break from what two authors reporting on the event called the "strictures" of "grotesquely oversimplifying problem solving structures" and tackled the pressing question of "not only how, but why."[5]

This rhetorical recalibration of the algorithmic design processes and tools developed during the 1960s had numerous repercussions and ripple effects — too many to account for in a short essay. A key one worth delaminating though was the retreat from narratives of complete algorithmic automation and the move toward a reintegration of humans into the operation of computational environments.

Cover for the Portsmouth design methods symposium proceedings. Source: Broadbent, Geoffrey, and Anthony Ward, eds. 1969. *Design Methods in Architecture [Symposium at Portsmouth School of Architecture, 1967].* London: Lund Humphries.

"Environments" is construed broadly here, spanning from interactive computer programs for designing architecture to actual physical architectures managed through data like the ones we saw described in *La ville totale.* Nicholas Negroponte, the founder and director of the MIT Department of Architecture's first computing facility that went by the name Architecture Machine, referred to this new agenda for research into design and computing as a "soft [...] computational paradigm"[6] — computation not as stifling, but as enhancing personal meanings and idiosyncrasies.

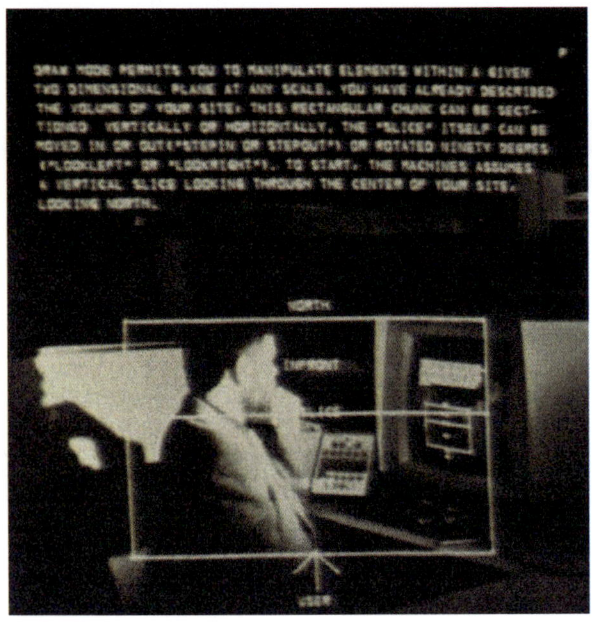

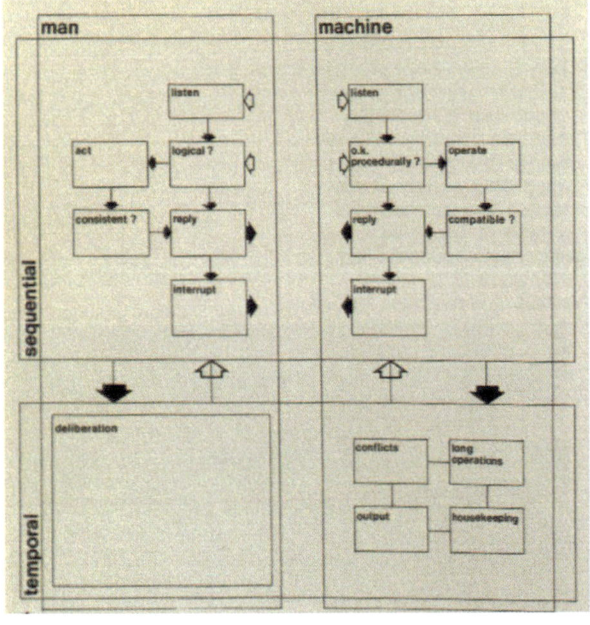

Top: The URBAN 5 system in use: MIT architecture and mechanical engineering graduate Ted Turano observes an explanatory text provided by the system, including a site diagram. The photograph also shows the system's IBM 2250, model 1 cathode ray tube and a set of function-key buttons on which different labels could be overlaid.

Bottom: URBAN 5's temporal and sequential organization.

Source: Negroponte, Nicholas. 1973. *The Architecture Machine: Toward a More Human Environment.* Cambridge, Mass.: MIT Press, 92; 86 respectively.

Introductory image for Warren Brodey's influential article on intelligent environments. Source: Brodey, Warren M. 1967 (May). The Design of Intelligent Environments: Soft Architecture. *Landscape:* 8-12.

A landmark project in recasting ideas of behavioural modelling and algorithmic design under an umbrella of "softness" was "Intelligent Environments." The Architecture Machine launched this project in the late 1960s under the support of the Graham Foundation for Advanced Study in the Fine Arts and Ford Foundation funding through MIT. Intelligent Environments speculated on a physical environment embedded with sensors and effectors and capable of computation that could change in real time according to its inhabitants' behaviour. The project advanced visions of fluid human-machine interaction nascent in earlier computer aided design prototypes by the Architecture Machine, such as the 1967 discursive urban design program URBAN 5,[7] with ideas about conversation and evolutionary learning promoted by influential figures such as Gordon Pask or MIT-trained cybernetician Warren Brodey, from whose writings Negroponte readily appropriated the monikers "soft architectures" and "intelligent environments."[8]

Intelligent Environments combined these cybernetic ideas with late-1960s experiments in natural language processing, face recognition, motion tracking, and semantic processing that were ongoing in the less than 10-year old field of artificial intelligence (AI).[9] Symbolic AI had been birthed in the late 1950s through a distinct break from earlier cybernetic approaches that were strongly entangled with the engineering of physical hardware. Instead, symbolic AI was preoccupied with the computational modelling of various human cognitive or perceptual capabilities as abstract mathematical structures and algorithmic processes.[10] Intelligent Environments remained in the sphere of speculation, mostly because of limitations in embodying fluid transformability in physical building systems. Nonetheless, they tapped into the vogue of "softness" and ephemerality that permeated the American counterculture and dominated the international "radical" architectural scene.[11] Negroponte was avidly pursuing such connections, in efforts to push computer research from the provinces of the "military-industrial complex"[12] to the front line of architectural techno-speculation. Such alliances bootstrapped the otherwise sober exposition of Intelligent Environments as a challenging, yet plausible, research agenda in computational modelling: a far-reaching goal propelling advances in "learning the user."[13]

Negroponte presented a sketch of an intelligent environments theory in the 1971 Design Participation Conference.[14] This was the first international conference of the Design Research Society — an interdisciplinary organization founded in 1966 in the UK to advance work on systematic design methods, and which the turn of the decade found in a state of stalling self-scrutiny about identity and theoretical position vis-à-vis its technocratic legacy. The DRS's impasse was recognized by Nigel Cross, a lecturer and part-time doctoral researcher at the University of Manchester Institute of Science and Technology, who was researching human and machine roles in computer aided design with a specific emphasis on how humans could simulate computer aided design processes without using computers. Circa 1969, Cross proposed to host a conference on the topic of participatory design in the Design Research Laboratory —a lab that design methods instigator John Christopher Jones had set up at UMIST— to address the role of design methods and new technologies in enabling "wider sections of society to actively participate in the processes of planning and design."[15] Fostering a general optimism toward the socially transformative effects of technology, a crucial one being the demise of professional authority, Jones had supported Cross's proposal.[16]

Entitled "Aspects of Living in an Architecture Machine" Negroponte's paper for the conference compared different attitudes toward computationally enhanced physical environments, specifically in relation to how they approached "learning" and "responding" to their inhabitants. The Design Participation conference also coincided with a pivot in the Architecture Machine's work toward a new research project seeking to overhaul architectural professionalism: computer aids to participatory architecture. One year after the conference, the Architecture Machine's eponymous research proposal received a two-year award from the National Science Foundation's (NSF) Institutional

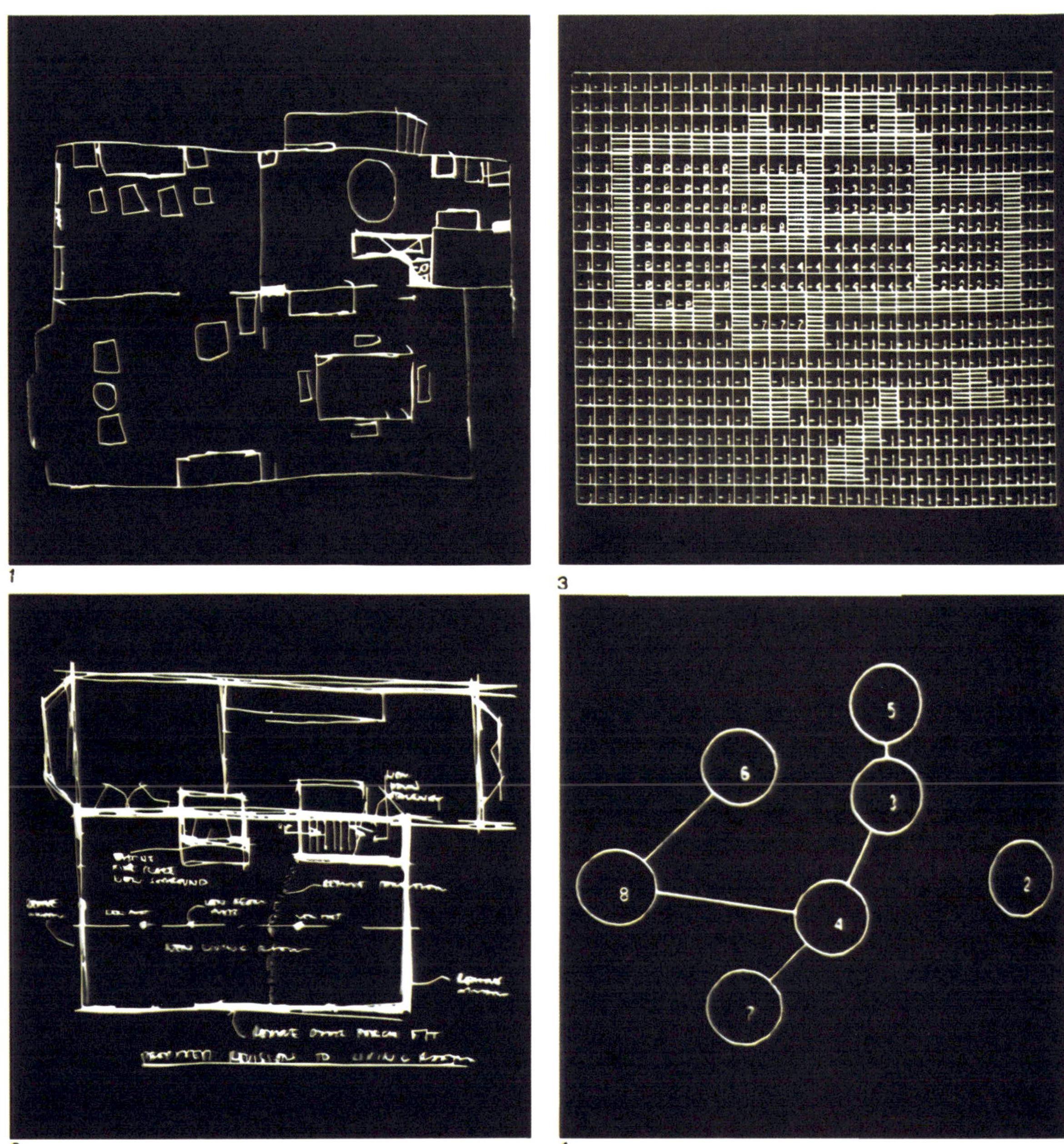

Sketch by someone without architectural training along with its interpretations by a professional architect (bottom left), by the computer as gridded plan (top right) and by the computer as planar graph (bottom right). Source: Negroponte, *Soft Architecture Machines*, 86.

Display and interface of a computer system for do-it-yourself architecture developed by the Architecture Machine. Source: Weinzapfel, Guy, and Nicholas Negroponte. 1976. "Architecture-by-Yourself: An Experiment with Computer Graphics for House Design." In *Proceedings of the 3rd Annual Conference on Computer Graphics and Interactive Techniques*, 74–78. SIGGRAPH '76. New York, N.Y.: ACM, 76.

Support for Science and Computing Activities. The research proposal submitted to the NSF described a "straightforward, free-wheeling, and congenial conversation" between the "proverbial man-in-the-street, who is both a novice in architecture and a novice with machines" and "a machine which has some 'knowledge' of architecture [...] not only appear[ing] to be a 'competent' architect, but [...] a sympathetic conversant, a good model builder, graphically dextrous, and friendly."[17]

The computer system delivering these lofty promises would adapt the technical repertoire of existing systems designed to algorithmically automate design, albeit with a key conceptual shift from "specification" to "recognition."[18] In other words, instead of mandating the input of well-defined constraints and criteria like traditional programs for automatic spatial layout did, it aspired to infer "stated or unstated criteria"[19] from the user's design acts. The conceptual shift toward "recognition" called for an "intelligent" machine that could go beyond the information provided and reason about its meaning on the basis of the information's context – in this case, an evolving model of the system's user.

Despite "draw[ing] very badly," Negroponte later wrote, the architectural novice was "extremely adept at describing physical relations and juxtapositions."[20] A sketch recognition computer routine called SQUINT extracted such implicit positional and relational requirements in a building's layout and represented them as topological diagrams — as graphs. These graphs provided "an initial, though crude, overview of the user's criteria,"[21] while also permitting the use of various graph-based layout generation methods that were proliferating in computer aided architectural design[22] and for which, as Negroponte and Groisser wrote in their research proposal, "these two kinds of criteria (positional and proximity) provide the bulk of the variables."[23] Unlike traditional automatic layout generation programs, the system did not output an optimum or sub-optimum design, but instead itgenerated alternative arrangements and prompted the user to alter them while storing and retrieving "'apparently satisfactory states'."[24] The goal was for the two entities — the user and the machine— to reach a convergence. These cyclical interactions were a modelling exercise: the system was "build[ing] a model of the user's new or modified habitat" while "simultaneously building a model of the user and a model of the user's model of it."[25] A graphics data structure of discrete geometric elements described in terms of position and size was overlaid on a design data structure of topological diagrams extracted from the user's sketches, and tied to a model of the user conceptualized as "a probabilistic chaining of functions and procedures, situations and responses."[26]

Apart from providing a telling example of the ways in which architectural research absorbs, culturally parses, and eventually technically recasts research into computing, the Architecture Machine's proposal carved a specific attitude toward machine intelligence. This attitude aligned with the middle category of the famous triptych "mechanical extension" (automation), "symbiosis" (augmentation) and "artificial intelligence" (replacement), proposed by computing patron J.C.R Licklider in the 1960s.[27] In fact, if early 1960s computer aided design systems sought to *replace* the architect by *automating* an imagined type of work (the generation and evaluation of alternatives),[28] the Architecture Machine cast the middle ground of *symbiosis* as the ultimate frontier of intelligent computing.

Revisiting some of these ambitious early visions is illuminating as questions about the applications of AI (where and to what end) come centre stage again today. From the vast collection of computational methods that have historically fitted the expansive label "Artificial Intelligence" (from decision-making techniques to pattern recognition, and from probabilistic inference to language processing, to name only a few), the genre that captures contemporary architectural imagination is machine learning — a process in which a machine emulates a thing or a task by processing a large number of its instances. As various programming languages dedicated to machine learning help lower the floor of "doing AI," various consortia boldly lay out an optimistic future of various industries and professions being disrupted by data and algorithms.[29] Among them are art and architecture, two areas whose subjective, meaning-rich, and context-dependent dimensions have been a steady challenge for mathematical and algorithmic abstraction.

A recent article featured opinions from various members of the American Institute of Architects (AIA), urging architectural firms to "embrace artificial intelligence" so that they don't "get left behind."[30] It described a future in which architects would accumulate, share, and leverage through machine learning data about the lifecycle of buildings — from the drawing board to full use. The article saw AI as a productivity aid, a way to make the design and construction of buildings or cities "faster and easier" through the learning and automation of various relevant tasks. Architecture, the article reassured, would remain in the hands of human designers because of computers' "limited purview into the nature and proclivities of human experience."

These pragmatic goals about working faster and more productively do not satisfy other groups of researchers who use machine learning to venture, once again, either toward the algorithmic automation of design or the enhancement of designers' imagination. Architectural researchers have been experimenting with training a machine to design floor plans in different architectural styles from scratch after being fed images of architectural drawings.[31] Other similar projects training the network based on the work of one single designer present striking affinities with ideas about emulating specific stylistic idiosyncrasies advanced by the Architecture Machine and allowing the machine to come up with unexpected alternatives.[32] The statistical processing of pixels makes architecture more vulnerable to the surface, style and penmanship than the 1970s topological abstractions did. However, the abstract topological underbellies that ensure the various efficiencies and rationalities of various design options generated by the network persist.[33]

As visions of AI-powered architecture proliferate and excite, we need to look back and understand the visions, challenges, failures, and unresolved —perhaps irresolvable— questions around architecture, design, and computing, and to find critical ways of asking these questions anew or expanding them to new realities. This is both a historical and a creative project. As I have argued elsewhere, in order to understand if computers will be able to design for us, we need to understand how they design, who designed how they design, and what implicit commitments and assumptions about what design is lay at their basis.[34] It is by asking these questions that we might arrive at a provisional response to a nagging suspicion about computers and architecture – a suspicion that architectural researcher Jos Weber once printed in a speech bubble coming out of one of Claude Bell's Cabazon Dinosaurs. Sitting on a desert route between Phoenix and Los Angeles with its metal frame exposed and waiting for its shotcrete coating, the replica of the prehistoric beast pondered: *A new concept for architecture or just a quicker working method?*

Metal frame for Dinny, the brontosaurus, one of Claude Bell's Cabazon Dinosaurs, featured in Jos Weber's mid-1970s report on computer aided design developments in Denmark, Holland, and Germany. Source: Weber, Jos. 1975. Denmark, Holland, Germany. In Negroponte, Nicholas (ed.) *Reflections on Computer Aids to Design and Architecture*, New York, NY: Petrocelli/Charter.

References :

1. Tange, Kenzo, Yona Friedman, Nicholas Negroponte, and R. Buckminster Fuller. 1973. "La Ville Totale." 2000 [*Deuxmille*] : *Revue de l'Amenagement Du Territoire et Du Developpement Regional*, no. 24: 5–7, 5.

2. For histories of design methods see, for example, Bayazit, N. 2004. "Investigating Design: A Review of Forty Years of Design Research." *Design Issues*, 20 (1): 16–29; Broadbent, G. 1988 [1973] Design in Architecture: Architecture and the Human Sciences. Fulton; Cross, Nigel. 2013. "A History of Design Methodology." *In Design Methodology and Relationships with Science*, edited by Marc J. de Vries, Nigel Cross, and D. P. Grant, 15–28. Springer Science & Business Media.

3. N. Cross, *The Automated Architect*, London, UK: Pion Ltd, 1977, 34.

4. Lowry, Ira S. 1965. "A Short Course in Model Design," *Journal of the American Institute of Planners* 31 (2): 158-166.

5. Cave, Collin, and Keith Elvin. 1968. "Design Methods: Not Only How But Why." *The Architects' Journal* 147: 63.

6. Negroponte, Nicholas. 1975. *Soft Architecture Machines*. Cambridge, Mass.: The MIT Press, 147.

7. Negroponte, Nicholas. 1967. "URBAN 5, an On-Line Urban Design Partner." *Ekistics*, 289–91.

8. Brodey, Warren M. 1967. "The Design of Intelligent Environments: Soft Architecture." *Landscape*, no. 17: 8–12.

9. For a detailed discussion of the relationships between the Architecture Machine and AI research see Steenson, Molly. 2017. *Architectural Intelligence: How Designers and Architects Created the Digital Landscape*. Cambridge, Mass.: The MIT Press.

10. For a description of the rift between symbolic AI and cybernetics see, for example, McCorduck, Pamela. 2004. *Machines Who Think: A Personal Inquiry into the History and Prospects of Artificial Intelligence*. 2nd edition. Natick, Mass: A K Peters/CRC Press; Edwards, Paul N. 1997. *The Closed World: Computers and the Politics of Discourse in Cold War America*. *Cambridge*, Mass.: The MIT Press

11. See, for example, Busbea, Larry D. 2017. "Soft Control Material: Environment and Design C. 1970." *Journal of Design History*; Turner, Fred. 2008. *From Counterculture to Cyberculture: Stewart Brand, the Whole Earth Network, and the Rise of Digital Utopianism*. Chicago, IL.: University of Chicago Press; Scott, Felicity D. 2016. *Outlaw Territories: Environments of Insecurity/ Architectures of Counterinsurgency*. New York, N.Y.: Zone Books.

12. Negroponte, Soft Architecture Machines, 99.

13. Groisser, Leon Bennett, and Nicholas Peter Negroponte. 1971. *Computer Aids to Participatory Architecture. Cambridge*, Mass.: Massachusetts Institute of Technology, 32.

14. Negroponte, Nicholas. 1972. "Aspects of Living in an Architecture Machine." In *Design Participation: Proceedings of the Design Research Society's Conference, Manchester, September 1971*, edited by Nigel Cross, 63–67. London: Academy Editions.

15. Cross, Nigel. 1972. "Preface." In *Design Participation: Proceedings of the Design Research Society's Conference, Manchester, September 1971*, edited by Nigel Cross, 6. London: Academy Editions.

16. Cross, Interview by Vardouli, published in Vardouli, Theodora. 2017. "Graphing Theory: New Mathematics, Design, and the Participatory Turn." Cambridge, Mass.. Massachusetts Institute of Technology

17. Negroponte and Groisser, *Computer Aids to Participatory Architecture, i.*

18. Negroponte, *Soft Architecture Machines*, 119.

19. Negroponte and Groisser, *Computer Aids to Participatory Architecture*, 23.

20. Negroponte, *Soft Architecture Machines*, 121.

21. Negroponte and Groisser, *Computer Aids to Participatory Architecture*, 28.

22. See, for example, Grason, J. 1970. A dual linear graph representation for space-filling location problems of the floor plan type. In Moore., G.T. (ed.). Emerging Methods in Environmental Design and Planning, Cambridge, MA: The Design Methods Group, 170-178.

23. Ibid.

24. Ibid., 19.

25. Ibid., 7.

26. Ibid.

27. Licklider, J.C.R. 1960. "Man-Computer Symbiosis." *IRE Transactions on Human Factors in Electronics* HFE-1 (March): 4–11.

28. Vardouli T and David Theodore. 2020. "Walking instead of Working: Space Allocation, Automatic Architecture, and the Abstraction of Hospital Labor" *IEEE Annals of the History of Computing* [Early Access] doi: 10.1109/MAHC.2020.2990111

29. See for example, Montréal.ai's AI-First Conglomerate Overarching Program [Online]: https://montrealartificialintelligence.com/#MONTREAL-AI's-Umbrella-Montreal-AI-First-Conglomerate

30. O'Donnell, Kathleen M. 2018. Embracing Artificial Intelligence in Architecture. [Online]: https://www.aia.org/articles/178511-embracing-artificial-intelligence-in-archit:46

31. Chaillou, Stanislas. 2019. AI & Architecture: An Experimental Perspective. [Online]: https://towardsdatascience.com/ai-architecture-f9d78c6958e0.

32. For an overview of generative deep learning methods in architecture see Newton, David. 2019. Generative Deep Learning in Architectural Design, Technology|Architecture + Design, 3:2, 176-189.

33. Landes, J., Dissen, H., Fure, H., and S. Chaillou. 2020. Architecture as a Graph: A Computational Approach. [Online]: https://towardsdatascience.com/architecture-as-a-graph-6a835d46f918

34. Faculty of Engineering Dean's Report. 2020 (Winter). Architecture Lab Aims to Understand How AI Systems Undertake Design. University Advancement Office at the Faculty of Engineering, McGill University

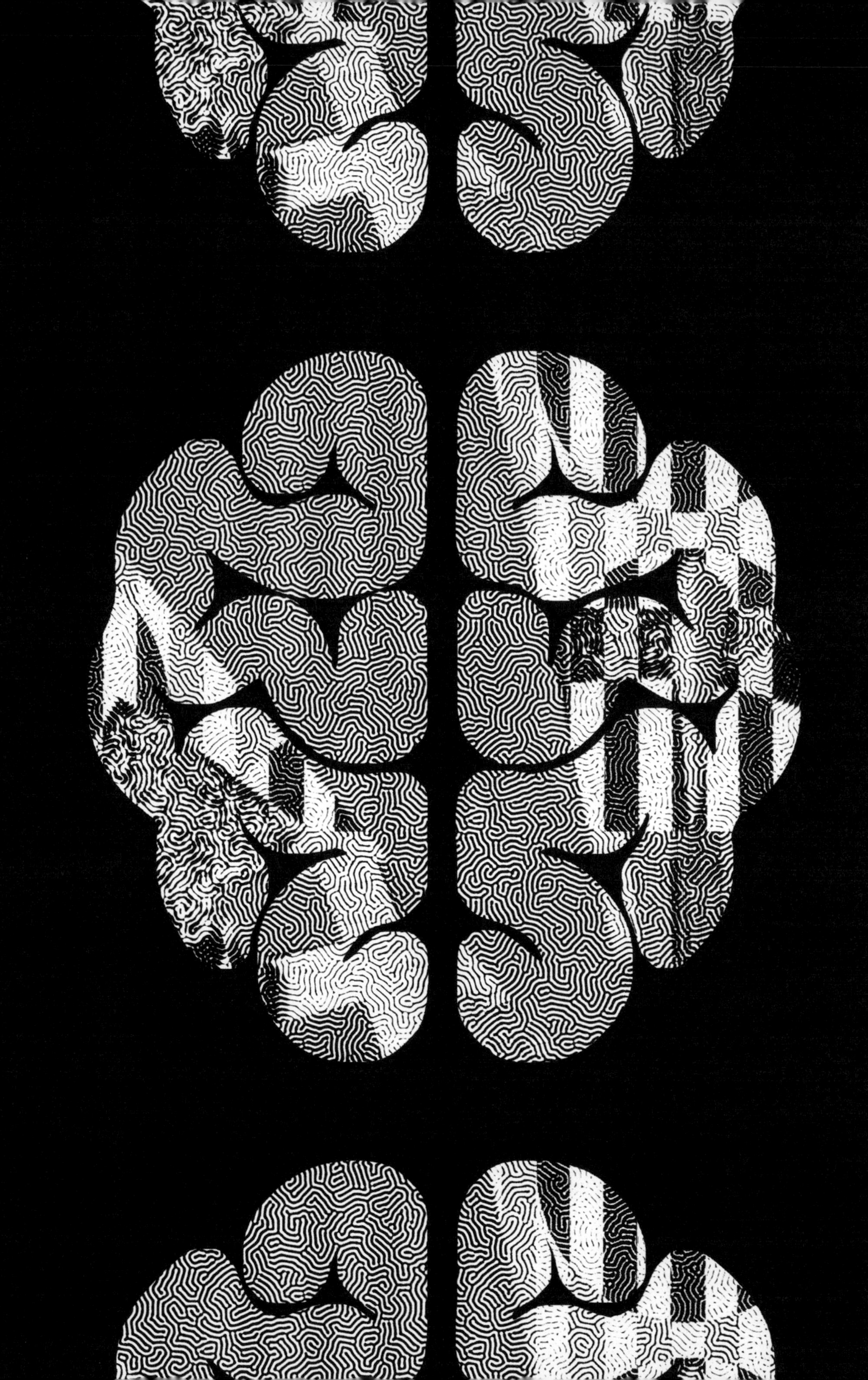

Semantics in Architecture From Words to Forms and Back Again

Stanislas Chaillou

This article reopens the parallel established between architecture and linguistics and posits semantics as a natural and necessary step forward for the architectural discipline. This analogy comes at a crucial point in time, as the intersection between artificial intelligence (AI) and architecture is, from a theoretical standpoint, still ill-defined. Overly documented and vaguely understood, the encounter between AI and our discipline has yet to find a name, or at least a framework. In this context, we believe that semantics offers the ideal analogy to address this junction. While borrowing once again from linguistics, semantics provides a powerful framework to apprehend what appears to us as a new era in Architecture.

Figure 1: GAN-Generated Masterplan. Source: Stanislas Chaillou.

In linguistics, semantics is devoted to the study of meaning. It is concerned with the relationship between the language and what it actually represents. It investigates reality through the documentation and modeling of significations. From the early work of Ferdinand de Saussure[1] to Tim Berners-Lee's Semantic Web[2], semantics has grown beyond the boundaries of linguistics to irrigate many other fields, providing them with an entirely new paradigm. And today, semantics allows us to go beyond the status quo, which dedicates grammar as the exclusive lens for considering architecture. Since Christopher Alexander[3] and *A Pattern Language*[4], this analogy between design and grammar has been a fruitful path. However, it is now showing the signs of its limitations, as discussed later in this piece. In light of this situation, we posit that the notion of "meaning" can unite discussions and research around a richer analogy.

Words, Grammar, Semantics

Linguistics has long been intertwined with adjacent disciplines. Over the past century, the work of logicians, philosophers and epistemologists has blossomed alongside linguists' efforts. From the Vienna Circle to the French Structuralists, the study of language has stood time and time again as an essential part of broader intellectual discussions. Language indeed remains the subject of profound debates among scholars, stretching beyond the scope of linguistics itself. Among the many fields that have borrowed from linguistics, architecture has benefited from its frameworks and its logics.

Linguistics offers taxonomies that are relevant to our discipline. The study of language unfolds on multiple levels, including words, grammar and semantics, to name the most important ones (see Figure 2). In most languages, words are the essential building blocks; their breadth, function and meaning constitute the investigative field of lexicology. From words to their assembly, language then aggregates sentences. Following rules, grammar and syntax formulate the process of forming these sentences as organized sequences. Defining the underlying logic of that aggregation is what motivates grammarians. However, beyond the strict grammatical effectiveness of discourse, however, lies its meaning. As linguists like Ogden & Richards[5] have realized, the additive logic of grammar fails to ensure the validity of the language significations. In fact, among experts, semantics has taken over, providing the tools to study and explain the structure of significations. By providing a more holistic attention to meaning, it has managed to round up its methodology and eventually surpass the empirical nature of the grammatical logic. By investigating the nature of relations and correlations, semantics unpacks signification as the relationships in context between the parts and the whole.

Words, grammar and semantics are some of the essential layers helping linguists to study languages. Not only useful in linguistics, such layers stand as distinct statements: when asked to represent reality, each one offers its own theory and methodology. Transposing their respective principles onto architecture has constituted radical frameworks to conceptualize our practice, which still define our approach to design today.

Semantics

Function → ***to Signify***
Form → ***the Field***
Mode → ***the Relation***

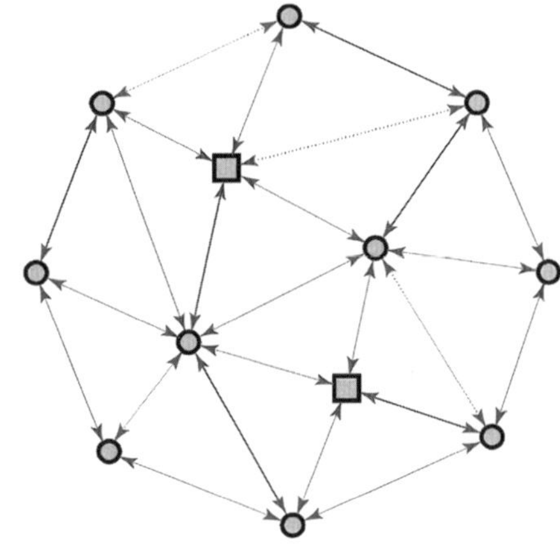

Grammar

Function → ***to Order***
Form → ***the Sequence***
Mode → ***the Rule***

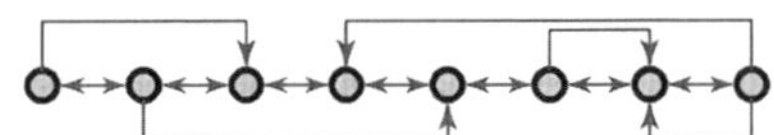

Words

Function → ***to Name***
Form → ***the Point***
Mode → ***the Unit***

Figure 2: From Words, to Semantics. Source: Stanislas Chaillou.

The profession is effectively living under the influence of the grammatical logic. Christopher Alexander's theory of the Pattern Language has been, in this respect, a decisive step forward. In short, this doctrine consists in applying a grammatical structure to the architectural expression. It has made it possible not only to abstract buildings as collections of objects, but also to bind them together through explicit rules and properties so as to form "patterns", in Alexander's words. Over time, this theory has emulated the way grammar typically assembles language into "object-oriented" software development, a paradigm which has been structuring how most practitioners still conceive buildings today. BIM remains the most vivid expression of this grammar-driven approach in our industry. In hindsight, we realize that the mindset of an entire generation of architects has been significantly shaped by Alexander's theory.

Although quite effective, this paradigm has led to an oversimplification. In our opinion, it has failed to capture the profound complexity inherent to architecture; much like grammar fell short of capturing meaning in linguistics, its principles did not suffice to grasp architecture's deep intricacies. At this stage, three simple observations sum up our position:

(1) buildings are more than the aggregations of their individual parts, (2) architecture is in essence highly contextual, and (3) the diversity of architectural forms associates multiple shapes with a single concept.

This evidence all points us towards a shift toward semantics as a new founding analogy, away from the current grammatical legacy.

The Multiple Contributions of Semantics

Semantics represents for architecture both an unprecedented promise and a proven methodology. This approach has indeed demonstrated a greater capacity than the grammatical one when it comes to abstracting and representing complex universes.

More practically, the semantic principles have found their best expression under the form of "semantic graphs". These graphs combine the triple benefit of being an abstract mode of representation, an expressive type of database and an effective design tool. Information theory has drawn great benefits from them. First, it has found the means to account for the complexity and contextuality of relations among elements in a system. Second, it has lifted standard representations of reality, like graphs, up to a brand-new level of expressivity. And, finally, it has enriched the way we formulate problems to computers and, more importantly, to AI systems. All three avenues are significant contributions of semantics that are especially relevant to the practice of architecture.

Relations & Context

Contextual and relational concerns are consubstantial to architecture. The form of a building always factors in the influence of its immediate context and its relationship with its surroundings. François Recanati, linguist and semantician, reminds us that, in language, "propositions only carry meaning in the context of their enunciation".[6] Conversely, reflecting this concern of semantics speaks to an essential dimension of architecture.

Semantic graphs, thanks to their structure, "de facto" qualify their constituents by defining and weighting the relationships each of them entertains with its neighbors. Evidently, none of them could exist without the support and relation to a broader set of items. By nesting this logic, semantic graphs model the transition across scales, reflecting the interdependence between the city, the buildings, their rooms, etc. As semantics defines fields across languages, semantic graphs can weave networks among built forms. In this way, they bring together architectural shapes and their surroundings and elaborate a more connected, holistic and expandable web of relations.

The Web is initially a flat relational collection of documents.

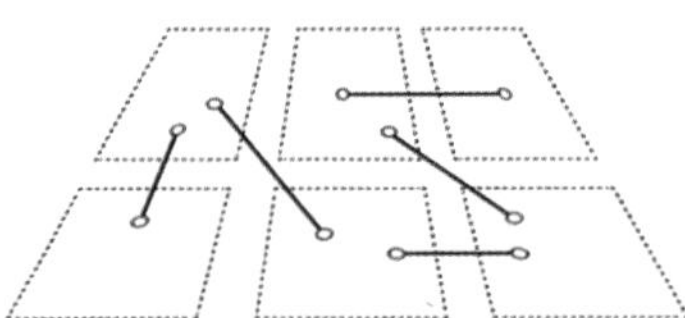

Users reason about the Web using their own set of abstract concepts, that the Web's structure does not reflect.

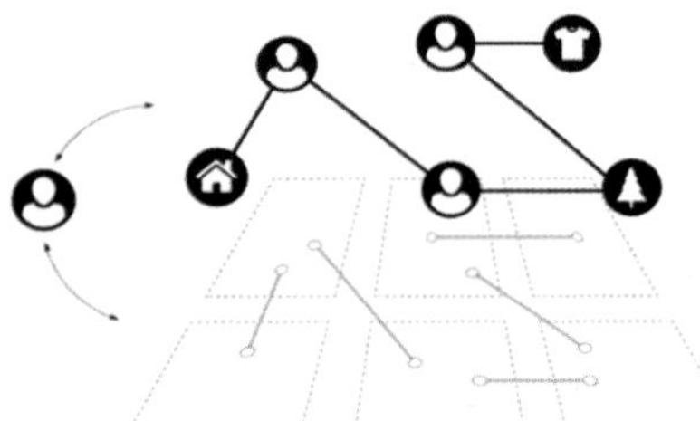

Tim Berners-Lee proposes to tie a semantic overlay to the Internet's architecture, thus providing, according to him, an "isomorphism between the Web and reality".

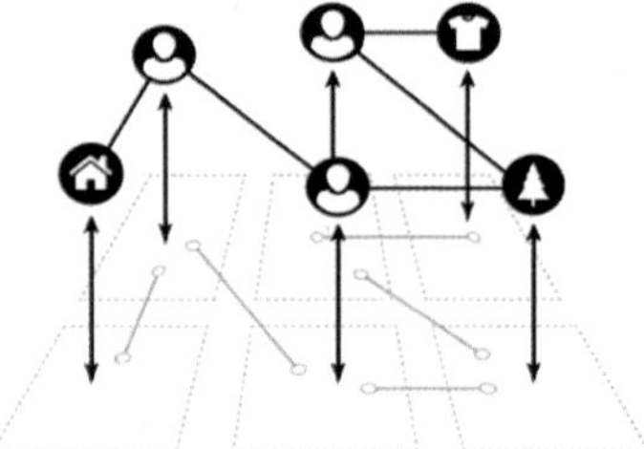

Figure 3: "The Need for Semantics in the Web", Tim Berners Lee at the Geneva WWW Convention 1994. Source: T.B. Lee, 1994.

Expressivity

Semantics can then open a new chapter for representation technics in architecture. To this day, the structural evolution of the Web's architecture stands as a striking precedent, showcasing the potential of semantic abstraction. In 1994, Tim Berners-Lee expressed the urgency of adding a "semantic layer" to the Internet (Figure 3).[7] Back in the early 90s, the Web simply offered an extensive constellation of undifferentiated documents. Berners-Lee's conviction was to reinforce this initial wireframe by bundling semantic descriptors to document every level of the Web's architecture so as to build an extensive semantic graph. By increasing the expressivity of its graph, the Internet, over the past 20 years, has incrementally been able to reflect, in its structure, the topics described by its content. Berners-Lee's hope, namely achieving an "isomorphism between the Internet and reality", is in fact today well underway. At its core lies the recourse to semantic graphs to depict reality.

Overall, we believe semantic graphs can provide the same expressivity to architecture. For our discipline, they are the opportunity to structure, organize and visualize knowledge. They make it possible to better document the importance and the variety of relationships and correlations across our built environment, while enriching the expressivity of our representations. Figure 4 illustrates, in the form of a semantic graph, what could be a typical translation of a standard plan into its corresponding semantic abstraction. The ontology, shown in the legend in Figure 5, defines the terminology used (families of nodes and connections) to establish the graph above it. Crafting the terminology of our graphs, by organizing relevant ontologies, will be one of the essential challenges of semantics in architecture.

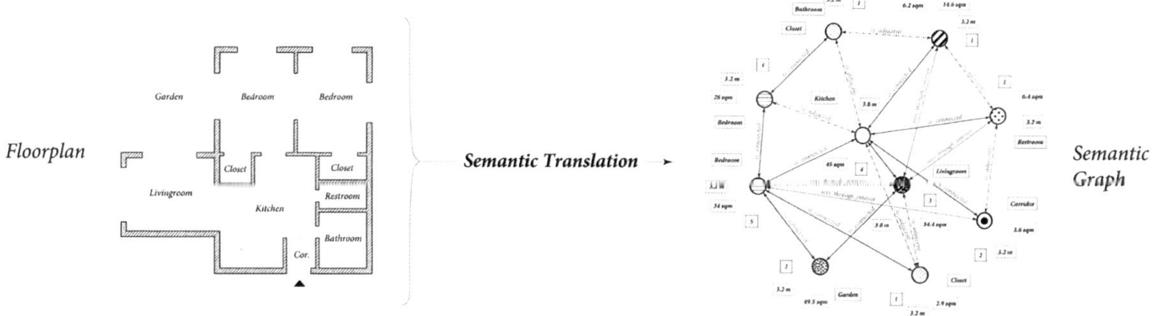

Figure 4: From Architecture to Semantic Graphs. Source: T.B. Lee, 1994.

The use of semantic graphs is far more than a modification of our representation modes alone. It allows architectural knowledge to be embedded in the very fabric of its representation. As nodes and edges in our graphs are tagged with architectural concepts, these webs become an expressive and useful abstraction of architecture, much like the Semantic Web lifted the confusion of the Internet to a richer level of expressivity.

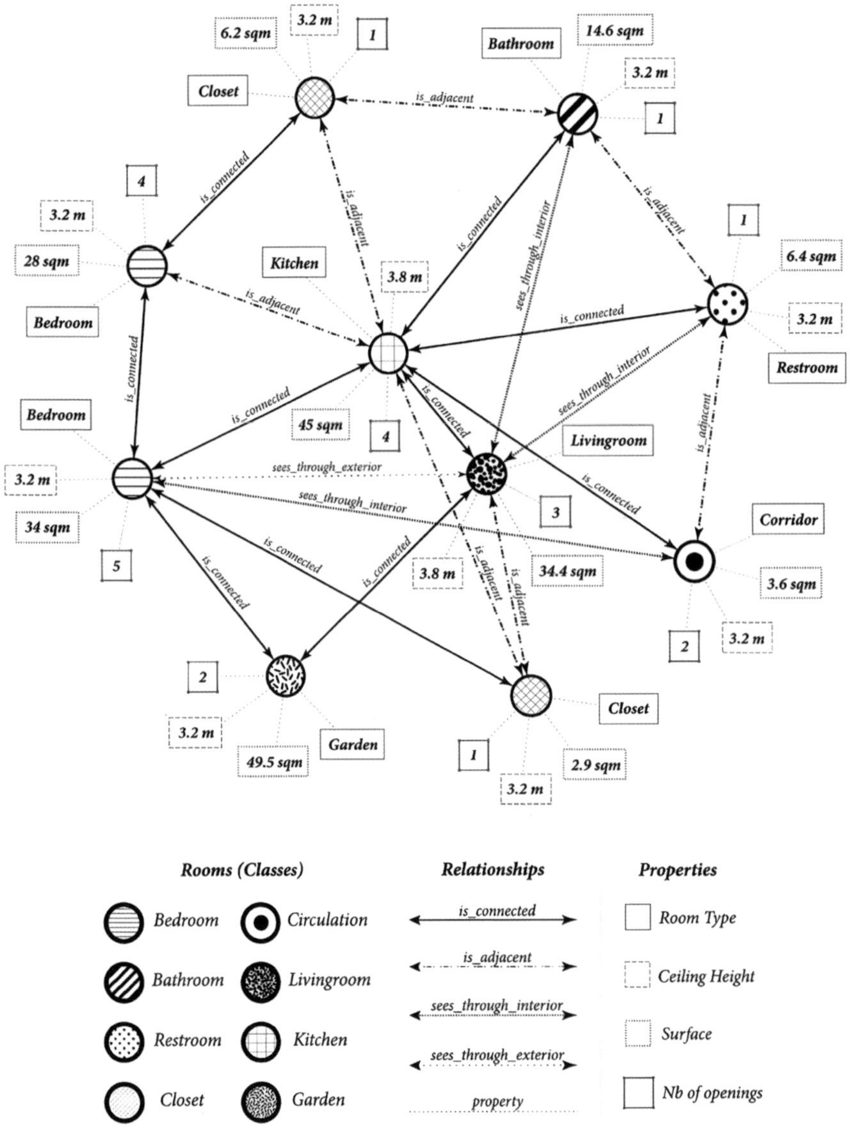

Figure 5: A Typical Semantic Graph in Architecture. Source: Stanislas Chaillou.

Artificial Intelligence

Unquestionably, AI is slowly entering the practice of architecture, beyond the strict realm of academic research. The contribution we expect from AI models will only be as rich as the information we communicate to the machine. Semantic graphs and their expressivity are, in that respect, an ideal springboard to formulate the signification and structure of architectural ideas. In return, artificial intelligence is expected to contribute to architecture in, at least, two distinct ways: namely, inference and generation (Figure 6).

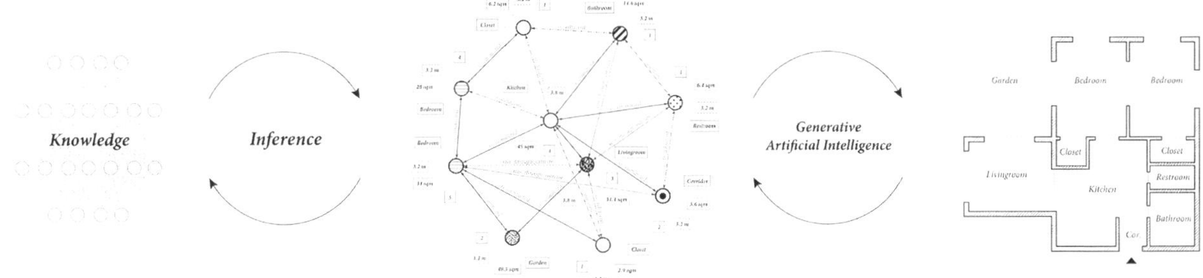

Figure 6: Knowledge < Inference > Semantic Graphs < Generative AI > Generation. Source: Stanislas Chaillou.

On the one hand, semantic graphs open the door to inference in architecture. By definition, inferring consists in admitting a proposition because of its link with a prior proposition held to be true. In computer science, an inference engine makes it possible to conduct logical reasoning and to derive conclusions from a baseline of facts and knowledge. Inference thrives, in fact, in fields of representation where knowledge is "a priori" structured. This point is crucial, and this is precisely what the abstraction of architectural forms into semantic graphs offers. The transition from our built environment to a more expressive and structured representation can help us automate tasks involving simple reasoning. In turn, inference should allow queries to reveal new induced realities beyond the existing elements of a built environment. The semantic graph, coupled with inference systems, is indeed a radical improvement over the profession's current practices. Today, within the "object-oriented" paradigm, a building is essentially indexed in the form of lists of objects and relationships between them. BIM models themselves are based on this indexing of objects, known as a "relational database" (RDB). Because these lists are "flat" and inexpressive, their format provides an abstraction that is not rich enough to allow machines to perform complex reasoning. Semantic graphs, however, bind complexity and hierarchy to the description of built forms. Conversely, inference engines can deduce new connections and propositions thanks to the richness of their structure.

On the other hand, a semantic representation of architecture allows artificial intelligence to ingest more high-level details about architectural taxonomies. A semantic graph can precisely convey to an AI model, for instance, not only a program but the relationships among rooms, the nature of these relations, etc. In turn, this enables current generative AI technics (Generative Adversarial Networks[8] & Variational Autoencoders[9]) to create more informed architectural forms. Artificial intelligence has, in fact, recently provided convincing

results, showing precisely how documented graphs provide an efficient representation to interface with most generative AI models. To name a few, projects like House-GAN,[10] Graph2plan[11], and others have demonstrated the value of graph-constrained generation. Figure 7A & 7B display, respectively, typical results from Graph2plan and House-GAN, where an annotated graph is turned into floor plans using a GAN-based approach. Although the input graph is not quite a semantic graph, this research outlines future developments where semantically enriched networks could abstract architectural concepts, to then be fed into generative AI models.

Figure 7 A: Graph2Plan results. Source: Graph2Plan, Hu et al., April 2020.

Figure 7 B: House-GAN typical results. Source: House-GAN, Nauata et al., March 2020.

Between inference and generation, the value of semantics graphs can translate into two very tangible outcomes. The state of current research lays down the technical feasibility of both avenues.

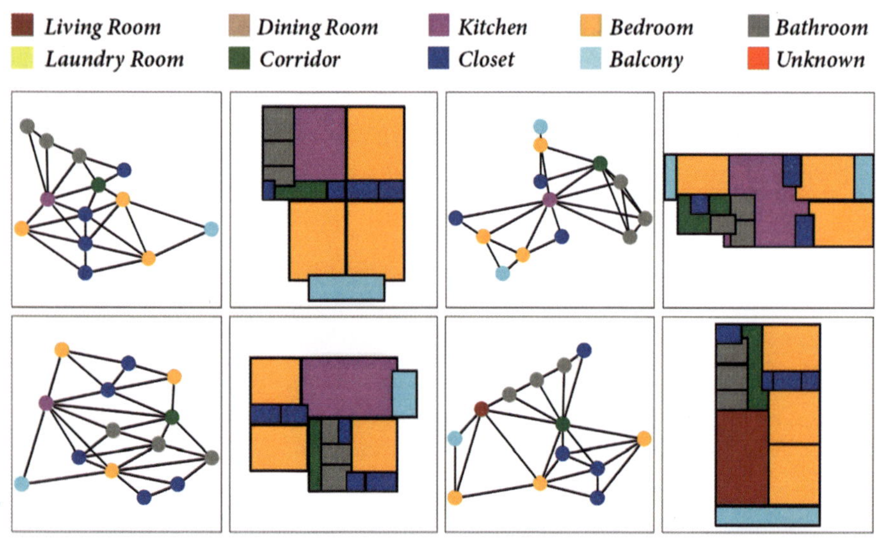

To conceptualize and control the immediacy of such applications, we believe semantics carries the right framework.

This article presents the potential of transposing semantics' principles onto architecture. However, to fully unpack the richness of this analogy, we invite further investigations on both its theoretical and experimental fronts. Formulating a consistent and rigorous discourse, borrowing from semantics' core axioms, can provide architecture with a new chapter in its theory. Then delving into the details of tangible applications will evidence the claim our article aims to put forward. The state of research shows early signs of the semantic principles applied to architecture using AI. These results, alongside the broader progress in artificial intelligence research across the board, are the foundation for our hope for the experimental demonstration of our theory in the years to come.

References

1. Ferdinand de Saussure (26 November 1857 – 22 February 1913) was a Swiss linguist, semiotician and philosopher. He is widely considered one of the founders of 20th-century linguistics and semiotics. His ideas laid a foundation for many significant developments in semantics.

2. "Information Management: A Proposal", Tim Berners-Lee, 1989, & "The Semantic Web Roadmap", Time Berners-Lee, 1998.

3. Christopher Wolfgang Alexander (born 4 October 1936 in Vienna, Austria) is a widely influential British-American architect and design theorist, and currently emeritus professor at the University of California, Berkeley. His theories about the nature of human-centered design have affected fields beyond architecture, including urban design, software, sociology and others. In software, Alexander is regarded as the father of the pattern language movement. The first wiki—the technology behind Wikipedia—came directly from Alexander's work, according to its creator, Ward Cunningham. Alexander's work has also influenced the emergence of agile software development.

4. *A Pattern Language*, C. Alexander, 1977, & *The Timeless Way of Building*, C. Alexander, 1979.

5. *The Meaning of Meaning: A Study of the Influence of Language upon Thought and of the Science of Symbolism*, Ogden & Richards, 1923.

6. "Philosophie du Langage et de l'Esprit", Leçon Inaugurale au Collège de France, François Recanati, December 2019.

7. "The Need for Semantics in the Web", Tim Berners-Lee, WWW Geneva Convention, 2004.

8. A generative adversarial network (GAN) is a class of machine learning frameworks designed by Ian Goodfellow and his colleagues in 2014. Two neural networks contest with each other in a game (in the sense of game theory, often but not always in the form of a zero-sum game). Given a training set, this technique learns to generate new data with the same statistics as the training set. For example, a GAN trained on photographs can generate new photographs that look at least superficially authentic to human observers, having many realistic characteristics.

9. An autoencoder is a type of artificial neural network used to learn efficient data encodings in an unsupervised manner. The aim of an autoencoder is to learn a representation (encoding) for a set of data, typically for dimensionality reduction, by training the network to ignore signal "noise". Along with the reduction side, a reconstructing side is learnt, where the autoencoder tries to generate from the reduced encoding a representation as close as possible to its original input, hence its name.

10. "House-GAN: Relational Generative Adversarial Networks for Graph-constrained House Layout Generation", Nelson Nauata, Kai-Hung Chang, Chin-Yi Cheng, Greg Mori, Yasutaka Furukawa, March 2020.

11. "Graph2Plan: Learning Floorplan Generation from Layout Graphs", Ruizhen Hu, Zeyu Huang, Yuhan Tang, Oliver van Kaick, Hao Zhang, Hui Huang, April 2020.

AI & Urban Environments

How can AI be used to enhance creativity in urban design?

What do we optimise for in design, when using codes and algorithms?

Will codes contribute to deeper learning of cultural phenomena?

Which technologies can help us monitor urban dynamic flows?

Can AI serve as a cartographic device that records aesthetic conditions in architecture?

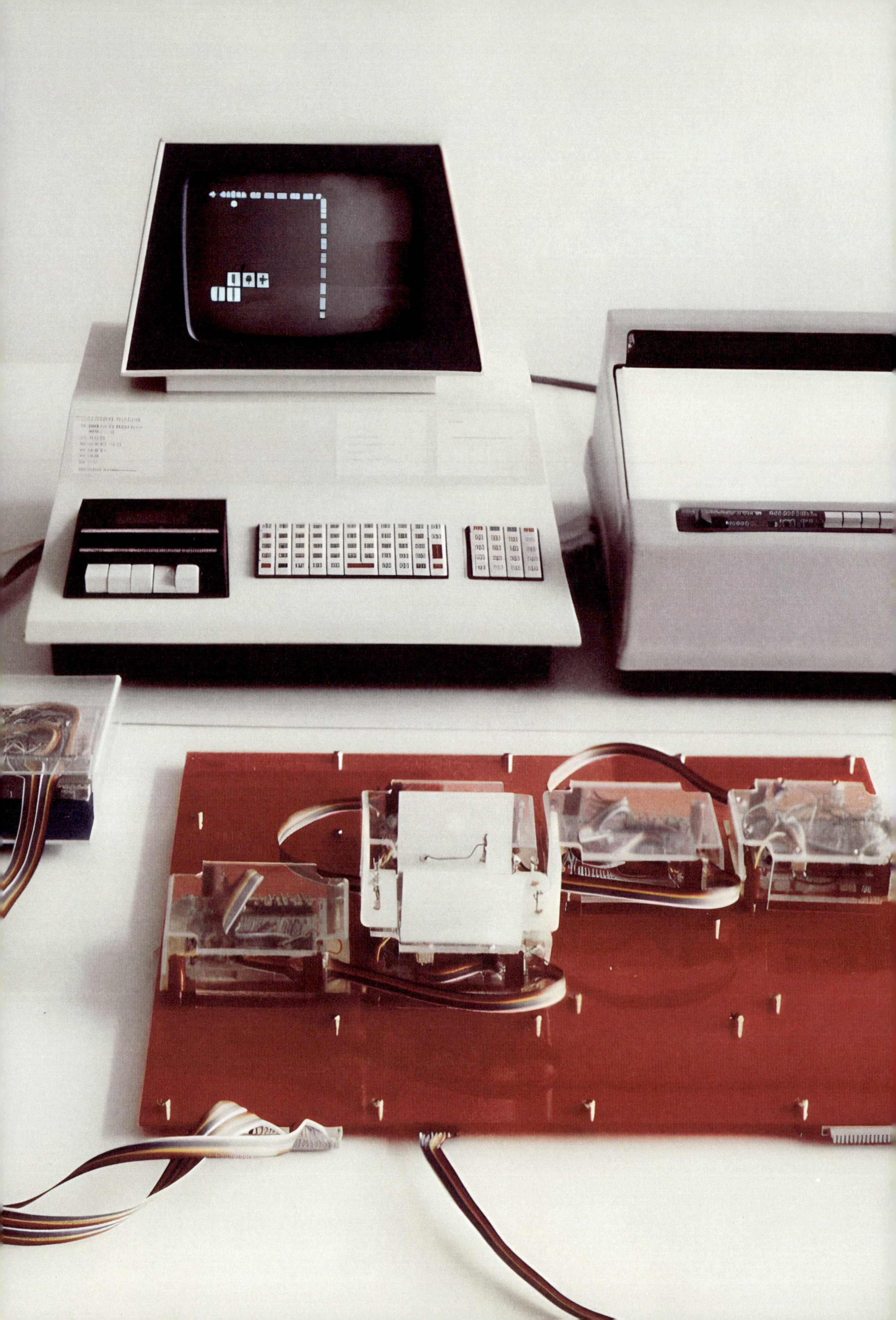

Architecture and Intelligence

Molly Wright Steenson
in conversation with
Areti Markopoulou and Jordi Vivaldi

In most of the work of researchers to define and describe the history of Artificial Intelligence in architecture, we observe a direct connection with architects and cybernetics back in the 1960. Molly Wright Steenson is a writer, designer and historial that has extensively researched the origins of Artificial Intelligence in Architecture and how research on cybernetics, computation and AI has been influenced by the work of visionary architects in the 1960s and vice versa. Steenson investigates how these architects pushed the boundaries of architecture and how their technological experiments pushed the boundaries of technology. Thinking and writing about the past, future and present of AI, architecture and design, Steenson discusses what is intelligence in architecture, our vision of AI as society and how we think and deal with forms of intelligence that might change what we design.

Previous page:
View of working electronic model of the Generator project, between 1976 and 1979. Cedric Price fonds Collection Centre Canadien d'Architecture/ Canadian Centre for Architecture, Montréal.

Areti Markopoulou: Along the effort of understanding the origins of Artificial Intelligence in Architecture, which are the most essential questions we should deal with?

I would like to start by asking you about the essence of your work in the last few years, particularly in relation to the potential and limitations of the use of artificial intelligence (AI) in architecture and, more specifically, in the urban field.

Molly Wright Steenson: I have been researching the intersection of AI and architecture since 2007, when I encountered one footnote in Christopher Alexander's Notes on the Synthesis of Form (Chapter 1, Footnote 19) where he referred to Claude Shannon, Marvin Minsky and Ross Ashby. Their work on AI, cybernetics and information theory didn't talk about the societal implications of those kinds of systems. I would say that, at that point in time, Alexander thought of cities as a diagram.

But for me it was the first mention I've seen of AIround 2007 everyone seemed obsessed with the idea of cybernetics, which differs in a number of ways from AI. Since then I have been chasing down the implications of that footnote. Everything has revolved around a few questions: what is intelligence in architecture? Why were architects in the sixties and seventies working with AI researchers closely? Why did AI researchers need architects? What is clear is that, in those early days, the idea of AI was already present in the architectural field.

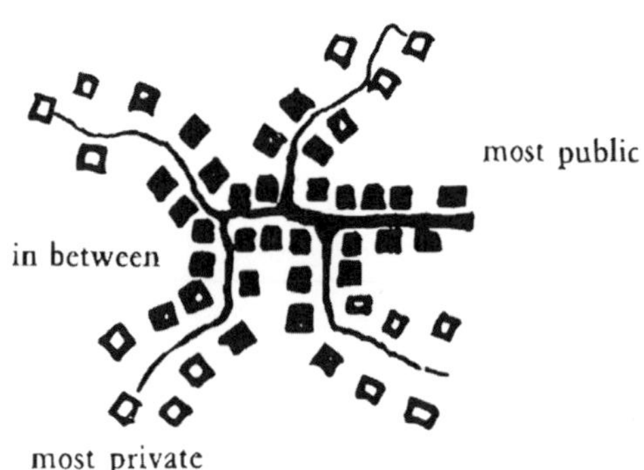

Diagram of the positioning of housing in an urban environment according to their level of privacy. Christopher Alexander, 1977.

People may not realise that we've been generally using the term "artificial intelligence" since 1985; Pamela McCorduck, one of the most well-known historians of the AI and the author of *Machines Who Think,* points out that actually, we've been talking about notions of intelligence and systems since the Egyptians.

So, when we look contemporarily to the issue of AI, I still go back to John McCarthy, who coined the term "artificial intelligence" and who said that machines could do tasks that would traditionally require people's intelligence to be done. And it is precisely in this idea of a "machine who thinks" where most researchers today find the definition of AI.

AM Indeed, in reality cybernetics and AI are different ways of thinking about intelligent systems. Although, it seems to be a common thinking that AI is an evolution of cybernetics, one could argue that cybernetics deals with a much more holistic view of intelligence, especially because it focuses on how systems could self-regulate and act in constant feedback with the environment which is far beyond computational. How would we define, today the idea of intelligence in space and what's the main difference of the ways AI has been applied in the architectural visions back in the early days compared to today?

MW Here it is crucial to understand how we define the term "intelligence". Many researchers that use the term AI seem to refer to the computational phenomena; one can see this happening in most of the students of our schools. It is also easier to say AI than it is to say "machine learning", "neural network" or "computation". In many cases, the use of the term AI just has come to stand for something that it actually doesn't mean. What seems to be also pretty common in the use of the term AI is its close relation to the question of the future: most of the use of the term by traditional press (New York Times, Washington Post etc) in United States and by academic journals and conversations about artificial intelligence almost always implicate the word "future" in the top 10 or 20 of its keywords.

This is something interesting: it indicates that AI is not only about using the computer, but about having a vision of it. If we talk about AI, we want to talk about a vision of what computation does today and could do in the future.

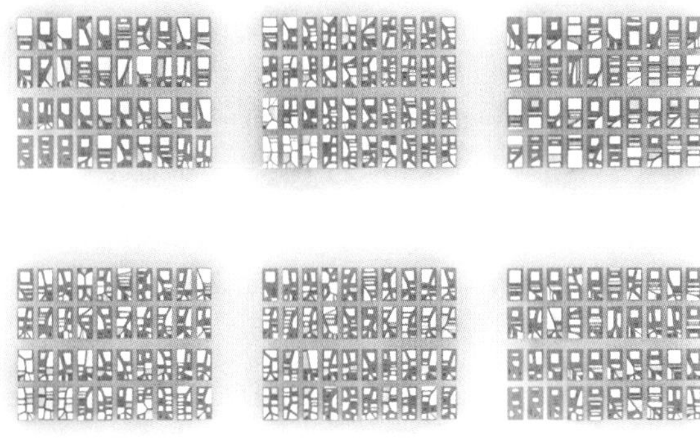

Manhattan, Development of Urban Tissue. IAAC, MaCT 2020/21 by students: Kshama Patil, Simone Grasso, Sinay Coskun, Stephania-Maria Kousoula and faculty: Milad Showkatbakhsh.

Under the definition of "artificial general intelligence" as a thinking machine, conventionally two big narratives seem to prevail: on the one side, the exciting intelligence that brings us new ways of being and new ways of thinking, on the other side, the "dark intelligence" that could take over the world and snuff us out. Those ideas of "ultraingelligence" have been present since 1964, and I point this out because I think that, as an historian of AI working on the contemporary implications of it, in many ways nothing is new and in other ways everything is new. These AI optimistic or pessimistic visions are certainly old, but what we can actually do is new.

I think that one key difference today is that storage has become very cheap. We also have very fast connectivity, way more mobility and the implementation of processes of miniaturization that were not present in the 60s or 70s. Today, we even started moving away from the term "big data"; we were very keen on that term in the early 2010s, but then from 2017 on it began to flip into AI. Data is still the new oil, since AI needs data to run: if you have no data, you have no AI. But now, if you look for example at how a university like ours is treating the big questions of AI, you realize that today engineers approach the AI as an infrastructure that can be physical or cyber, as occurs for example in the AI of autonomous vehicles. They are thinking in terms of engineered systems, not only in terms of computer science, that is, not only in the sense of building algorithms and looking at aspects of machine learning, of natural language processing and at the chips that are going to be required to develop these protocols.

In this sense, it is interesting to compare, in light of AI's instrumentalization, how computer scientists might get trained and how an architect, designer or maybe even a business strategist would get trained. For example, Carnegie Mellon University's School of Computer Science has the first AI major in the country for undergraduates. So you can major in artificial intelligence as something different from computer science by studying computer science and math core courses, but also human computer interaction and ethics. But training in AI from the perspective of design reverses this order: we start with ethics, that is, we start with people and with the locations where they live, then we look at their interactions, and finally, maybe you look at programming languages together with math and science.

Jordi Vivaldi: In relation to the visionary vocation of discourses orbiting around AI, in the field of architecture and urbanism AI usually seems to be connected with processes of optimisation, automatisation, efficiency, prediction, monitoring... In brief, processes of problem-solving. However, since we are speaking about intelligence, one cannot but think how this intelligence, precisely because of being intelligent, could transcend these tasks and impact the field of architecture in a deeper manner.

I have in mind other historical episodes in which the arrival of certain techniques radically changed the practice of architecture. The generalisation of the arch in the roman period or of concrete and steel technologies during the 19th century are good examples of it, crystallizing in novel architectural typologies as for example the skyscraper. Can the arrival of AI in the field of architecture and urbanism have a similar impact?

MW I would like to go through some of the things you said, which I think are good to pull out through this discussion. The question of automation is certainly a big question for AI: which kind of labour can AI automate? At the end of the day, this is actually very much a human question: people get disintermediated when certain things are automated. The question of automation is very much at the core of corporate interests in AI around the world and, more specifically, in the world of engineered systems. But you also highlighted the question of problem-solving, which is very much the language of "problem finding", "problem fitting", and, above all, "problem worrying", which is one of my favourite terms from the late MIT architecture professor Stanford Anderson. The question of problem-solving is related with that of heuristics and has its genesis in the 1970s, if not in the 19th century. Herbert Simon and Allen Newell got the notion of heuristics from George Pólya's book How to Solve It and that's from where early design thinking takes inspiration. In this sense, I keep myself at a distance from reducing architecture to questions of form or type; I like to rattle those edges a little bit because I think that the formulas on which we got stuck in for the last 30 years haven't been very productive for humans and cities.

Following page: "Organisational Plan as Programme", from the minutes of the Fun Palace cybernetics committee meeting, 27th January 1965. Cedric Price fonds Collection Centre Canadien d'Architecture/ Canadian Centre for Architecture, Montréal.

Following double page: Diagram of electronic communication network, Oxford Corner House, London, 1965. Cedric Price fonds Collection Centre Canadien d'Architecture/ Canadian Centre for Architecture, Montréal.

Organisational Plan as Programme

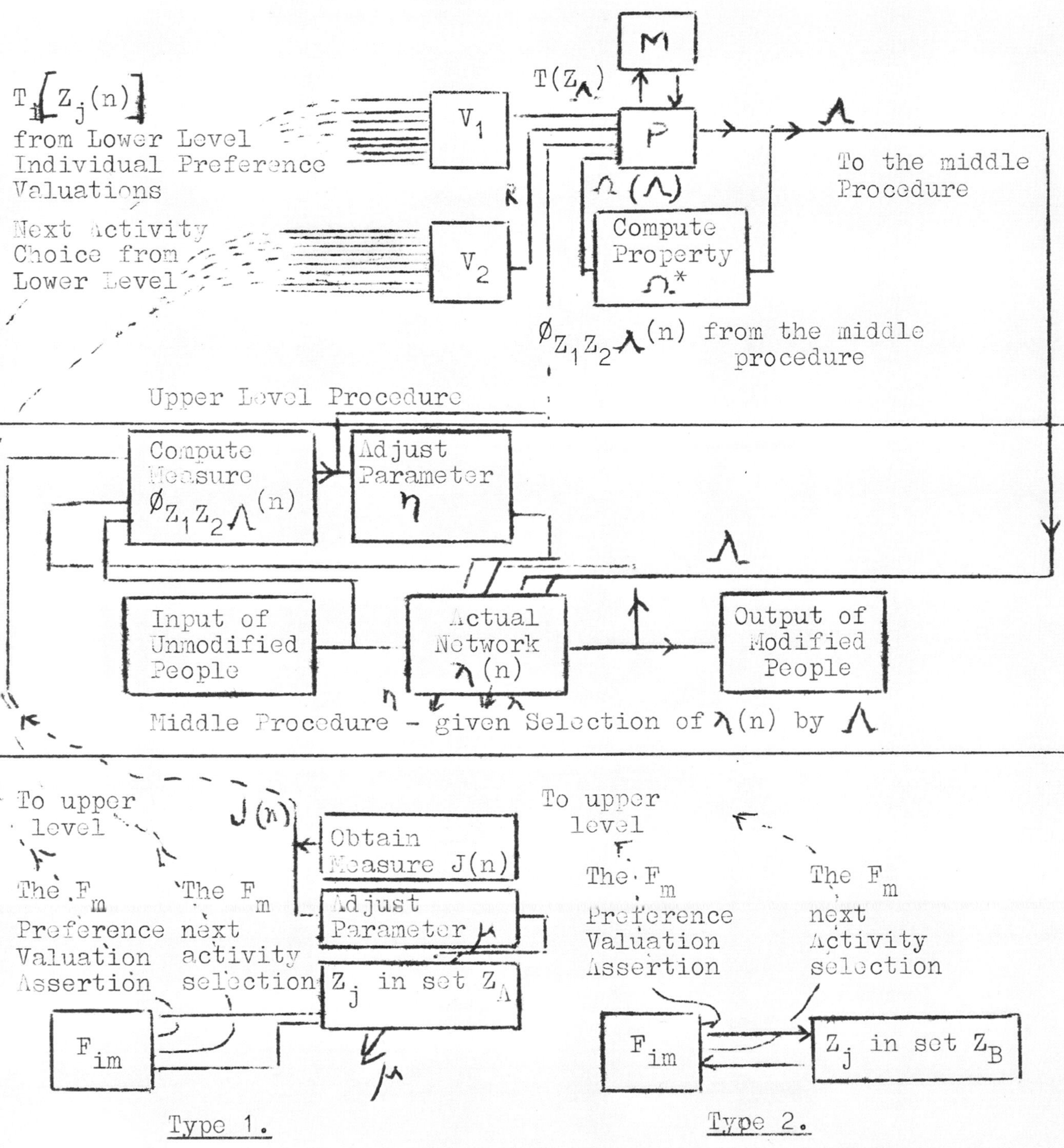

Lower Level Procedure - given individual F_m choosing r_i and $\Lambda(n) = r_i(n)Z_j(n)$

DIAGRAM 1.

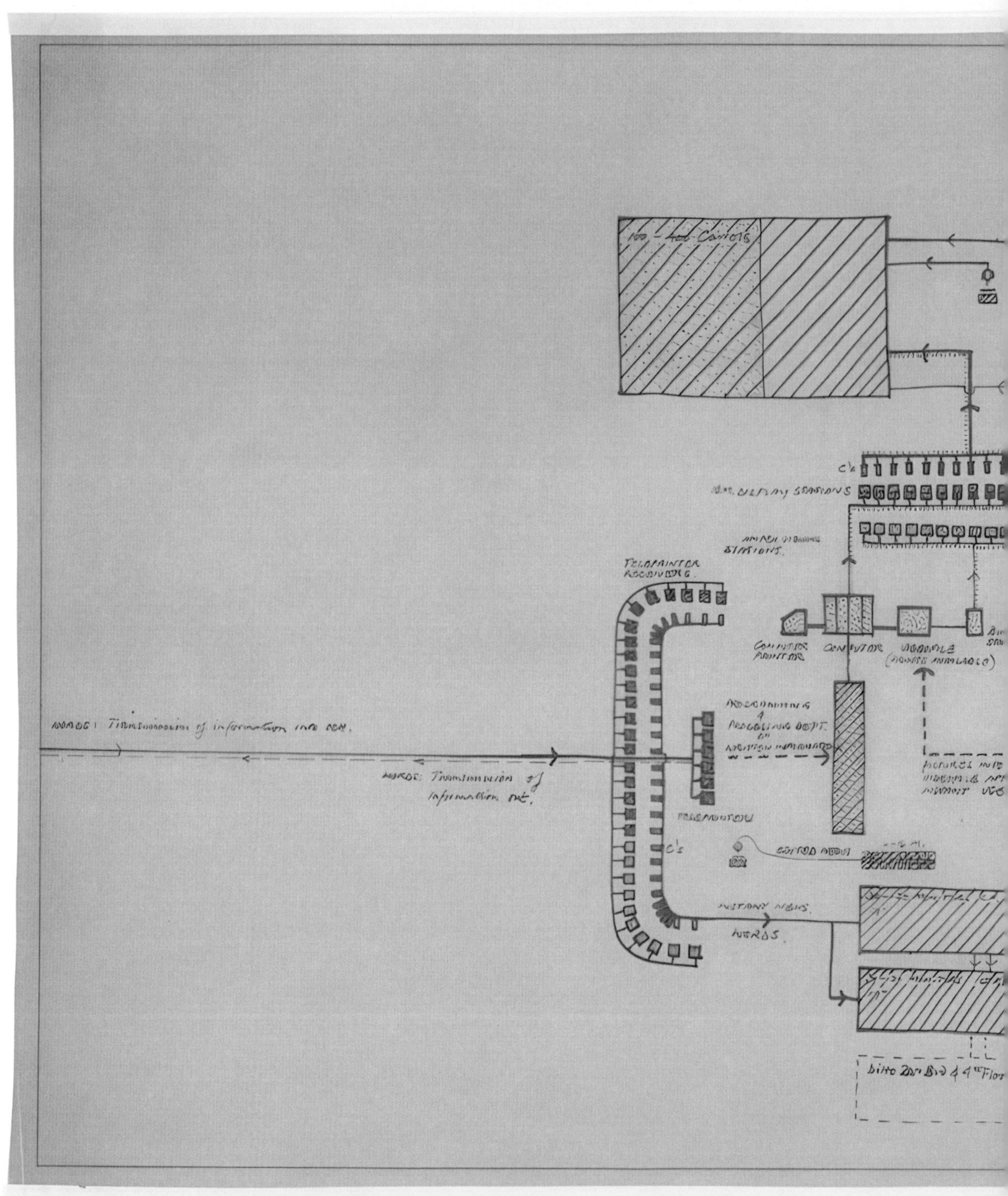
C's
COMPUTER
PRINTER
COMPUTER
C's

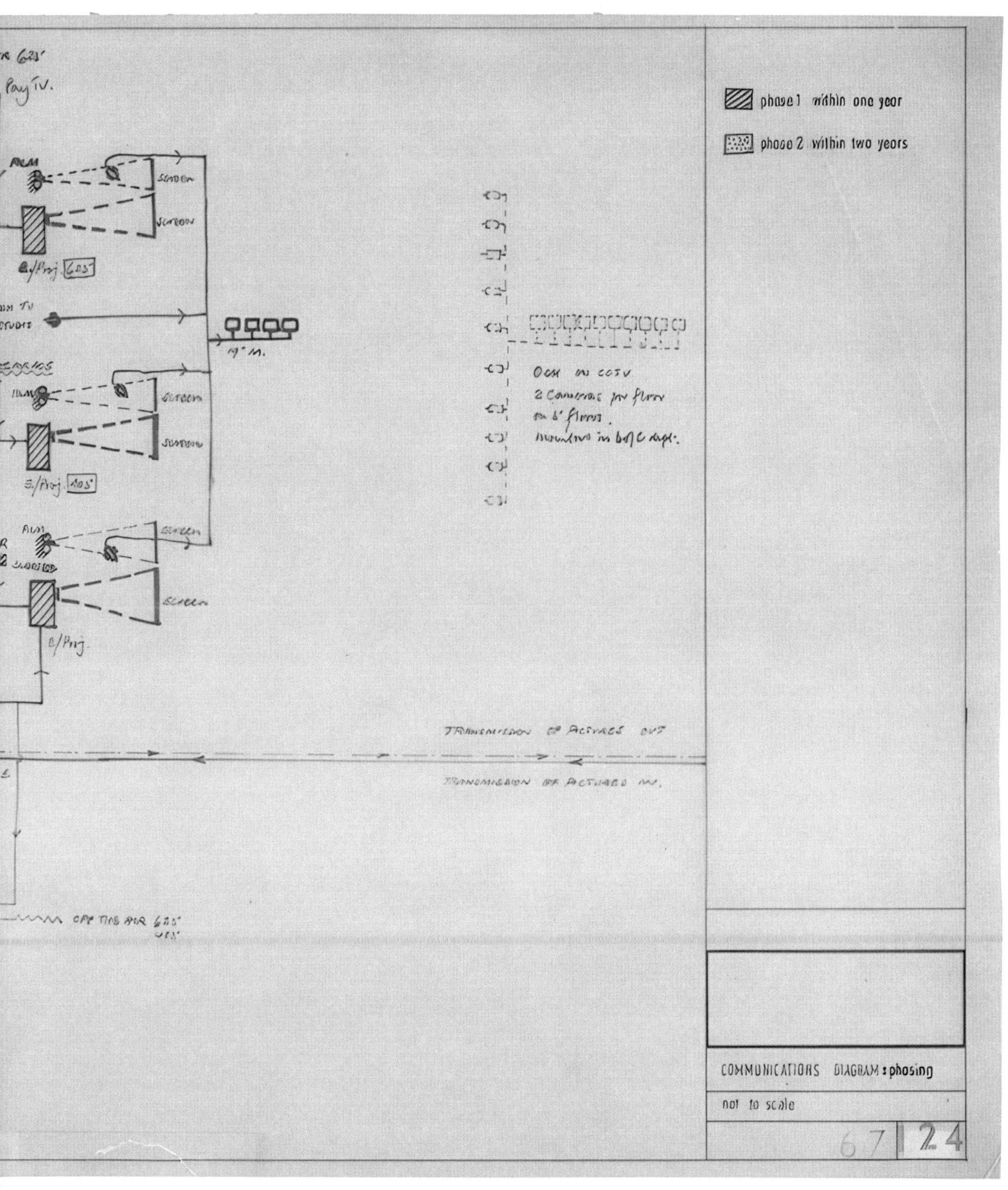
phase 1 within one year
phase 2 within two years
COMMUNICATIONS DIAGRAM : phasing
not to scale
67 24

I'm in the midst of preparing a talk that I'm giving about architecture in the future, and I just did a Google image search on architecture which gave me a bunch of these pixelated buildings that are so fashionable today. Is that where we want to end up? Because it would be extremely reductive to exhaust the impact of AI in pixelated dematerialising buildings that to a certain extend replicate the blocks' world from the 1970s, as for example the working cubes designed by Cedric Price in "The Generator" or the cubes of Negroponte in "Urban5", which replicated the form of intelligence that was at play. And to merely replicate these models seems dreadfully limiting.

I think that actually the really big and interesting questions lie in how we think and deal with forms of intelligence that might change what we design rather than merely automate, index and reformulate architecture. The interesting part of this adventure lies in the question, not in form.

JV When computer-aided design (CAD) appeared in the offices of architecture, for a long time its potential was not applied in the architectural design itself but in the way we represent that architectural design. Is the arrival of AI exhausted also in questions of representation and evaluation? How can the social and professional role of the architect change in light of AI's generalisation?

MW Have you ever seen a picture of what a large tech office looks like? For example, if you visit Facebook you don't actually end up back in the areas where people's tasks are; you just stand up in the larger social spaces and conference rooms. I think that increasingly architecture firms look more like Facebook. They look less like the messy kind of studio desks that you might have seen 10 or 15 years ago. I think that these transformations are particularly associated with the arrival of new workflows brought by computation. Although I don't work in an architectural office and I don't teach in an architecture school but rater in a design school, it seems hardly deniable that the need to design algorithms transforms the design of workflows. And the latter look a lot different than what architecture education has potentially done previously.But from my perspective as a historian, there is something else that I would like to mention:

Facebook Headquarters in California (2018).

There is an opportunity for historian practitioners and urbanists to find different points of departure that are no longer limited to being white and male.

I am really interested in the idea of Maria Göransdotter, a Swedish designer and vice director of the Umeå Institute of Design in Sweden. She talks about transitional design histories; the point of origin that we choose, determines the futures we can envision. If Nicholas Negroponte is the point of origin for everything, it enables a certain set of futures; if Christopher Alexander is that point of origin, it enables a different set of futures; if Sara Ishikawa—Alexander's longtime collaborator and colleague--is the point of origin, then maybe we see another understanding of the world. If we take a look at other locations and people, if we consider the work of someone like Charlton D. McIlwain, who wrote the book Black Software and looks at different histories of AI and technology with Black protagonists as a point of departure, maybe we have different futures and maybe we will stop talking about Negroponte, Alexander...

JV Science fiction has traditionally been a crucial way of thinking about the future. As occurred with Frankenstein at the beginning of the last century, today many movies instrumentalize the imaginary of artificial intelligence, like for example movies such as “Her” or “Ex Machina”. How do these fictions form our understanding of artificial intelligence and how can they affect the way the latter is instrumentalized by architecture?

This is Tomorrow exhibition, London, 1956, plaster sculpture wall. Author: Zelechin artwork by Sarah Jackson.

MW We have certain ways that we've tended to talk about the relation between intelligence and people. When I taught a class last year called "AI and culture" and had my students curate different kinds of speculations of what things look like, the best set of AI and culture examples came from a student who looked at dance performances connected with AI. I think it's important that architects and designers have access to a broad cultural imaginary, and for that it is crucial to address the whole field of artistic expression. I found myself thinking of the 1956 "This is Tomorrow" exhibition at the ICA in London, where groups of architects, sculptors and artists worked together to produce exhibits at the museum.

We have the ability as architects, designers and urbanists to change the materiality that we used to think through these questions. So what does it look like if it's completely organic? What does it look like if it's made of dirt or mud?

In the ways that we create speculative narratives, we can provide an alternative to Patrik Schumacher's agent based design filled with digitized human figures moving through buildings. What would it look like if it were the opposite? We have the ability to tell those stories too and to tell them differently with different kinds of people in the room. So if we start telling those stories, what kind of futures might we be putting out there? What might these speculations look like? How would they differ from the future celebrated by Ex machina?

AM Going back to the mainstream idea of smart city, we observe that the term has been very much associated with the corporate world, although lately new terminology such as "smarter city" or "smart citizens" has started to arise in order to cover that corporate notion.

A big part of what an intelligent city or a "smarter" city is actually trying to achieve is to monitor mobility, traffic, pedestrian flows, temperature, humidity, GDP, density, or public space use among others, through vast amounts of data coming from a technological infrastructure. Monitoring this data in order to plan and design more optimised cities certainly demands sensors and actuators. But is data enough for the future of urban planning and design? With which kind of data do you think that we should feed our algorithms? Doesn't the measurable data remain too minimal to analyze or understand cities? Our issue claims that deep knowledge on how people feel and perceive space might not be necessarily easy to quantify but it is extremely relevant to help researchers understand how people occupy and interact in cities. What kind of quantitative or qualitative data do we need to feed our AI algorithms for future urban planning and design?

MW It's interesting: some of the words that you just used in talking about the ways that smart cities are talked about is data for planning, monitoring and optimizing. You have said that it was about smarter cities, but I might have thought that it was about surveillance. In our first year Masters program in design, students are probably thinking about the latter when they sit down to design something. I feel like it is common to think about smart cities through a kind of surveillance capitalism mindset.

The term smart city has been used since the 1990, and it follows the smart boom that occurred in the 1970s, the smart chip that appeared in 1977, the smart card and the smart highways emerging in 1982, etc. And then, now we get smart grids, smart fabrics, smart cars and smartphones.

Software developed by China's SenseTime scans a city crosswalk and Tabulates pedestrian and car information. Image from SenseTime, 2017.

Interestingly, we started instrumentalizing the notion of smartness in urbanism or architecture after we had the infrastructure in place and after we had the weapons in place. This follows very much the same way we talked about robotics, AI and ethics;

We don't get to mobility concerns associated with the notion of smartness until the early 2000s. But, how do you make cities safer not through top-down surveillance and CCTV cameras everywhere? How do you use smartness as an input to make more beautiful, sustainable and life-giving public spaces? Architects tend to be quite allergic to the notion of place, but urbanists and designers really love that term. Is there something that we could learn together about how to make better places? There's an urban informatics undergrad program about to be launched at Michigan: "Urban computing has existed for 20 years". It poses the question of interaction design at the aforementioned levels, but again like I was saying, we've been talking about this idea since 1913 in The City as a Laboratory.

AM Thus, do you believe for instance that we can use AI for creating better places? That would mean that we can use AI for place making, for creating the identity that, as Jane Jacobs was emphasizing, people are giving to spaces by the way they occupy them.
Learning from the intelligence of people's self organization in spaces would allow us to produce information that could eventually be quantified in different ways in order to feed a machine. Would that be possible or relevant at all? In what ways can computational intelligence coexist with crowd intelligence instead of treating these as two separate approaches?

MW It is just a question of whether we choose to engage with that or not, if this becomes material for designers or not. But, can AI help us to design this? Could we work together to formulate, represent and bring different imaginaries that allow people whether architects or residents or policymakers to better understand the implications of what they're wanting to do? We know that we can come up with more beautiful forms with data, we're really good at that part.

That's not a question of making the magic algorithm: it's a question of understanding the myriad stakeholders and the kinds of data that are relevant, it is a question of bringing them together into the ways that we come together to make decisions and that seems to me to be a matter of citizenship, of human existence.

AM Thinking about transparency and bi-directional educational models in planning, it is crucial that we, as citizens, have more information about how the data produced by us is being used for certain analytics. This is fundamental in order to gain awareness of the impact of our way of living and possible change behaviours. In this sense, it's not only planners that need to be educated about people's desires and needs but also we, people need to be educated about what is the impact of such desires or lifestyle. I find a huge opportunity on how computational intelligence could be used in more engaging ways with communities in order to raise awareness about behaviours and regulate negative impacts in the collective.

MW I'm thinking about Richard Saul Wurman again and his conception of the city as a learning entity: it isn't that I educate you, but we are in a city and as such all of us within the city we educate each other. And transparency is not enough, because transparency isn't transparent at all: I can be very transparent and I can give you tons of data, but this would not be operative for you because it's way more than what you need for a proper interpretation.

I feel like the question of interpretation is one of the questions of design, the kind of decisions that we make whether we're designing a public space for building, or an algorithm, or an interface, or a tapestry, etc. These are all conversational human kinds of educational questions.

I'm quite curious about how large master planning firms or landscape architecture firms are taking on these questions. I don't know the answer, but I find myself wondering about how they think about the experience of feeling and the formal design in addition to the data that they're trying to parse.

JV Beside the question of what it means to design with AI, it seems also necessary to ask the question about what it means to live with AI. For example, how domestic spaces could be designed in order to open space for a coexistence between human beings and the algorithmic agents?

MW They're embodied in very small ways. For example, how many times today have we looked at something through a search engine? How many times have we used a map? In the maps that we use, in the tools that we use, AI is all around us all the time right now. It is in the devices that surround us. And that might not be what you're asking, but that's still going to be my answer. We're there.

JV So the arrival of AI has no special impact in our domestic environments because we are already there and our domestic environment seems to be the same. Is this what you mean?

MW It is already here. I'm in the house of the future and my house is 130 years old. You have this wonderful space behind you, which I figure is probably an older building. You are in the house of the future. I don't need to accommodate a rotary dial phone, my messages are not coming by pneumatic tube, but we're there.

Mark Weiser said in 1991 that the best user interface is the one you don't even notice. We think that to bring this about means to activate the world of the human scale, we see it as taking the virtual world inside the machine in bringing it out into the everyday physical world. And when we did that we found out that it's the same, it's a simulacrum.

AM What is "learning city" for you?

MW I actually have a quotation related to this expression. I found a George B. Ford's quote from 1913: "in the science of city planning the whole city is our laboratory". As I said before, this sounds so similar to how Richard Saul Wurman would have thought of cities. But there is a difference: I don't think he would have thought of it as a laboratory, he would have thought of it as a learning space. And I think there's a pretty beautiful and optimistic way of seeing the world in which we are all learners. We are all students of the world, we are all students of our city. I think many of us have been privileged enough to feel like our city teaches us beautiful and expensive things but I'm saying that as a white middle-aged woman who grew up in a midwestern city. I might have a different statement to say if I had grown up differently, if I was a person of colour, if I had grown up in a lower class than middle-class. I think at their best, cities bring us into contact with one another, bring together people who are unlike in a way that we can learn from each other and from the environment that surrounds us. And those of us who work on questions of cities, we do it because we love cities, because we believe in cities. This is what drives us when we look at AI and when we look at data to support other people in having those kinds of experiences and determinations for the cities that they want to live in.

City maps based on artificial intelligence.

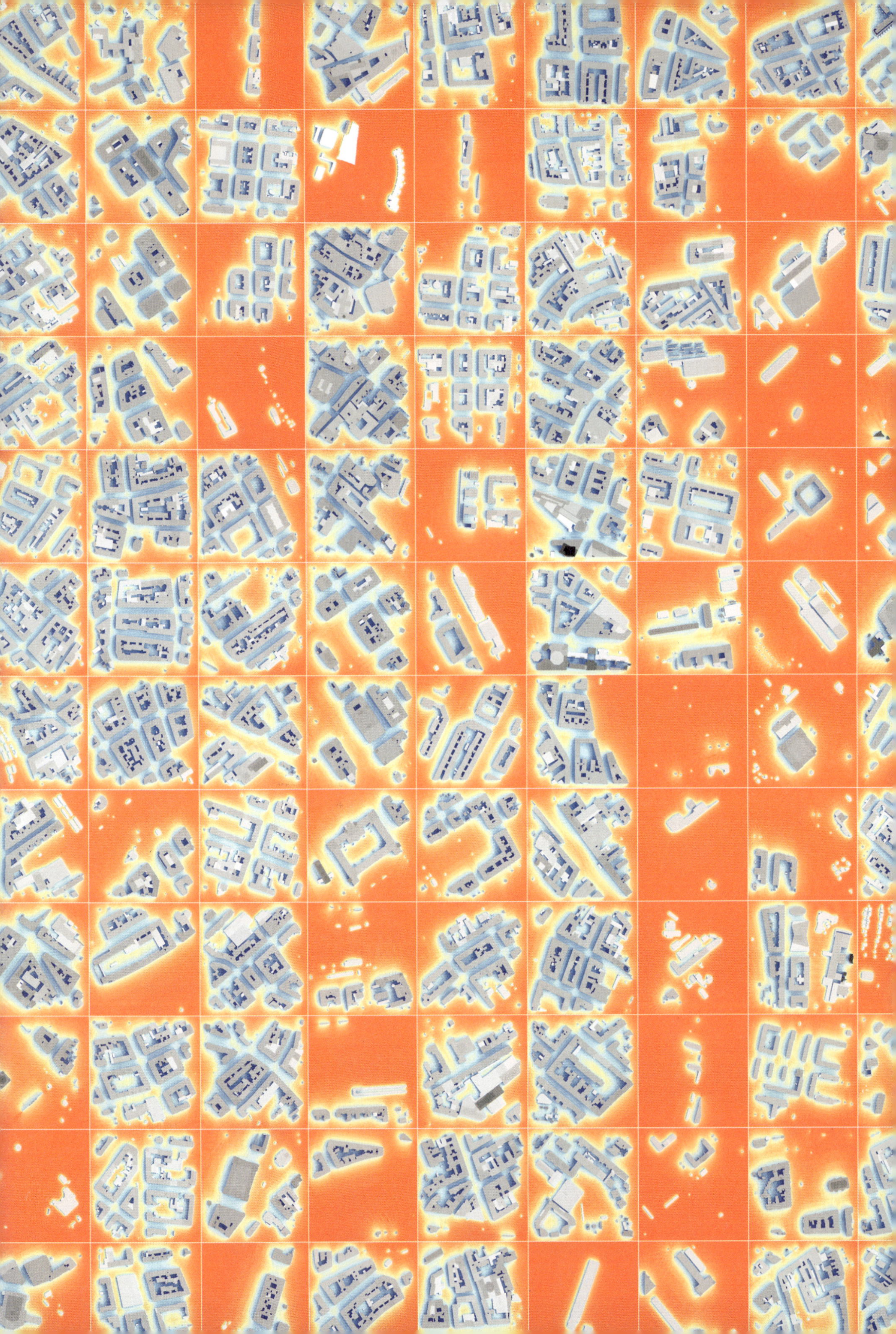

InFraRed: An Intelligent Framework for Resilient Design

Angelos Chronis

Climate resilience is no longer just an interesting research subject; it is an indisputable global emergency. Buildings are still a major contributor to climate change, as they are responsible for nearly half of the world's annual energy consumption and carbon dioxide emissions[1]. Architects, planners, environmentalists and developers urgently need innovative ways to respond to the climate crisis; they need to generate resilient urban projects by incorporating environmental performance simulations and analyses into their design methodologies.

Building performance simulation (BPS) tools have been developed increasingly in recent years to provide access to more environmentally informed design systems. One of the main challenges of contemporary architectural and urban planning practices, however, is the negotiation of these simulation metrics in a meaningful way and within fast and intense design cycles.

The City Intelligence Lab (CIL) of the Austrian Institute of Technology (AIT) is focused on an innovative approach for an Intelligent Framework for Resilient Design (InFraRed) which employs parametric and generative design, machine learning (ML) and augmented reality (AR) to enable a seamless design-decision framework with real-time performance feedback (Figure 2). The system allows architects, planners and other stakeholders to negotiate various design parameters and performance objectives in a fast and effective way, promoting sustainability goals in the design process. InFraReD is comprised of both a back-end real-time ML simulation prediction and a front-end AR interface which supports a natural interaction with physical models. Further to the real-time design-decision framework, the generative design capabilities of the system allow for the exploration of vast performance solution spaces that can produce higher performance designs.

Previous page: Figure 1: InFraReD training set. Copyright: City Intelligence Lab, Austrian Institute of Technology GmbH.

Figure 2: InFraReD in the City Intelligence Lab.

The widespread growth of the community-based development of computational design tools has given rise to an ever-increasing amount of simulation integration tools, especially for simple environmental studies such as solar radiation, daylight, energy simulations, etc. The importance of such tools in early design stages has been argued for repeatedly, and their efficiency in relation to the eventual achievable design performance is well documented. It has been shown, however,[2] that early design stage simulation tools are still not well aligned with design practice due to various reasons. These include the lack of actual design practice case studies in the context of BPS tool research, as well as typical simulation barriers, such as lack of simulation data, domain expertise and, very commonly, time-consuming simulation engines. In our framework, we aim to address these barriers by increasing the agility of the proposed simulation framework using machine learning and large simulation datasets – for real time performance prediction – as well as innovative and interactive interfaces – for eliminating the domain expertise gaps of the different stakeholders.

Further to the need of more integrated, accessible and agile performance feedback for design-decision support, the advent of generative design methods brought about by the available computational design systems is also posited[3] as a key driver for more sustainable design of buildings and cities by allowing an unprecedented and exhaustive exploration of design spaces. The ability to produce large design spaces, however, also requires exponentially faster simulation methods to be able to meaningfully assess the numerous design alternatives. Whereas simple simulations such as a solar radiation analysis take several minutes, and more complex simulations such as a wind analysis can take up to few hours, iterative generative studies would need a few factors of magnitude more time, making them completely unattainable in any design cycle. Our design framework utilizes a machine learning simulation prediction model that can predict simulation results in real time for several key environmental metrics such as solar radiation, wind comfort and overall thermal comfort, thus enabling the exploration of unprecedented design and performance spaces.

InFraReD

InFraReD is an open-ended system, which can be identified as a collection of components that all come together to create a powerful intelligent decision-support framework. In its current state, the framework can be divided into three main parts that integrate its different capabilities, each supported by sub processes which can be recombined and adapted to support different design workflows. The three components presented here are employed to support an actual design case study and include a parametric design model, backed by the ML simulation prediction, a design explorer of the entire parametric design space and an AR collaborative design component.

Parametric Urban Block – Machine Learning Simulation Prediction

The initial part of the framework is a parametric model generating urban designs for a typical urban block, backed by the real-time ML simulation framework. The parametric model is controlled by a few simple but fundamental parameters that allow for the exploration of the design space in a meaningful way. These include the density of the buildings, the maximum height, parameters that control the position and the amount of space between the buildings, green space and the orientation of the streets in relation to the buildings.

Every change to the parametric design model triggers real-time performance feedback for important climate simulations such as wind speed, temperature and outdoor thermal comfort. The framework is developed with state-of-the-art ML models that have been trained using large simulation data sets developed by the CIL. The ML models have been pre-trained and tested with simulation datasets specifically for the city of Vienna and provide an accurate result for early design stages.

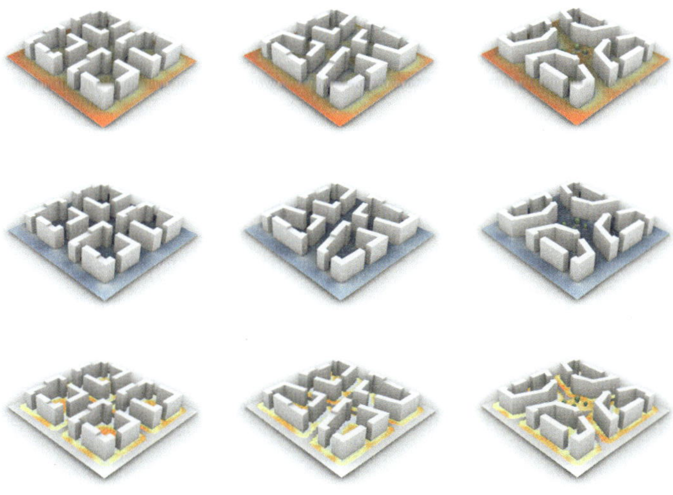

Figure 3: Parametric Urban Block and Machine Learning Simulation Prediction.

Following double page: Figure 4. InFraRed, all components.

The simulation results, which are acquired in real time, are summarized as a ratio of the urban block's area to satisfy specific comfort criteria (typical wind comfort and thermal comfort range). These are presented to the user in a graph, which makes it easy to identify the performance of the different objectives (Figure 3).

This first component offers an intelligent parametric model with real-time performance feedback that allows us to approach a design challenge in a completely new way, zeroing simulation times and thus fostering collaboration between stakeholders. In our case study, the participants can quickly identify the relationship between design parameters and their performance outcomes, demonstrating the potential of informed decisions for performance objectives that are not trivial, such as wind and thermal comfort, which would normally take hours or days to compute. The available performance metrics are only a subset of the potential of the system, as many other performance metrics can be integrated into the framework.

Parametric Design Explorer

Given the ability to instantly predict the performance of each parametric design iteration, we can then algorithmically generate, if not an exhaustive design space of all the possible parameter combinations – which would be costly and counterintuitive, a very large and representative sampling set of all design parameters for that design space. We can compute instantly, for each design, the environmental and spatial metrics that our design task includes. However, to make sense of the complexity of the requirements and design goals embedded in this design challenge, a more intelligent approach is needed. Using a common design space exploration tool, it is possible to narrow down and select designs based on different performance goals and design parameters.

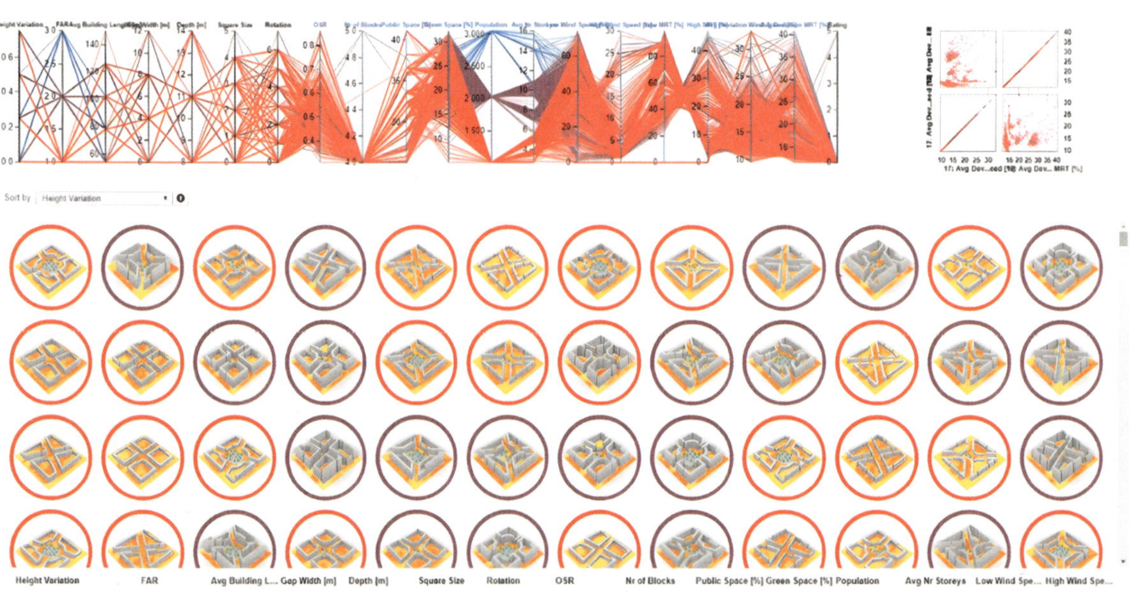

Figure 5: Design Explorer.

In our case study, we have generated around 1,000 representative design iterations and computed the aforementioned performance metrics using the ML simulation prediction. The design explorer presents the whole range of generated solutions, which can be filtered, ranked and easily navigated according to design parameters, spatial metrics and environmental performance metrics. The design explorer also works as an online tool that can be shared with different stakeholders, fostering a collaborative or participatory design process (Figure 5).

The generative design explorer further allows the planners, architects, consultants and other stakeholders to undertake an informed exploration of possible design solutions in a much more efficient way by focusing on ranges of design parameters and performance goals, thus allowing them to quickly identify correlations between spatial configurations and climate or spatial performance.

This also makes it possible to quantify and easily demonstrate arguments regarding the climate quality and sustainability of proposed designs and the importance of design parameters in the resilience of the urban scenarios. As mentioned in the single block component, the system can incorporate other climate-resilience metrics such as energy requirements or rainfall that would further enhance the design-decision framework. Nevertheless, in our design case study the potential of a generative design component with embedder performance feedback has been proven instrumental, and thus further development is envisioned.

Augmented Collaborative Design Interface

Digital models and simulations are fundamental in driving a resilient design-decision framework. However, all the digital information that is produced will remain inaccessible if it is not communicated to stakeholders through their natural forms of interaction. Traditionally, physical models have been the medium for communicating designs; therefore, an augmented physical model is a more natural form of interaction than a screen. As another layer of communicating design parameters and performance, a custom AR platform has been developed that allows us to visualize the generated designs and performance metrics and overlay them on a physical context model. Users can interact with the digital model by both visualizing the metrics and directly interacting with the design while being able to get real-time feedback on the environmental and spatial performance.

In our case study, multiple users using both an AR headset and tablets can interact with the parametric model of an entire neighborhood.

Figure 6: Augmented Physical Model (Tablet).

Figure 7: Interactive AR Model (AR Headset).

Users can visualize individual blocks and add or remove components (parks and typologies) and get real-time feedback on environmental, spatial and accessibility metrics (Figure 6 and Figure 7). The collaborative interactivity of the augmented physical model fosters the discussion of performance, which is crucial for environmentalists when it comes to conveying the benefits of more sustainable design approaches.

Discussion & Further Work

The development of the InFraReD system serves as a first step towards an open, integrated and continuously growing decision-support and recommendation framework that aims to promote informed sustainable design solutions by providing easily accessible, real-time and informative performance feedback. In this first iteration and through the presented case study, the system shows significant potential in promoting performance-driven design. The most significant advantages of the system are derived from its ability to provide real-time simulation prediction, thus zeroing the computational bottleneck of the simulation, especially in the case of wind and thermal comfort.

The real-time ML models also allow for vast exploration of an unprecedented performative design space. Another significant advantage of the system is its accessibility in terms of the interaction components, which are developed with the aim of allowing stakeholders to interact with it in natural ways. Finally, the modularity and open architecture of the system mean that its components can be reconfigured for different design problems and strategies.

As the system is very novel, a few important pitfalls have been identified as well: mainly, for the design-decision framework to reach its full potential, a range of other metrics are needed. In this effort, the focus has been on the main microclimate features of a typical urban scenario (solar, wind and thermal comfort) as well as basic accessibility functions (walkability), but there are many more that the system can support. Further work is already focused on providing more metrics, such as rainwater, noise, extreme climate resilience and more. In order to enhance the analytical power of the decision framework, it is also imperative to further abstract the performance feedback and make more concise and actionable design recommendations to the users.

The aim of our system is not to increase the burden of simulation and analytical tools that designers and planners have available today but to employ them to make meaningful suggestions and enable meaningful interactions that will lead to more sustainable designs.

This study presents an Intelligent Framework for Resilient Design (InFraReD), using machine learning models for simulation prediction, generative design methodologies and interactive and augmented interfaces to enable more informed design decisions and thus more sustainable designs for our cities.

The results from our case study show how impactful this framework can be at the planning negotiation table, especially in the early stages of design; it also shows that employing novel ML and AR methodologies can drive a meaningful and intelligent decision framework with a potential significant impact for the sustainability of our city planning.

References

1 (UNEP), N.E.P. (2016). *The Emissions Gap Report 2016*, United Nations Environment Programme (UNEP).

2 Purup, P.B. and Petersen, S. (2020). "Research Framework for Development of Building Performance Simulation Tools for Early Design Stages." *Automation in Construction* 109, 1–15.

3. Soares, N., Bastos, J., Pereira, L. D., Soares, A., Amaral, A. R., Asadi, E., Rodrigues, E., Lamas, F.B., Monteiro, H., Lopes, M.A.R., Gaspar, A. R. (2017). "A Review on Current Advances in the Energy and Environmental Performance of Buildings towards a More Sustainable Built Environment."

4. *Renewable and Sustainable Energy Reviews* 77 (February 2016), 845–860.

Urban Fictions
SPAN

Matias del Campo & Sandra Manninger

Vienna is the home of one of the world's oldest clusters of research on Artificial Intelligence – the OFAI, the Austrian Institute of Artificial Intelligence, founded in 1969[1]. About 30 years later, in Summer 1998, Sandra Manninger and myself were sitting around in a Schanigarten, in the court of the Baroque ensemble that houses the OFAI. We were discussing the possibilities of integrating Artificial Intelligence into Architecture design with Prof. Trappl, the director of the OFAI, and Dr. Arthur Flexer. Of course, this was a purely hypothetical conversation as Neural Network based in computational processes were in its infancy. A couple of years later, in 2006, SPAN conducted the first Machine Learning workshop at the Angewandte in Vienna[2]. After the move to the University of Michigan a collaboration with Michigan Robotics and Computer Science paved the way to a series of new design techniques. In particular the director of Michigan Robotics, Jessy Grizzle and PhD Student Alexa Carlson, have been crucial in this collaboration. The project presented in this essay *Urban Fictions* (Figure 1) is a direct result out of this collaboration.

Previous page:
Figure 1: Urban Fictions - using Vienna as Style, and a rendering by SPAN as the Target image.

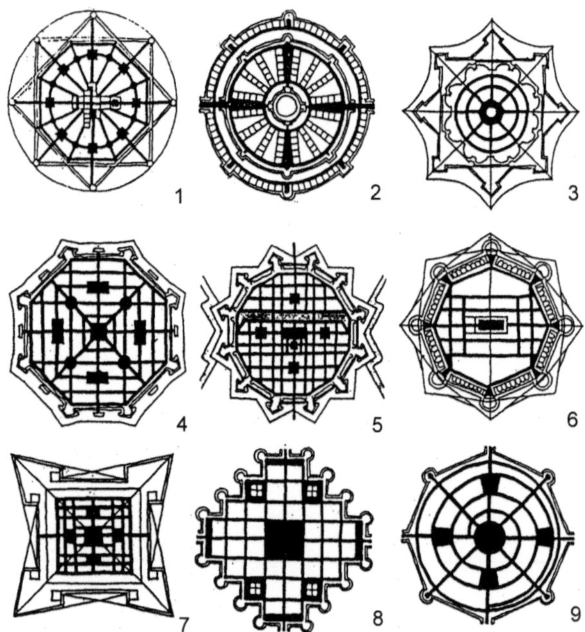

Figure 2: Ideal cities from the Renaissance with the emphasis on defense (city walls). 1. La Sforzinda by Filarete (1460 – 1465); 2. Fra Giocondo (Giovanni of Verona), c. 1433 – 1515; 3. Girolamo Magi (or Maggi) (c. 1523 – c. 1572) (1564); 4. Giorgio Vasari (1598); 5. Antonio Lupicini (c. 1530 – c. 1598); 6. Daniele Barbaro (1513 – 1570); 7. Pietro Cattaneo (1537 – 1587); 8/9; Francesco di Giorgio Martini (1439 – 1502).

Following page:
Figure 3: Zaha Hadid Architects. The Kartal-Pendik masterplan is a winning competition proposal for a new city center on the east bank of Istanbul. It is the redevelopment of an abandoned industrial site into a new sub-center of Istanbul, complete with a central business district, high-end residential development, cultural facilities such as concert halls, museums, and theatres, and leisure programs including a marina and tourist hotels. The site lies at the confluence of several important infrastructural links, including the major highway connecting Istanbul to Europe and Asia, the coastal highway, sea bus terminals, and heavy and light rail links to the greater metropolitan area.

Of ideal cities and other strange things

It is almost impossible to judge the planning of urban textures on a purely pragmatic level. They always simultaneously discuss aspects that include planning processes, economic environments, material preferences, political conditions, stylistic fashions, aesthetics and the general culture of the time the design was created. Wither this be in the rigorous structure and geometrical purity of Renaissance Ideal cities (Figure 2), as exemplified in the concept of the *ideal town* as proposed by Leon Batista Alberti in *De Re Edificatore*[3], or in the intricate voluptuous geometry of parametrically designed settlements such as Zaha Hadid's *Kartal-Pendik Masterplan* for Instanbul[4] (Figure 3). In both cases it is not surprising that the intrinsic matter of urban planning in a large scale involves aspects of ideology and utopia. Both examples mentioned above can be identified as representatives of ideologies that span areas beyond shape and geometry and involve political, social and economic conditions[5]. It might not surprise that in this extent they also represent a vessel and repository of the history of urban planning imaginations, and as such can be considered an enormous mine for new ideas on the nature of the city[6]. What is meant by this? Traditionally urban planners (and architects for that matter) are trained during their studies to operate like data miners. Every new project is based on the hundreds and thousands of images ingested during the training received in architecture school.

This of course is an oversimplification of a highly complex pedagogical model, but admittedly in the very core there is a kernel of truth to it. Learning the trade of planning is a profoundly visual matter,

Figure 4: Nolli Map based on Vienna and a generative pattern. Neural Style Transfer SPAN 2020.

amplified in the age of social distancing with Instagram, Slack, Zoom, at.studio and Miro boards. This image-based tradition is exploited in the 2D to 2D style transfer approach presented with the project *Urban Fictions* (Figure 1, Figure 3).

What goes beyond the ability to simply ingest imagery, is the inherently human ability to perform pattern recognition. One of the things the human mind is particularly skilled in, is to recognize events and objects, separate fore- and background. The ability to even recognize that an error or mistake inhabits the potential for a creative solution to a problem[7]. How can this, computationally rather difficult to grasp problem be harnessed to differentiate between successful and unsuccessful image to image style transfer? This is where the aspects of the neural network's learned features come into play. (Factually, what it has learned are salient pixel patterns within a given image – just saying). We can use trained neural networks to successfully quantify and define textures within images, and in the context of urban maps, we can create a 'city texture' and hallucinate[8] its specific features in other images of city plans.

Figure 5: From SPAN's Urban Fiction series. A Neural Style Transfer between a pattern, generated using a naïve algorithm and a series of satellite images of Detroit, Michigan, USA (SPAN 2020).

SPAN has developed a specific technique, harnessing the ability of Neural Style transfer not to just create a mash up between existing cities, and thus interrogating the underlying rulesets in terms of its material and symbolic culture, but expanding it to their own inherent sensibilities. Historically SPAN has shown an acute interest in patterns and ornaments. This curiosity emerged out of a critical interrogation of the relationship of Adolf Loos to the contemporary project in which the claims of Adolf Loos[9] have lost their edge, due to technological, cultural and social developments. Breaking away from the traditional assumption in architecture about patterns as appliqué to volumetric objects, but rather exploring the organizational and esthetic value inherent in these geometrical configurations[10]. Projects such as Barcelona recursion[11], Recursion III[12] and Blocks[13] are evidence in SPAN's oeuvre for an obsession with Algorithmically generated textures that are interrogated for their architectural qualities. On another note: these projects demonstrate another obsession within the work of SPAN - the continuous questioning of the role of the architect spanned in a field of tension between top down authorship and the emergent agency of computational processes[14].

Within this lineage the project *Urban Fictions* presented in this essay interrogates the ability of Neural Networks to serve as a cartographic device that measures and records underlying aesthetical conditions in the work of the architect.

In this case it is not intended as a tool of expediency that serves purposes of optimization or rationalization, but rather serves as a, quasi intelligent, machine of exploration. More specifically this machine explores the combination between sensibility and input images.

Figure 6: Barcelona Recursion 2011; an example of the use of recursive algorithms in the work of SPAN; SPAN (Matias del Campo, Sandra Manninger) courtesy of the FRAC collection.

Lines, surfaces and quasi intelligent machines

As laid out in the introduction to this essay the urban map is a cultural staple of the architecture discipline. It is the vessel that best captures the intentionality of the urban project in an abstract medium as a two-dimensional surface. In architecture discourse the line, the plan, the abstract representation of materiality has played a major role, and it always has been interpreted as the result of human cognition and mind. This can be illustrated as a core idea in the architectural theory of for example Leon Battista Alberti, as expressed in the *De re aedificatoria*, pertaining to the distinction between "lineament", the line in the mind of the architect, and "matter," the material presence of the building[15]. This particular distinction plays a key role in architectural design, and the conceptualization of the architectural project, throughout the history of western architecture. Le Corbusier described this at the heyday of modernism in the twentieth century like this: "Architecture is a product of the mind[16]." The distinction between mind and matter can be found in Vitruvius, in the distinction between "that which signifies and that which is signified[17]"; at the Accademia di San Luca in Rome, between *disegno interno* and *disegno esterno*[18]; or in Peter Eisenman's distinction between deep aspect and surface aspect[19] in architecture, to name just three examples that profoundly describe the planning process as a particular ability of the human mind. What position does the discipline have when it comes to understanding the potentialities of applications such as NN's that are able to produce results that question the sole authorship of human ingenuity? Well, there is always the chicken & egg problem: NN's origin in the human mind. That they are able to autonomously generate plan solutions is in itself not yet proof for thinking or even intelligence. However, if we take the philosophical standpoint of materialism it would allow to create an even field between these two thinking processes. In a materialist tradition though itself is just the result of material processes in our brain, neurochemical reactions able to form thought. If this position is taken, then the conclusion is that AI's can think as much, and form original language[20] or shape[21] as humans can, the only difference being that their neural processes are not based on neurochemical processes but computational processes within another material paradigm. But we digress. *Urban Fictions* interrogate the possibility to utilize AI applications for the generation of design processes. In particular the application of style transfers with NNs.

This approach on the one side critically interrogates the unique position of the human mind when it comes to creative processes and in addition questions aspects of creativity in planning processes. In a design ecology where the boundaries between human and computational cognition are increasingly blurred, the presented process combines the ability of neural networks to read and recognize features of a style image and combine them with a target image.

Following double page: Figure 7: From SPAN's Urban Fiction series. A Neural Style Transfer between a pattern, generated using a naïve algorithm and a series of satellite images of Canberra, Australia.

An overdue re-evaluation of urban density

Urban Fictions is an experiment in exploring the combination between patterns created, and curated by SPAN, and urban textures of existing cities. In short SPAN's renderings serve as the target image, and satellite images of selected cities serve as target image. Producing images that oscillate between tangible realism and unlikely scenarios. Exactly this thin line between utopia and reality is what makes these images a compelling proposal for a re-evaluation of the urban condition.

Urban Fictions can also be read as a response to the current criticism towards the city in the light of the current Covid-19 crisis[22]. Instead of joining the choir praising the life on the countryside as the remedy in the times of social distancing, *Urban Fictions* celebrates urbanity and its density as a possible, or rather *necessary* future. The reasons why could fill tomes, but in short:

> architects understand that the city is -apart from being a symbol of human culture- a necessity concerning the responsible consumption of the resources of this planet. Instead of painting a gloomy dystopia (controlled by a pathogen), *Urban Fictions* relies on the possibility to laud urbanity and advocate for a reevaluation of city with the aid of Machine Learning.

In an outlook it can be stated that this is only a first attempt in the area of the critical interrogation of planning in architecture in the age of AI. In fact, there is still a lot to be done. The first, alien, results achieved in this paper can only be seen as a first tapping into the potentialities of this approach. From tapping into novel design direction that rather talks about how machines see our world - with all its wonderfully strange results in terms of morphologies, chromatics and possible theories, to profoundly pragmatic approaches. Further research needs to be done to dive deeper into the opportunities presented in this approach to urban design. In this extent the work on this problem can be considered a work in progress. The refinement of the algorithm allows to continue the conversation laid out in this design methodology. We have already started to refine this approach, and to expand the code to understand semantic information – crucial for a well-informed design method- and are looking forward to the in-depth interrogation of this posthuman design ecology.

References

1. OFAI is a research institute of the Österreichische Studiengesellschaft fuer Kybernetik (OSGK), a registered scientific society founded in 1969. **http://www.ofai.at/about.html** (visited 21.08.2020)

2. On invitation by Rainer Zettl, Matias del Campo and Sandra Manninger gave a workshop on Machine Learning together with Dr. Arthur Flexer in July 2006. The workshop was part of the Postgraduate *Urban Strategies* of the University of Applied Arts, Vienna, Austria.

3. Alberti, Leon Battista. De re aedificatoria. On the art of building in ten books. (translated by Joseph Rykwert, Robert Tavernor and Neil Leach). Cambridge, Massachusetts: MIT Press, 1988.

4. Zaha Hadid Architects, London, *Kartal-Pendik Masterplan Istanbul*, 2006

5. *Just think about Patrik Schuhmacher's Theoretical oeuvre and the schism it has created in the discipline by provoking with neoliberal statements. In the process creating a counter-culture in Digital Design opposing the neoliberal position and adopting instead a leftist, Accelerationist Ideology.*

6. See also the discourse put forward in Michel Foucoults *Archaeology of Knowledge*, which forms the basis for a critical interrogation of methodologies that use systems based on scraping the internet for data that forms the basis of a design. Foucault argues that the contemporary study of the history of ideas, although it targets moments of transition between historical worldviews, ultimately depends on continuities that break down under close inspection. The history of ideas marks points of discontinuity between broadly defined modes of knowledge, but the assumption that those modes exist as wholes fails to do justice to the complexities of discourse. Foucault argues that "discourses" emerge and transform not according to a developing series of unarticulated, common worldviews, but according to a vast and complex set of discursive and institutional relationships, which are defined as much by breaks and ruptures as by unified themes.

7. See also Greg Lynn's entire conversation on "Happy Accidents"

8. $\boldsymbol{\ell}(\boldsymbol{m}) = -|\boldsymbol{f}(\boldsymbol{R}(\boldsymbol{m}, \boldsymbol{\phi}))|_F^2$

(as a comment: this essay does not really discuss machine hallucinations but clearly talks about 2D to 2D Neural Style Transfer)

9. Adolf Loos, Ornament und Verbrechen, Cahiers d'aujourd'hui, 5, 1915.

10. See also Matias del Campo, *Moody Objects,* in AD 06 | Vol 86 | 2016, Evoking through Design – Contemporary Moods in Architecture, Wiley, London, 2016 pp.54-57

11. SPAN 2011, first shown in the MAK in Vienna and subsequently acquired by the FRAC collections Orleans

12. SPAN 2012, first shown in the MAK in Vienna and subsequently acquired by the FRAC collections Orleans

13. See also Matias del Campo, *Moody Objects,* in AD 06 | Vol 86 | 2016, Evoking through Design – Contemporary Moods in Architecture, Wiley, London, 2016 pp.54-57

14. See also Matias del Campo, *Autonomous tectonics: the work of SPAN, between autonomous behavior and cultural agency,* Dissertation Doctor of Philosophy, PhD at RMIT *http://researchbank.rmit.edu.au/view/rmit:162717* (visited 21.08.2020)

15. Hendrix, John S., "Leon Battista Alberti and the Concept of Lineament" (2011). School of Architecture, Art, and Historic Preservation Faculty

16. Le Corbusier, Towards a New Architecture, New York, Praeger, 1970, pp. 202

17. Vitruvius. *On Architecture, Volume I: Books 1-5.* Translated by Frank Granger. Loeb Classical Library 251. Book One, Chapter One: The Education of the Architect, 3. Cambridge, MA: Harvard University Press, 1931. P.7

18. Hendrix, John S., "Leon Battista Alberti and the Concept of Lineament" (2011). Architecture, Art, and Historic Preservation Faculty Publications. 30. https://docs.rwu.edu/saahp_fp/30 (visited 21.08.2020)

19. Eisenman, Peter D. "Notes on Conceptual Architecture: Towards a Definition." *Design Quarterly,* no. 78/79 (1970): 1-5. Accessed August 21, 2020. doi:10.2307/4047397.

20. See for example the *Bob & Alice* experiment by the Facebook AI Research group. Two chatbots were programmed to discuss economic problems with each other. Once the test ran overnight the two bots started to develop their own language.

21. See for example the artwork Portrait of Edmond de Belamy created by Paris based art collective *Obvious* using a Generative Adversarial Network. It was sold at Christies for the sum of $432.000, and was promoted by the auction house as *the first painting solely created by Artificial Intelligence*

22. See for Example: Article in Time: Architect Rem Koolhaas Says Redesigning Public Spaces was necessary before the Pandemic https://time.com/5836599/rem-koolhaas-architecture-coronavirus/ (visited 21.08.2020)

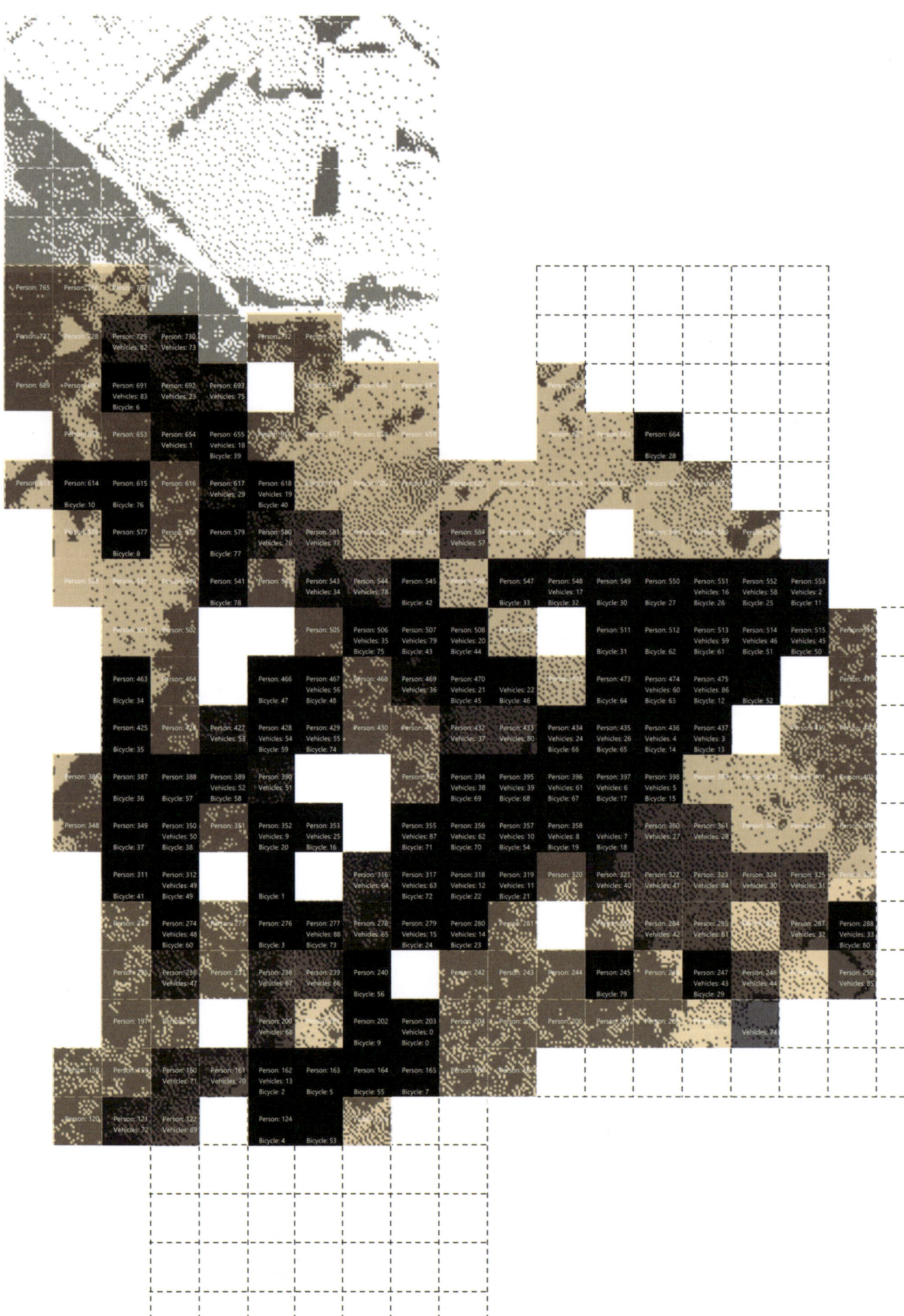

Person: 765
Person: 727
Person: 729 Vehicles: 82
Person: 730 Vehicles: 73
Person: 732
Person: 689
Person: 691 Vehicles: 83 Bicycle: 6
Person: 692 Vehicles: 23
Person: 693 Vehicles: 75
Person: 696
Person: 653
Person: 654 Vehicles: 1
Person: 655 Vehicles: 18 Bicycle: 39
Person: 658
Person: 659
Person: 664 Bicycle: 28
Person: 614 Bicycle: 10
Person: 615 Bicycle: 76
Person: 616
Person: 617 Vehicles: 29
Person: 618 Vehicles: 19 Bicycle: 40
Person: 577 Bicycle: 8
Person: 579 Bicycle: 77
Person: 580 Vehicles: 76
Person: 581 Vehicles: 77
Person: 584 Vehicles: 57
Person: 541 Bicycle: 78
Person: 543 Vehicles: 34
Person: 544 Vehicles: 78
Person: 545 Bicycle: 42
Person: 547 Bicycle: 33
Person: 548 Vehicles: 17 Bicycle: 32
Person: 549 Bicycle: 30
Person: 550 Bicycle: 27
Person: 551 Vehicles: 16 Bicycle: 26
Person: 552 Vehicles: 58 Bicycle: 25
Person: 553 Vehicles: 2 Bicycle: 11
Person: 501
Person: 502
Person: 505
Person: 506 Vehicles: 35 Bicycle: 75
Person: 507 Vehicles: 79 Bicycle: 43
Person: 508 Vehicles: 20 Bicycle: 44
Person: 511 Bicycle: 31
Person: 512 Bicycle: 62
Person: 513 Vehicles: 59 Bicycle: 61
Person: 514 Vehicles: 46 Bicycle: 51
Person: 515 Vehicles: 45 Bicycle: 50
Person: 463 Bicycle: 34
Person: 464
Person: 466 Bicycle: 47
Person: 467 Vehicles: 56 Bicycle: 48
Person: 468
Person: 469 Vehicles: 36
Person: 470 Vehicles: 21 Bicycle: 45
Vehicles: 22 Bicycle: 46
Person: 473 Bicycle: 64
Person: 474 Vehicles: 60 Bicycle: 63
Person: 475 Vehicles: 86 Bicycle: 12
Bicycle: 52
Person: 425 Bicycle: 35
Person: 427 Vehicles: 53
Person: 428 Vehicles: 54 Bicycle: 59
Person: 429 Vehicles: 55 Bicycle: 74
Person: 430
Person: 432 Vehicles: 37
Person: 433 Vehicles: 80
Person: 434 Vehicles: 24 Bicycle: 66
Person: 435 Vehicles: 26 Bicycle: 65
Person: 436 Vehicles: 4 Bicycle: 14
Person: 437 Vehicles: 3 Bicycle: 13
Person: 386
Person: 387 Bicycle: 36
Person: 388 Bicycle: 57
Person: 389 Vehicles: 52 Bicycle: 58
Person: 390 Vehicles: 51
Person: 394 Vehicles: 38 Bicycle: 69
Person: 395 Vehicles: 39 Bicycle: 68
Person: 396 Vehicles: 61 Bicycle: 67
Person: 397 Vehicles: 6 Bicycle: 17
Person: 398 Vehicles: 5 Bicycle: 15
Person: 400
Person: 402
Person: 348
Person: 349 Bicycle: 37
Person: 350 Vehicles: 50 Bicycle: 38
Person: 351
Person: 352 Vehicles: 9 Bicycle: 20
Person: 353 Vehicles: 25 Bicycle: 16
Person: 355 Vehicles: 87 Bicycle: 71
Person: 356 Vehicles: 62 Bicycle: 70
Person: 357 Vehicles: 10 Bicycle: 54
Person: 358 Vehicles: 8 Bicycle: 19
Vehicles: 7 Bicycle: 18
Person: 360 Vehicles: 27
Person: 361 Vehicles: 28
Person: 311 Bicycle: 41
Person: 312 Vehicles: 49 Bicycle: 49
Bicycle: 1
Person: 316 Vehicles: 64
Person: 317 Vehicles: 63 Bicycle: 72
Person: 318 Vehicles: 12 Bicycle: 22
Person: 319 Vehicles: 11 Bicycle: 21
Person: 320
Person: 321 Vehicles: 40
Person: 322 Vehicles: 41
Person: 323 Vehicles: 84
Person: 324 Vehicles: 30
Person: 325 Vehicles: 31
Person: 274 Vehicles: 48 Bicycle: 60
Person: 276 Bicycle: 3
Person: 277 Vehicles: 88 Bicycle: 73
Person: 278 Vehicles: 65
Person: 279 Vehicles: 15 Bicycle: 24
Person: 280 Vehicles: 14 Bicycle: 23
Person: 284 Vehicles: 42
Person: 285 Vehicles: 81
Person: 287 Vehicles: 32
Person: 288 Vehicles: 33 Bicycle: 80
Person: 236 Vehicles: 47
Person: 237
Person: 238 Vehicles: 67
Person: 239 Vehicles: 66
Person: 240 Bicycle: 56
Person: 242
Person: 243
Person: 244
Person: 245 Bicycle: 79
Person: 247 Vehicles: 43 Bicycle: 29
Person: 248 Vehicles: 44
Person: 250 Vehicles: 85
Person: 197
Person: 200 Vehicles: 68
Person: 202 Bicycle: 9
Person: 203 Vehicles: 0 Bicycle: 0
Person: 204
Person: 206
Vehicles: 74
Person: 158
Person: 160 Vehicles: 71
Person: 161 Vehicles: 70
Person: 162 Vehicles: 13 Bicycle: 2
Person: 163 Bicycle: 5
Person: 164 Bicycle: 55
Person: 165 Bicycle: 7
Person: 120
Person: 121 Vehicles: 72
Person: 122 Vehicles: 89
Person: 124 Bicycle: 4
Bicycle: 53

Sensing Public Spaces
Image Analytics for Urban Planning

Aldo Sollazzo

Rising levels of air pollution demand urgent actions by administrators and urban planners. To face this unprecedented threat, cities need to reshape their urban patterns by reprogramming mobility, public spaces, and urban infrastructures towards safer, healthier, and more ecological solutions.
The city of Barcelona currently ranks among the most polluted in Europe [1,2](Cyrys et al. 2012; Eeftens et al. 2012b). To revert this trend, in 2016 Barcelona introduced a new urban planning model called the Superblock. This planning approach treats the urban fabric as a programmable surface, regulating access to cars and vehicles while enabling the extension of walkable areas and cycling paths.

Concurrently with the development of new urban strategies, novel data-driven instruments have been emerging, providing different approaches to inform spatial planning. This chapter will highlight several techniques triggered by computer vision and machine learning algorithms for use in analysing image-based data, extracting meaningful metrics to inform spatial transformations and estimate CO2 emissions in an urban environment. This methodology can enrich emergent urban planning approaches, such as the Superblock, with a novel set of metrics and criteria based on real-time spatial usage and carbon footprints to guide and orient future urban transformations, ultimately supporting the implementation of more resilient, ecological, and sustainable urban models.

The Urgency of a New Urbanism

Environmental pollution is set to redefine all ecosystems. The geological era of the Anthropocene is the ultimate cause of a new shift in weather patterns affecting the climate, biodiversity, and geomorphology – and consequently our cities and built environments. Rising levels of air pollution demand urgent action by administrators and urban planners to address the need to adapt urban organisms to this invisible enemy hanging over our parks, schools, offices, and houses, ultimately deteriorating the wellbeing of the entire population. Air pollution has been associated in numerous studies with congenital anomalies, mostly in connection with exposure to traffic-related gasses.[3]

In this regard, the Air Quality Index (AQI) categorises the risks associated with air pollutants based on different scales. Warnings begin at 51-100, while levels at 201-300 bring a 'significant increase in respiratory effects'. Above that, in the 301-500 range, it is possible to detect 'serious aggravation of heart or lung disease, and premature mortality'. To confront this unprecedented threat, cities need to reshape their urban patterns and reprogram mobility, public spaces, and urban infrastructures towards safer, healthier, and ecological solutions.

The plan for the extension of the city of Barcelona, proposed by Ildefonso Cerdà, was originally designed to reframe built and natural environments into a hybrid urban pattern balancing lighting, ventilation, public spaces, greenery, and mobility. Nonetheless, today Barcelona is ranked among the most polluted cities in Europe.[1,2] This is partly attributable to its geography, high traffic density – four times higher than London, and large proportion of diesel-powered vehicles – currently 50%.[4]

To revert this trend, in 2016 Barcelona introduced a new urban planning model called the Superblock. It aims to reclaim public space for people, reduce motorised transportation, promote sustainable mobility and active lifestyles, provide urban greening, and mitigate the effects of climate change.[5] This planning approach treats the urban fabric as a programmable surface, regulating the access to cars and vehicles on streets while enabling the extension of walkable areas and cycling paths.

Concurrently with the development of new urban strategies, novel data-driven instruments have been emerging, providing different approaches to inform spatial planning. This chapter will highlight several techniques, triggered by computer vision and machine learning algorithms, to analyse image-based data, extracting meaningful metrics to inform spatial transformations and estimate CO2 emissions in an urban environment.

Different methodologies for image analytics will be compared and evaluated to determine the most efficient algorithms for the correct analysis and interpretation of spatial dynamics. Maps and visual representations of spatial occupancy will be generated through the application of those instruments, clustering and classifying the spatial associations among the different actors operating in the urban environment. Consequently, pollution levels will be estimated based on detected objects, calculating the carbon footprint for each agent populating the scenes under analysis.

In conclusion, this approach can provide a deeper understanding of urban dynamics, adopting image-based information for clustering and classifying the spatial dynamics produced by multiple actors operating in the urban environment and calculating their environmental footprint. This methodology can enrich emergent urban planning approaches, such as the Superblock, with a novel set of metrics and criteria based on real-time spatial usage and carbon footprints to guide and orient future urban transformations, ultimately supporting the implementation of more resilient, ecological, and sustainable urban models.

Towards Spatial Analytics

As technology improves and extends its capabilities, it becomes all the more relevant to establish decision-making protocols that promote more resilient, participatory, and responsive public spaces, in which urban configurations can be defined and redefined by a city's inhabitants.[6] These approaches become relevant for offering a clearer interpretation of spatial dynamics, beyond pre-established TPA datasets based on GPS and mobile data.

Today, at the city scale, the emergence of novel technologies is providing a variety of datasets and solutions to monitor and evaluate urban phenomena, offering a new range of opportunities to determine metrics and inform the transformation of urban spaces.

In this context, **Big Data** becomes the reference domain representing a wide spectrum of observational or informal data produced through transactional, operational, planning, and social activities. In the urban environment, these datasets establish a new operational area called **Urban Informatics**, focused on the exploration and understanding of urban systems by leveraging novel sources of data. The major potential of Urban Informatics research and applications is in four areas: (1) improved strategies for dynamic urban resource management; (2) theoretical insights and knowledge discovery of urban patterns and processes; (3) strategies for urban engagement and civic participation; and (4) innovations in urban management, and planning and policy analysis.[7]

With the growth of **multimedia data** generation and consumption, image-based data analytics plays an increasingly important role in big data analytics systems. Regarding image analytics, machine learning and computer vision algorithms provide a foundation for a variety of image-based applications.[8] In recent years, **image analytics** emerged as a disruptive technology to sense, capture, and describe complex **spatial dynamics**. In fact, today's most popular methods for representing spatial dynamics rely on a few, generic data sources. Data stored by mobile devices represent a limiting source when it comes to providing deeper insight into spatial dynamics. Those datasets present positioning inaccuracies due to incorrect GPS signals and can't provide useful insights regarding transportation means or most articulated individual behaviours.

Image analytics sensing technologies can introduce new workflows informing design solutions through spatial-sensing data. Information-rich descriptions of behaviour can support the development of **design and visualisation tools**, enabling the development of architecture that accounts for the interactions between occupants and space based on factual observations of existing and similar interactions.[9]

In the following section, this chapter will describe emerging solutions that can generate datasets from video frames by means of computer vision and machine learning, introducing convolutional neural networks to determine and classify video and image contents, providing useful insights on spatial dynamics.

Deep Learning and Spatial Analytics

The increasing quantity of publicly available labelled data, and the appearance of GPU computing, boosted deep learning algorithms, improving the performance and efficiency of neural network applications. Substantial breakthroughs in deep learning architecture date back to 2006, when Hilton et al. introduced the unsupervised training logic. These improvements paved the way for many computer vision applications implemented for object detection, image recognition, motion tracking, pose estimation, and semantic segmentation, among other algorithms. Guiding the training of intermediate levels of representation using unsupervised learning, performed locally at each level, was the main principle behind a series of developments that brought about the last decade's surge in deep architectures and deep learning algorithms.[10]

With regard to spatial analytics, deep learning algorithms are finding widespread applications. To date, image data has been used for the following purposes, among others: the behavioural analysis of crowded scenes in the context of crowd management, implemented to avoid crowd-related disasters and ensure public safety; public space design, providing indicators and metrics to inform spatial solutions; virtual environments, to validate and improve the performance of digital representations and simulations of digital crowds; visual surveillance, for automatic detection of anomalies and alarms; and culminating in intelligent environments, to reorganize flows and crowd distribution in given environments.[11]

In the Superblock framework, analysing mobility and patterns of spatial occupancy becomes a crucial parameter to calibrate instruments necessary for the activation of areas with restricted accessibilities for cars and heavy vehicles. There is a need to develop a model of mobility and more sustainable public space in order to guarantee a more accessible, comfortable, safe, and multifunctional public space in which citizens can exercise their rights to interchange, culture, leisure, expression, and demonstration, besides the right to freedom of movement.[12] Through these technologies it is possible to introduce a responsive approach to adapt, reconfigure, and extend public spaces, regulating mobility based on data-driven criteria for intervention.

Novel Methods for Image Analytics

Operational Setup

Image analytics can render spatial dynamics by detecting the locations and movements of different objects in space. Existing methods based on image analytics can be distinguished according to two main categories: computer vision and machine learning approaches.

Several algorithms have been deployed in computer vision based processes, such as optical flow, background subtraction, edge detection, etc.[13] While these approaches are able to detect the motions of different objects, they lack individual discrimination and robustness in different lighting conditions, such as in the case of weather changes. Machine learning methods can compensate for these issues, improving the accuracy of detection while also adding robustness in different lighting conditions. Some of the existing machine learning methods in image analytics include image classification, image segmentation, and object detection.

This section will focus on a comparative evaluation of recent algorithms for object detection to determine and calibrate the most accurate available solution to describe spatial dynamics, mobility, and pedestrian behaviour in public space. The experiment will be run using

Object Detection performed in a Barcelona intersection. Source: Noumena.

video frames recorded from intersections in the city of Barcelona. This context can serve as a unique testing ground for evaluating detection algorithms' performances, measuring time capabilities, identifying classes, calibrating image data sources, and outputting spatial resolution for mapping transposition.

Object Detection Algorithms

Deep learning technology has been widely used in object detection. Although deep learning technology greatly improves the accuracy of object detection, we also have the challenge of a high computational time.[14] These kinds of algorithms can be categorized according to two main characteristics.

One type includes single-stage detectors, such as YOLO (You Only Look Once) and SSD (Single Shot MultiBox Detector), which treat object detection as a simple regression problem by taking an input image and predicting the class probabilities and bounding box coordinates. A second category refers to two-stage detectors, such as Faster R-CNN or Mask R-CNN, which use a RPN (Region Proposal Network) to generate regions of interest in the first stage and send the region proposals down the pipeline for object classification and bounding-box regression. Two-stage detectors provide regions of the segmented object compared to bounding boxes from single-stage detectors. However, these algorithms also require more computation time compared to single-stage detectors. In this chapter we will focus on single-stage detectors since we are prioritising real-time capability to ensure responsive spatial solutions.

Carbon Footprint Calculation

According to studies performed by ISGlobal CREAL over an area of 56 municipalities including Barcelona, air pollution has been deemed responsible for 3,500 premature deaths per year, 1,800 hospitalisations for cardiovascular reasons, 5,100 cases of chronic bronchitis in adults, 31,100 cases of paediatric bronchitis, and 54,000 asthma attacks among both children and adults.[15] Today, the impact of air pollution on health is the most serious problem caused by the current model of mobility.

Having developed a robust method for object detection, our system introduces a computational method to define and estimate carbon dioxide emissions generated by the different actors populating the urban scene.

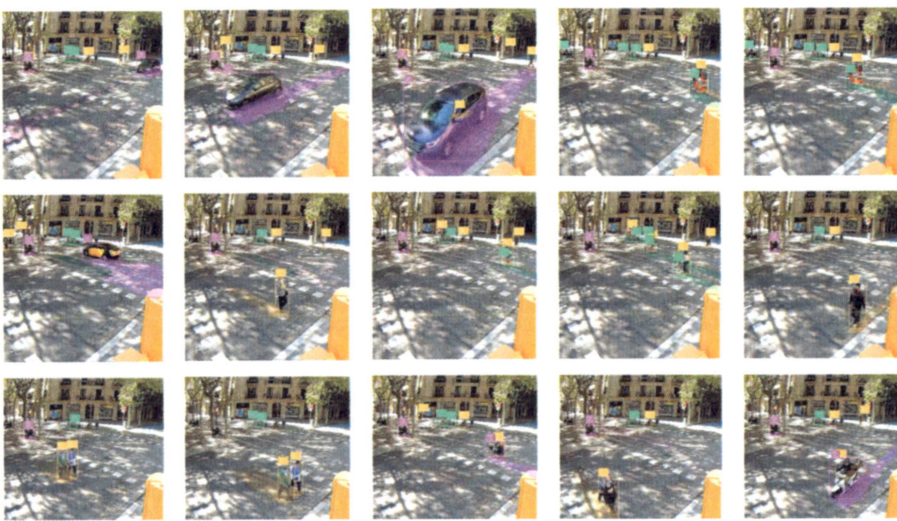

Frame analysis sequence. Source: Noumena.

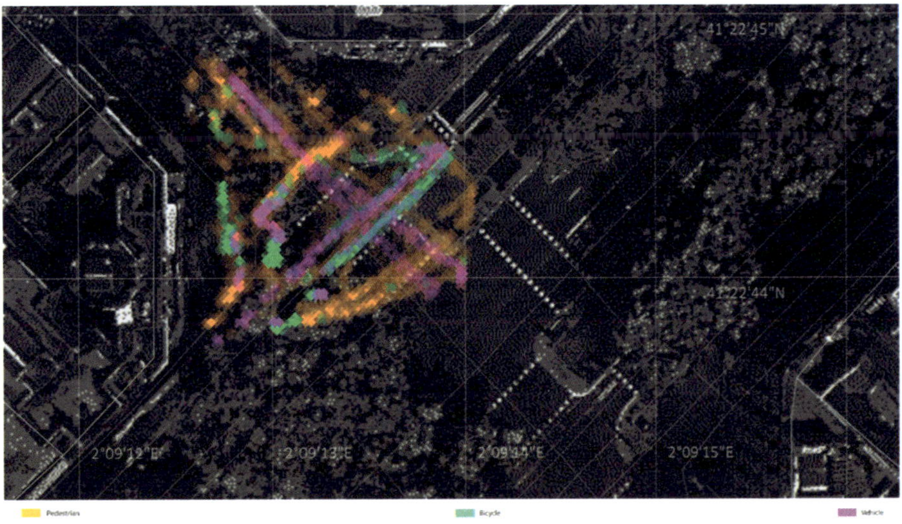

Orthomosaic representation of spatial occupancy. Source: Noumena.

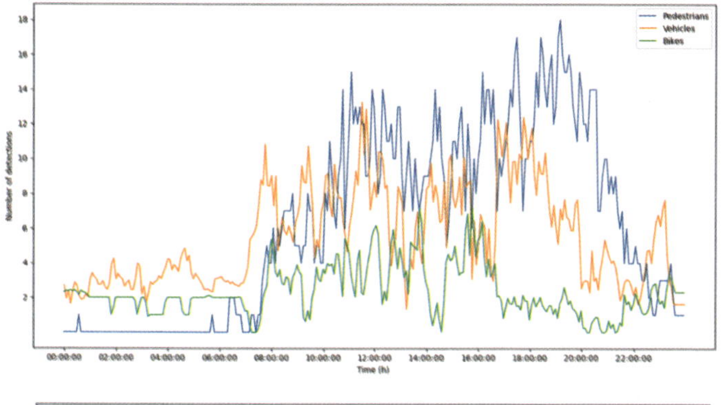

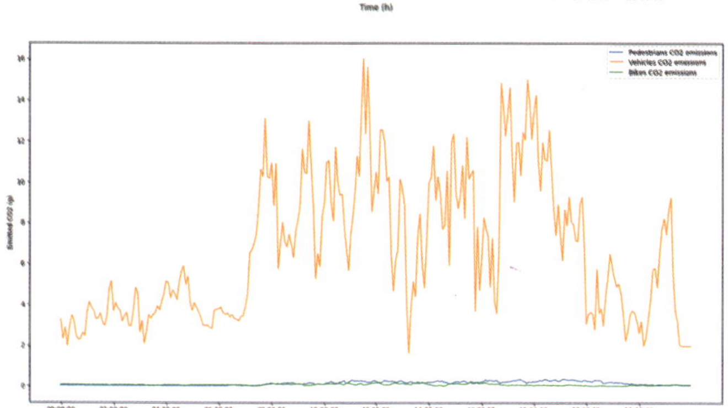

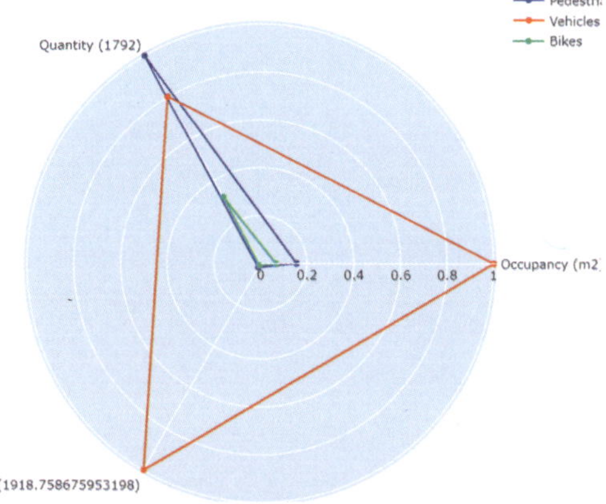

Occupancy timeline classified by different classes (pedestrian, bicycle and vehicle). Source: Noumena.

CO2 emissions timeline classified by different classes (pedestrian, bicycle and vehicle). Source: Noumena.

Radar chart of the occupancy, the quantity and the CO2 emission of the three different classes over an entire day. Source: Noumena.

The evolution of urban models such as the Superblock is defining a novel approach to city planning, driven by ecological methods intended to build healthier and safer habitats. In this context of increasing complexity, it is necessary to adopt new tools for decision making.

This chapter serves as an operational baseline, promoting machine learning techniques to evaluate the implementation of urban models such as the Superblock, establishing data-driven criteria for activation based on actual observations performed in public spaces.
In fact, AI-driven techniques can provide a deeper understanding of spatial dynamics, offering extensive insights related to spatial occupancy and carbon emissions. Nonetheless, in a panorama of rapidly evolving technologies, it becomes increasingly necessary to adopt comparable approaches to estimate more performative solutions, introducing methods such as the one described here.

Furthermore, as technology paves the way for novel applications, it becomes necessary to calibrate those instruments within a legal and administrative framework, in order to guarantee privacy, ethical coherence, and citizen participation. As a result, it becomes crucial to evaluate opportunities and implications derived from the application of these instruments, establishing a critical approach to measure novel methodologies and operational strategies.

Additionally, in parallel to technological improvement, it will be necessary to ensure the coherence of technological applications with human norms and values. Today, evaluating and calibrating these models makes up a substantial portion of the research around machine learning. The alignment problem represents the beginning of a new challenge to ensure that machine learning models will capture our norms and values.

The looming threat of a climate crisis makes it necessary to elevate our decisions, improving awareness regarding dependencies and implications of the actions we perform for the purpose of manipulating our habitats. It offers a new challenge in reshaping cities through responsive and resilient solutions.

Acknowledgments:
Noumena Data analytics: Soroush Garivani, Oriol Arroyo, Cosme Pommier, Maria Espina, Salvador Calgua
Barcelona Regional: Marc Montlleo, Director of Environmental Projects

References

1. Cyrys, J., Eeftens, M., Heinrich, J., Ampe, C., Armengaud, A., Beelen, R., Bellander, T., Beregszaszi, T., Birk, M., Cesaroni, G., Cirach, M., de Hoogh, K., De Nazelle, A., de Vocht, F., Declercq, C., Dėdelė, A., Dimakopoulou, K., Eriksen, K., Galassi, C., … Hoek, G. (2012). Variation of NO2 and NOx concentrations between and within 36 European study areas: Results from the ESCAPE study. *Atmospheric Environment,* 62, 374–390. https://doi.org/10.1016/j.atmosenv.2012.07.080

2. Eeftens, M., Tsai, M.-Y., Ampe, C., Anwander, B., Beelen, R., Bellander, T., Cesaroni, G., Cirach, M., Cyrys, J., de Hoogh, K., De Nazelle, A., de Vocht, F., Declercq, C., Dėdelė, A., Eriksen, K., Galassi, C., Gražulevičienė, R., Grivas, G., Heinrich, J., … Hoek, G. (2012). Spatial variation of PM2.5, PM10, PM2.5 absorbance and PMcoarse concentrations between and within 20 European study areas and the relationship with NO2 – Results of the ESCAPE project. *Atmospheric Environment,* 62, 303–317. https://doi.org/10.1016/j.atmosenv.2012.08.038

3. Schembari, A., Nieuwenhuijsen, M. J., Salvador, J., de, N. A., Cirach, M., Dadvand, P., Beelen, R., Hoek, G., Basaga, ña X., & Vrijheid, M. (2014). Traffic-Related Air Pollution and Congenital Anomalies in Barcelona. *Environmental Health Perspectives,* 122(3), 317–323. https://doi.org/10.1289/ehp.1306802

4. Reche, C., Querol, X., Alastuey, A., Viana, M., Pey, J., Moreno, T., Rodriguez, S., González Ramos, Y., Fernandez-Camacho, R., Verdona, A. M., de la Rosa, J. D., Dall'osto, M., Prevot, A., Hueglin, C., Harrison, R., & Quincey, P. (2011). New Considerations for PM, Black Carbon and Particle Number Concentration for Air Quality Monitoring Across Different European Cities. *ATMOSPHERIC CHEMISTRY AND PHYSICS,* 11, 6207–6227. https://doi.org/10.5194/acp-11-6207-2011

5. Mueller, N., Rojas-Rueda, D., Khreis, H., Cirach, M., Andrés, D., Ballester, J., Bartoll, X., Daher, C., Deluca, A., Echave, C., Milà, C., Márquez, S., Palou, J., Pérez, K., Tonne, C., Stevenson, M., Rueda, S., & Nieuwenhuijsen, M. (2020). Changing the urban design of cities for health: The superblock model. *Environment International, 134,* 105132. https://doi.org/10.1016/j.envint.2019.105132

6. Ho, T. K., Matthews, K., O'Gorman, L., & Steck, H. (2012). Public space behavior modeling with video and sensor analytics. *Bell Labs Technical Journal,* 16(4), 203–217. https://doi.org/10.1002/bltj.20542

7. Thakuriah, P. (Vonu), Tilahun, N. Y., & Zellner, M. (2017). Big Data and Urban Informatics: Innovations and Challenges to Urban Planning and Knowledge Discovery. In P. (Vonu) Thakuriah, N. Tilahun, & M. Zellner (Eds.), *Seeing Cities Through Big Data: Research, Methods and Applications in Urban Informatics* (pp. 11–45). Springer International Publishing. https://doi.org/10.1007/978-3-319-40902-3_2

8. Chang, H.-, Jiang, I. H.-, Hofstee, H. P., Jamsek, D., & Nam, G.-. (2015). Feature detection for image analytics via FPGA acceleration. *IBM Journal of Research and Development,* 59(2/3), 8:1-8:10. https://doi.org/10.1147/JRD.2015.2398631

9. Jørgensen, J., Tamke, M., & Poulsgaard, K. (2020). *Occupancy-informed: Introducing a method or flexible behavioural mapping in architecture using machine vision.*

10. Voulodimos, A., Doulamis, N., Doulamis, A., & Protopapadakis, E. (2018, February 1). *Deep Learning for Computer Vision: A Brief Review* [Review Article]. Computational Intelligence and Neuroscience; Hindawi. https://doi.org/10.1155/2018/7068349

11. Silveira Jacques Junior, J., Musse, S., & Jung, C. (2010). Crowd Analysis Using Computer Vision Techniques. *IEEE Signal Processing Magazine,* 5562657. https://doi.org/10.1109/MSP.2010.937394

12. Rueda, S. (2019). Superblocks for the Design of New Cities and Renovation of Existing Ones: Barcelona's Case. In M. Nieuwenhuijsen & H. Khreis (Eds.), *Integrating Human Health into Urban and Transport Planning: A Framework* (pp. 135–153). Springer International Publishing. https://doi.org/10.1007/978-3-319-74983-9_8

13. Kam Ho, T., Matthews, K., O'Gorman, L., & Steck, H. (2012). Public Space Behavior Modeling With Video and Sensor Analytics. *Bell Labs Technical Journal,* 16(4), 203–217. https://doi.org/10.1002/bltj.20542

14. Lu, S., Wang, B., Wang, H., Chen, L., Linjian, M., & Zhang, X. (2019). A real-time object detection algorithm for video. *Computers & Electrical Engineering,* 77, 398–408. https://doi.org/10.1016/j.compeleceng.2019.05.009

15. Künzli, N., & Pérez, L. (2007). The public health benefits of reducing air pollution in the Barcelona metropolitan area. *Undefined.* https://www.semanticscholar.org/paper/The-public-health-benefits-of-reducing-air-in-the-K%C3%BCnzli-P%C3%A9rez/58f8e45158eca9b2634483244b1da24a96fb939e

Crowd Wisdom and Participation

What is the connection between quantitative and qualitative data when we design the urban environment?

How do we map people's emotions, desires and needs?

Could the role of citizens and commons in AI drive towards more inclusive and participatory design processes?

How digital and social platforms can affect decision-making and urban planning?

Who trains the algorithms?

How can we "harvest" crowd wisdom to feed our design processes?

On Evolutionary Digital Design Processes & Citizen Involvement

John Frazer
in conversation with
Areti Markopoulou and Jordi Vivaldi

When we explore concepts of intelligence and evolution in the architectural and urban environments, the influential architect, writer and educator John Frazer is a key figure whose work has contributed to a radical redefinition of the operation and performance of built space. A pioneer of computer technology in design research, architecture, and urbanism, John Frazer is widely recognized as the godfather of architectural computation. He has written and published extensively on generative and evolutionary computing for sustainable and intelligent design systems, embracing the domains of participatory design, co-operative design and public involvement in architecture and urban planning.

Previous page: Experimental neural network computer. *Image by Miles Dobson, 1991.*

John Frazer's first response to our description of the current issue of "Learning Cities" was a spontaneous retrieval of The Groningen Project: a project he participated in during the 1990s with a goal to develop a co-operative urban computer model that would allow citizens to participate directly in the urban planning and development of their city. Starting with a description of the virtual model for the (until now) unpublished Groningen Project, our discussion revolves around topics of urban intelligence and prediction, as well as crowd-wisdom and participation in architecture and urban design.

The model for the Groningen Project

John Frazer: Groningen enjoyed a reputation for urban design and planning innovation, and contributors included Rem Koolhaas, Will Alsop, Zaha Hadid, Bernard Tschumi, Henri Ciriani, John Hejduk, Daniel Libeskind, Paul Virilio, Philippe Starck, Coop Himmelb(l)au, Allessandro Medini, and Mecanoo among others. Groningen now has a development plan, deepening into new urban strategies for the 21st century.

I was invited into this future planning project , in collaboration with my wife Julia, colleagues and students from the Architectural Association in London, to demonstrate the potential for an intelligent, interactive, evolving, co-operative computer model of a sustainable urban environment which would enable the citizens of Groningen to interact and influence the development of their city. Julia and I had been working on these ideas with students at the AA for about five years by then.

Whilst working on the Groningen Project, we produced a generative computer model which could mediate different parameters in scale, space and time:

- In scale, between the urban context and the fine grain of the housing typologies.
- In space, between the existing fabric of Groningen and specific dwelling units.
- In time, between the lifestyle of the medieval core and the future desires of citizens of the next century.

It is, in reality, an evolutionary model able to explain the transition from the past to the present and project trajectories for future possibilities.
A "what if" model for exploring urban futures and evaluating them.

More specifically, we developed a model which simulated the historical development of Groningen in a dynamic and predictive manner by searching in the local context for local rules which would generate self-determining emergent properties for the whole. We looked specifically at the way in which the implications of changing lifestyles and work patterns could be incorporated into the model, and we developed a structure for the model which was strategically modular - in the sense that, say, a tree's branching structure is modular without being geometrically constrained. Finally, we embodied all the ideas for the housing typologies and the site organisation, including environmental influences.

Central to the Groningen model is the idea that the computer program inhabits an environment, enters it, reads it, understands its developmental rules and history, grasps its topography, latitude and climate, models its society and economy – and then starts to solicit suggestions and make proposals for possible features.

The computer model becomes, for all intents and purposes, an inhabitant of the city. It maintains a discourse with other, human inhabitants and tries to understand and interpret their desires, aspirations, urges, expectations, and reactions to their existing environment and projected future environments. On the basis of this interaction with the actual inhabitants, the "virtual inhabitor" patiently modifies its criteria for evolutionary development and selection, endlessly repeating the process of refining and modelling prototypical futures. As it does so, it occasionally produces experimental genetic mutations or amplifies variety.

The "inhabitor" models the desires, aspirations, urges, expectations, reactions of the inhabitants to their environment and is able to project new future environments; it can inhabit at any level from cell to room, tohouse to district to cit to, regions to continent and planet. It can inhabit past and present environments and propose possible re-inhabitation of past and present habitats based on the interaction of citizens who provide feedback.

The core of the "inhabitor" is the "evolver", an evolving genetic model. The "evolver" is a recursively self-similar program which employs the same strategies at each level of interaction. It provides starting configurations, or seeds, for genetic algorithms which learn on the basis of feedback from specific sites.

The criteria for genetic selection are determined by citizen interaction with the "enabler", which, in its turn, has connections to an interactive map and an active output model. This is the basis for dialogue between the virtual "inhabitor" and the real inhabitants.

The "generator" is a hierarchically self-similar data structure that models the environment at the regional, urban, district and site scales . It can interact with other sites sing specific data. hese levels are mapped to specific situations and respond to exogenous influences.

To paraphrase Stafford Beer, the public is conceived as a system, a model of which is contained in the computer. The public supplies minimal information, which the computer then synthesises in the model. This amplifies variety as required to help the public, and attenuates variety to help the manager, thereby meeting the requirement of the law of requisite variety for each of them.

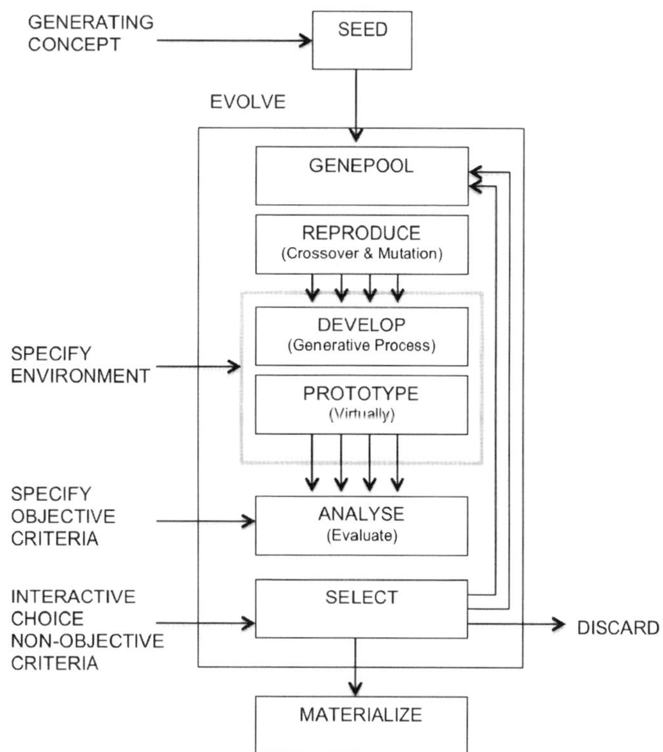

Initial Evolutionary Digital Design Process of the Groningen Model, *Diagram by John Frazer.*

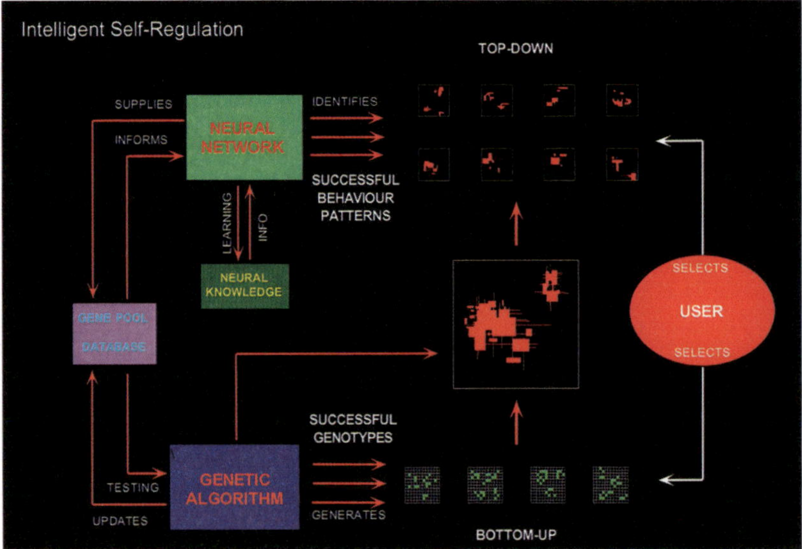

The Groningen Model and the Emerging Model of a Future, Groningen, *John Frazer and Cristiano Ceccato.*

Jordi Vivaldi: I would like to start with a famous quote from Cedric Price: "Technology is the answer, but what was the question?". What was the question that the work that you developed in the second half of the 20th century tried to answer? Do you think this question is still relevant today?

John Frazer: Let me start with the notions of "choice" and "the choice of choice". Cedric Price would talk about menus and appetites, and how we had the wrong menu. I used the word "choice" and "choice of choice", but I think Cedric's terminology of menus is nicer. The question is how to give people more choice and how to let them exercise that choice. When I was doing architecture in the 60s, the world was extremely constrained by the planners. The question on how to change the role of the architect was also relevant. I was uncomfortable with the way the architectural profession operated. Instead, I enjoyed working where agents for real social change were operating, although they weren't represented in the profession. I had a dreadful shock around 1970-72: The Royal Institute of British Architects hosted a conference on the environment. They invited me to make a presentation, which I did, but it wasn't well received by most of the participating audience! It was well received only by a very small core of people who were very excited.

It was perfectly obvious from the conversation that none of these architects in their practices saw that it was important to be worrying about the environment. They were not at all interested in the work we were doing on autonomous servicing, solar collectors, wind, energy and resources (we were doing the Cambridge autonomous housing project at that time). So that was a very unpleasant discovery.

But I was keen to change the role of the architect and I was also keen to change the role of the consumers – that is, the citizens – so that they could be more involved.

And I was keen to change the understanding of the role of the computer, which I thought was being grossly misunderstood since, at the very best, it was being used by architects as some sort of drafting aid.

Artificial intelligence was being trivialised, just like generative design has been trivialised recently.
I find that most people just pick certain things that suit them, like the ability of generative programs to produce complex shapes. Those same people pinched that bit and forgot that generative design was for a purpose - as a means to understand evolutionary modes and behaviours and optimise design accordingly - using generative techniques such as the rule-based systems of poly-automata; evolutionary techniques: genetic algorithms, learning systems, interactive systems, electronic modelling, semantic modelling, and so on.

There were all these tools available. Julia and I used those tools for Cedric Price's project called "Generator" in 1974. Cedric was wonderful to work with because he really understood the point. He was as happy as a small child when we wrote him an electronic model for his project. We flew to London from Belfast (where we were living then) with a working electronic model in a suitcase - which caused massive security problems at the airport. Cedric hired a Commodore computer from a local shop and he was so delighted by the fact that we could just fly from Ireland and plug in this model and reproduce his

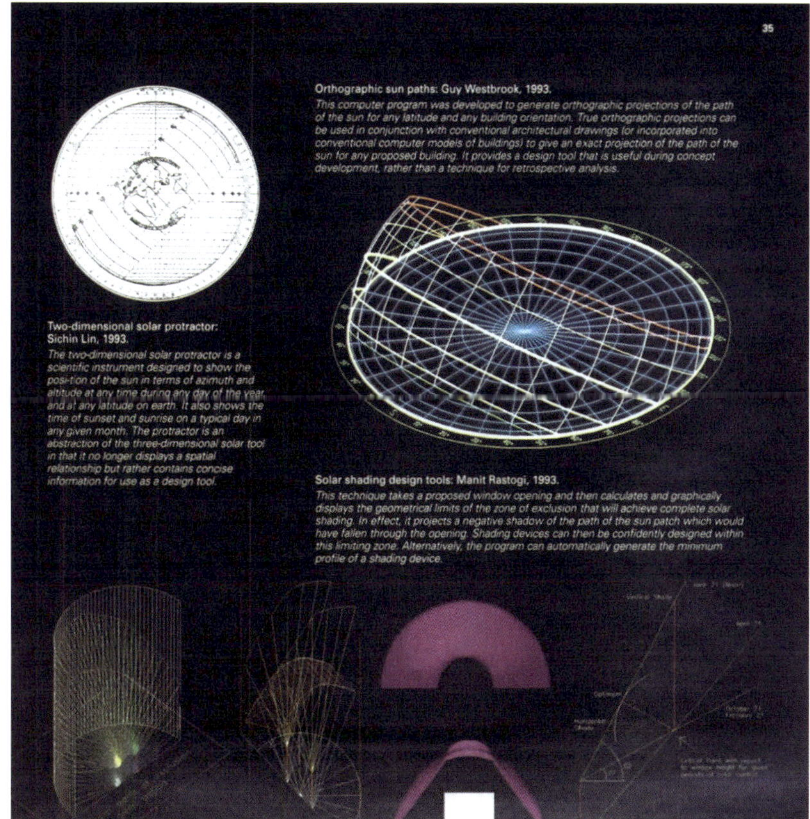

Orthographic sun paths, Two-dimensional solar protractor and Solar shading design tools, *Guy Westbrook, Sichin Lin and Manit Ratogi, 1993.*

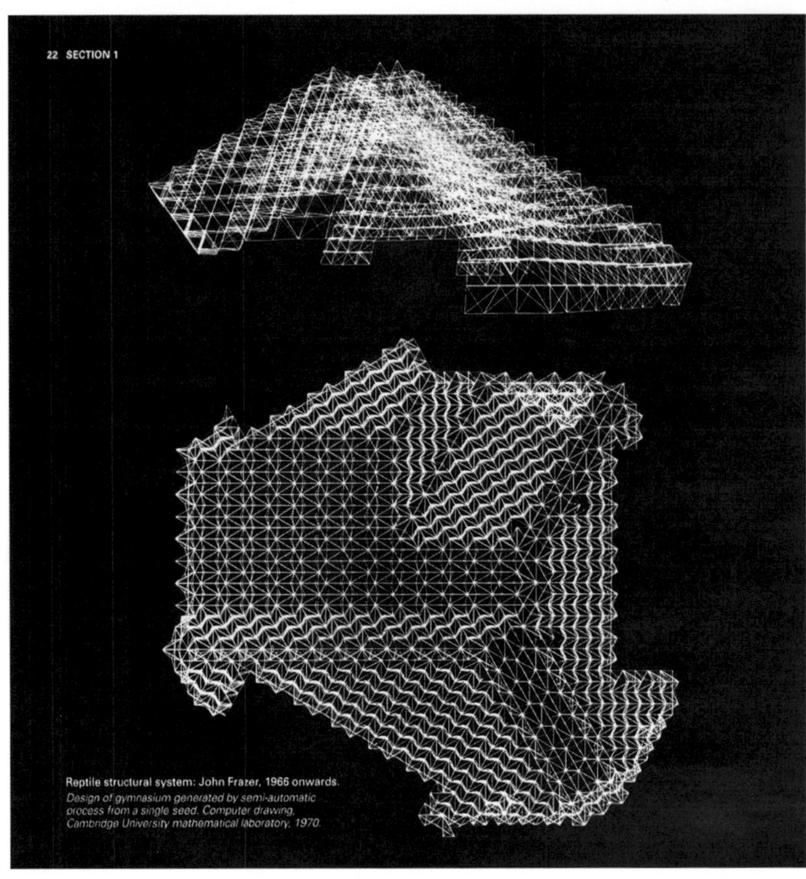

Reptile structural system: Design of gymnasium generated by semi-automatic process from a single seed, *Cambridge University mathematical laboratory, 1970.*

Following page:
Folding blanket input device, *Tim Jachna, 1993.*

Generator on the screen. He was extremely excited and thrilled, but it was perfectly obvious that he would never ever touch the computer himself.

He understood the implications of technology but refrained from using it himself. For example, he did not use an answerphone machine as he said he did not want to waste the morning on yesterday's problems. He also had a fax machine and he said it was out of paper so he could only send out faxes, not receive them. In this sense, he was highly selective about his level of personal involvement with electronic and digital technology, whilst talking very intelligently about the implications of it. . We decided to call this "computing without computers". First, one just imagines the capacity to access computers of immense power. Then one sees in which sense this is inspiring, seeing how that changes the way one thinks, without necessarily getting stuck in trying to actually design things with the computer. So, when we ran a unit of the Architectural Association, people always assumed that in order to be one of my students you had to be able to program and so on. But this was incorrect; only a small percentage of them could, some of them couldn't at all, and some of them never touched the computer.

They just used it under this idea of "computing without computers".

JV You've mentioned questions about the role of the architect and questions about the notion of evolution. In the introduction to your book An Evolutionary Architecture (1995), Gordon Pask affirms that your text prompts a line of thought that leads to a fundamental change in the understanding of the thinking of the architect: "The role of the architect here, I think, is not so much to design a building or city as to catalyse them: to act that they may evolve." The conventional association of the term evolution and the work of Darwin might lead us to think that evolution is an extremely slow process of production for our daily needs.

How might we speed up this process in order to make it operational in the architectural design field?
Does it suggest the need for a new role of the architect in the age of AI?

Is collective intelligence – organic and inorganic – crucial for this purpose?

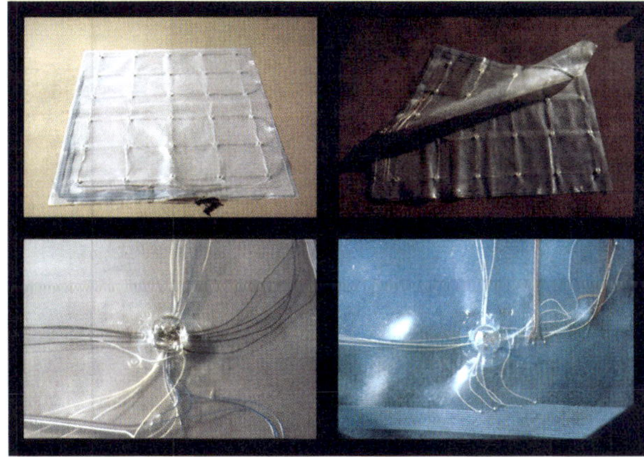

JF First of all, and in opposition to natural evolution, in architecture we don't tend to build prototypes that may collapse. They did it in the Middle Ages when a Gothic cathedral fell down because they were pushing the limits of their understanding of geometry.
That's got to be out of fashion! We are not too keen on having buildings failing as structural experiments, but with a computer you can do virtual prototyping and evaluate things in a virtual environment, and with increasing computer power that can become very fast. So, my first answer to the question is : you only do a virtual prototype when looking for simplification or optimisation to call for a basis. ature literally has all the time in the world to do its prototyping. An architect hasn't, as she's got to keep her clients.

The urgent need for speed is there. But then, so is the availability of massive computing. If we could instrumentalize all this power, we would certainly be able to generate alternative designs for cities. We can already do alternative designs for buildings. We've done them and built them. We have done yacht design, by running the evolutionary computer program overnight - f the program is well conceived, thealgorithms are effective and have clear objectives and structure - then you can produce a designvery quickly.

I think it's important to explain the relation between top-down and bottom-up processes. There are people out there who claim that one can generate something out of nothing, expecting that things will simply emerge. I think, apart from life, it is very unlikely that buildings are going to just emerge – not in the foreseeable future at least! There are two reasons underpinning this argument: one lies in the amount of power available in the structure of our knowledge, and the other lies in the reading of human intentionality as something that is of real interest. I like the idea of seeding programs top-down with intentionality and then observing the generated concept. But then I want to let it go. I do not want to start with nothing and expect something to happen. It is important to start with something and then let other people come in and interact with it. So, if you structure the program well, then you have a powerful generating model capable of producing constructive outcomes.

Evolving sequence from the Universal Constructor, *Stefan Seemüller, 1991.*

In order for the model to be operative, first of all, you've got to have an intention. You can't really say nature has an intention (unless you are religious) which raises a problem. Richard Dawkins, struggling with this, decided to call the intention in what we know to be our civilization, "The Selfish Gene". Dawkins offered the idea that a gene had the idea of its own selfishness in order to thrive. Although I find that very hard to agree with, the important aspect is that at its base there is an intention. A model that is capable of both evolution and development has an intention at its core. There are a few architects who have ideas which are susceptible to all kinds of evolution and development - Cedric Price is an extreme example with The Generator project.

For the majority of architects, their ideas are stuck in time: a concept is one concept,one building, without any ability to be anything else. I am not arguing that such approaches aren't useful, but this is definitely a different world and game than the one we are discussing now.

To go back to the top down seeding of the program: the seed is encoded in computer terms - a person's (or designer's) intentionality has been captured and encoded. This is very much the most difficult part of the process, at least as far as I'm concerned. And then you breed the seed using genetic algorithms and evolutionary algorithms. You have an environment, you start multiplying these factors, you develop a population of different variants in that environment, you explore those variations, and then you generate virtual prototypes in order to analyse the performance of those prototypes using objective criteria. But this process also allows users, and indeed architects, to use subjective and non-objective criteria as well to aid design decisions Just to digress on Darwin for moment - he faced the problem of explaining natural selection. He starts in chapter one of 'On the Origin of Species' by talking about unnatural selection or artificial selection. And then in chapter four he gets out of it by saying, "If you've got all the time in the world and billions of years, you can evolve by natural selection". Darwin clearly differentiates between natural selection and artificial selection. This is also the difference between convergent evolution and divergent evolution, which are also important aspects of this process

One of the reasons why we have a little bit of error in the copying of DNA lies in the fact that you can produce divergent evolution, so we don't all get stuck in a rut. However, most of the time, evolution is converging on improving something. Most people who use these kinds of algorithms coming from engineering expect convergent natural selection (natural meaning objective in this case), forgetting there are other divergent possibilities. Well, now there is a lot of fun to be had there, particularly if you as the designer interferes in the process. Instead of simply letting an algorithm breed some results, you can adjust the perameters - turn up the random number generator for instance, to produce more and more errors in the code and, therefore, produce more divergent evolution.

We used to turn up the random number generator, producing all kinds of wild ideas very quickly, which is great fun, but not necessarily the best way of doing serious work. The best option is usually a mix of a very small amount of random numbers.

Once one has produced the virtual prototype, then it is necessary to analyse the performance and select successful outcomes with both objective and subjective criteria. Then, one can recycle those in the gene pool: one can select some of them for materialisation in order to build them as actual prototypes. One can run pretty accurate analyses of the structural and environmental performances for example, but also in relation to some aspects of mobility, traffic, or accumulation of goods, among others. I do believe, therefore, that evolutionary speed could be very high!

JV Matters of speed are usually also associated with processes of A.I. As a sort of recursive myth, A.I. has been abundantly conjured up in different geographies and epochs. It seems that, especially in the Western world, there is a desire for emulating the activity of a God capable of producing not only life, but also intelligence. Why do you think that we keep coming back to A.I. as a society in general, and, more in particular, on the architectural scene? Why in the 70s and 80s? What are the dangers of posing it as new today? What could be lost?

JF Let me place here two different perspectives: a general one and a personal one. The general perspective is that there seems to be some urge to try to play God, as it were, and there's a lot of misunderstanding about that. The other urge is greed, of course.I lived for seven years in China and got quite friendly with the director of a university research centre where they were doing a lot of work on genetic algorithms and eventually, after a series of visits, he showed me the very top floor of his lab and I was stunned to find they were using genetic algorithms to predictively model the behaviour of the world's stock markets!

The cause of this fascination also lies in human laziness and occasional lack of energy. I realised I couldn't possibly do by hand all the work these genetic algorithms are doing. And to do that, the obvious thing is to have programs which learn. And they were already learning right in front of me when I first started, when I didn't know about genetic algorithms. My first program emulated the use of Donald Michie's work at Edinburgh University where he developed a technique for rewarding the outcomes of learning programs: you reward successful outcomes and you punish unsuccessful outcomes, so gradually the algorithms learn according to these systems of rewards. After this initial approach, I came across genetic algorithms and I understood that this might be the best way to optimize the process. In my case, therefore, using artificial intelligence (in the slightly limited sense of machine learning at least) is a manner to achieve the automation of these processes, which otherwise I was doing tediously and painstakingly by hand.

Areti Markopoulou: I wanted to open up a little chapter about risks and fierceness in relation to A.I. because, of course, there are a lot of doubts that go hand to hand with the idea of A.I. and architecture. One of the first criticisms, or fears, that we see in many people is that machine learning and machine thinking will take over a big part of designers' decisions while it will also automate or even eliminate important creative processes from designers'minds related to subjective choice, personal abstraction, customisation and more. I know that you have been talking about the idea of human intentionality, but I would like you to elaborate a bit on how far you see these fears as valid; or are the parameters of the design process so complex that, to some extent, no machine could eventually replace them?

JF There are genuine reasons for fear. One is that the architectural profession has refused to get involved in a sensible dialogue about these technological advancements, and they left them to the technical experts. I think this is very unfortunate because they don't necessarily share the same set of values. There is also another reason to be afraid: some of these insights have been implemented in such incorrect ways that when you actually look at the result you may think that it might eliminate the need for some architects - and that maybe this wouldn't be a bad thing in some cases. But how is anyone going to distinguish or discriminate? I think there's genuine worry there.

The Universal Constructor, working model of a self-organizing interactive environment, *Group Project, 1990.*

Another point to take into account is that architects' attitude towards the possibilities and limitations of the use of A.I. has been ambiguous, or better said, ambivalent. Right from the beginning, at the point when we started with drafting machines such as CAD, architects were horrified that it was going to take over the design process from them. They thought they could draw, and instead they had to teach the machine how to draw. For them, in this situation the fun is over because the only thing that they actually enjoyed has been replaced. They certainly feared that. Moreover, the same architects were disappointed to discover that they still had to sort information into a CAD system, and introducing information into AutoCAD was extremely tedious, or a boring process to do. They were rather disappointed by the fact that it wasn't more automated, and this is why I think there has been a mindless ambivalence to this all along. No one is taking enough interest to get deep into better analysing and understanding the processes of A.I., and while there is much negative press about it, it also creates much hysteria.

AM Let me pose another scenario now. Following some of Nicholas Carr's views, the most revolutionary consequences of the internet and thinking machines will not be that computers will mimic and think like humans, but rather that we will come to think like computers. What about the risk of a scenario in which the artificial intelligence that we are creating actually may turn out to be our own? What about witnessing a kind of rising extensive use of machines that take decisions for us? Could that bring about an unprecedented weakness in human creative and critical thinking?

JF I think all that is possible, indeed. I think the human race seems to have enjoyed mechanistic allergies for centuries, starting with cogwheels. It has gradually moved into electronics, under the premise that the human brain works like a computer. Well, it doesn't. Anyone who knows a bit about how computers or human brains operate, knows that.

I do, though, agree with the worry about how this algorithmic process might genuinely influence the act of thinking; this might indeed be a cause for concern. Another cause for concern would be that we don't know what is inside and outside the algorithm. When the algorithm makes some of these decisions, we usually don't know how it is doing it. I bought a car recently that's got too much intelligence in it for me to cope with. I don't understand what it is trying to do when I am slithering around on the ice and it thinks it knows better than me how to control the car. I don't know what it is trying to do, and I think that not knowing could be very dangerous in a more general sense. We, therefore, need more transparency about how these systems are working and which are the bases of their operation.

Of course, there is also an issue related to laziness: it's just so easy to capitulate over machines and computers (as it is over politicians) that tell us what and how to do things. Although this has been going on for 50 years or so, in some cases, as for example in relation to software interfaces, there is not enough imagination to anticipate what people might do wrong. People can easily claim that it's the machine's fault, although it might be the programmer's fault for leading algorithms through a particular way. Or, as in other cases, they might assume that we want to be approached in a linear manner, when, in fact, one might want to go back and change his or her mind about something.

And this can actually make the whole process and objective collapse: for example, you finish by either ordering no cans of baked beans or one hundred cans by mistake! There is a serious issue in this case which I think is clearly related to education. We should be teaching more in schools, not only about programming (because it is like Latin, just in another form) but mainly about understanding logical thinking processes – that is, what constitutes a logical process, and how do machines learn.

If we get to teach people how computers learn then we will probably avoid much of these fearful arguments. It's not the computer that is scary, but human nature; it is human ignorance that is scary, not artificial intelligence.

Gordon Pask with the Universal Constructor. Diploma 11 installation, AA end-of-year exhibition, June 1990.

64 SECTION 2

Emergent forms under solar influence: Guy Westbrook, 1993.
An initial circular form (which considers all possible sun angles) is allowed to 'grow' with different constraints on its response to the movements of the sun. Lines and surfaces have the potential to grow and/or move under the influences of the mathematical environment created by solar geometry. The surfaces grow outwards in the directions of greatest solar radiation, while the edges and planes respond to undesirably high levels of solar radiation, forming extensions that protect the sensitive core of the form. Just one criterion, such as solar shading, was used in these studies to make the implications clearer. Multi-criteria studies followed later.

Emergent forms under solar influence, *Guy Westbrook, 1993.*

JV Before you mentioned the expression "too much intelligence". I would like to introduce here some press comments on Cedric Price's The Generator (1976) which state the following: "But the real breakthrough by Price's computer consultants John and Julia Frazer is to give the Generator a concept of boredom. If the site is not reorganised for some time or conditions change, it will get bored and start to suggest its own plans." One might think that too much intelligence might lead to boredom and, thus, be counterproductive, particularly in the field of architecture.
How can we overcome this phenomenon?

JF Cedric Price was worried that people wouldn't change the building enough for a very simple reason: they weren't used to the building being able to change. So, I asked myself the following: why doesn't the building provoke some sort of change? Since the algorithm was learning from people's reactions and desires, this would also be part of the learning process for all. This is related to Gordon Pask's "Musicolour Machine", a machine that turned on flashing lights in response to changes in the tempo and rythmn of a jazz band. Although this might sound irrelevant today because every rock group on the planet has used that gadget for the last 60 years, the truth is that it didn't really exist before Pask. He was the one who got this started, particularly the fact that the lights changed in response to the rhythm, although he decided that alone might be a bit boring. He started, therefore, to build in the concept of boredom to his machine: eight algorithms were prepared to detect the possibility of repeated patterns in the song of the band and, if that happened (i.e. it repeated too many times), the lights slowly turned off. Then the band was provoked into producing more variations. While the entire process was more complex than that - there were also dancers involved that were responding mostly to the lights and the jazz group, the musicians then responded to the dancers responding to the light, which created a complex feedback loop. I thought that was an absolutely brilliant idea in order to keep bands on their toes; and so part of what Cedric, Julia and I were thinking about was how to keep the users of Generator on their toes.

Experiments with neural networks, *Miles Dobson, 1991.*

AM I think we have been talking a lot about the minds of architecture, and now I would also like to discuss the body of it. I've sometimes observed that the AI applications in architecture are purely mechanical, and I'm not sure they are intelligent or evolutionary, at least the way that you were framing it. You describe it as a form of artificial life, where architecture attempts to evolve its form and structure in an emulation of the evolutionary processes of nature, such as morphogenesis, genetic coding, replication, selection, etc. I wonder to what extent this evolution can happen when the body of architecture, especially its materiality, is limited to concrete, steel or glass. In order for architecture to think and behave cognitively like humans, doesn't it require a body that is similar to a living organism's body? How could that body eventually relate to the mind?

JF I wrote a paper called "The Intelligent Teacup", which was about starting experiments in which the intelligence would be embedded in the object: that is, what we call,a data structure. It is a structure which has waves of logic going out from cells. The structure is generated in the clay in a manner analogous to forming transistors. Faults are created which can replicate and the faults, or dislocations, are how information and logic are stored.The cup, then, will be able to start computing alterations to its own design and ideally would be able to actually move and change. There are several points to say about that. One of them is that we have a lot of experiments with intelligent cubes which plug together. They are physical modelling systems, all cubes with intelligence embedded within them. Occasionally, someone sends me a cube in the post - with their own intelligence embedded in it... This experiment has been done many, many times. Why are they repeating our experiment? Because they are exploring intelligent materials. There's a group in France exploring intelligent materials that use our modelling systems to simulate the behaviour of the material at a molecular level. As we move to quantum computing, I envisage the physical construction of computers with this intelligence and understanding embedded within them. .
Although, what has actually been achieved with this today is somewhat limited. It would be useful to reference here a brilliant and largely analog experiment of one of my PhD students who was a weaver. A weave is in fact a linear series, an automata; while in the formulation, one stitch can be described by the next stitches on either side of it. We can therefore describe this as a linear automata: it's one row after another. When my student started developing weaves for an exhibition, the experienced weavers that saw them were amazed simply because they saw completely new weaves and patterns produced in a way they had never imagined. They could be described as the outcome of the physical errors in the system and, although, as I mentioned we are still a bit away from such applications, we could eventually think of the outcome at the level of a sweater or blanket or as a building or a city.

AM I would like to discuss the circular feedback thinking and its relation to the model of big data in the current mainstream idea of smart cities. Drawing on Gordon Pask's conversational theory, we know that a big change of information and feedback among objects, environments and machines can lead to the creation of knowledge that will allow both the environment and the objectís user to alter their behaviour. But if we observe how the big data in city models works, we actually observe a profoundly linear approach. How could we apply a multiple feedback evolutionary model to future cities and in the planning in order to break with that linearity?

JF The Groningen model indicated to some extent how that could be done with models at lots of different scales. It was a recursively self-similar model. The Living Systems book by J.G. Miller proposes a self-similar diagram, while it presents several subsystems in each level of the cell: the organ, the organism, the group, and the organisation, among others. We took as a reference this brilliant approach and tried to apply a similar idea to our system. One of the things we did was to make our model identical at each level, arguing that it was our belief that if you looked at a room in the city, it behaved the same as a building in the city, which behaves the same as a street path in the city. In Groningen we had lots of well observed examples. The way the salt pot was arranged on the table in the the cafe actually reflected the way the street was organised. And although the process followed was not exactly evolutionary, the point was that, in the computer system, we said that we thought this was a good basis for the assumption. Having done that, it basically means that all you've got to be able to do is get control of the system at any one of the levels - or one could say scales. If you have an output at one level or scale, then you can influence what's going on up and down from that, since you were up and down in the same recursively self-similar system. This, additionally, greatly reduces the amount of programming required: it greatly reduces the time it takes to run the program because you can run it at just the level you are interested in. If you're interested that day in the design of doorknobs, you don't have to bother to run the whole city model and vice versa.

The first building procured from a building information model was One Isalnd East in Hong Kong. There were no traditional drawings produced as such, but all constructional data was derived directly from the model.

Although this case study came twenty years after the Groningen model, we had dealt back then with similar problems. We actually got to finance some of our research in the early days by selling drafting systems (we sold the first drafting system Autoplan two years before AutoCAD). One of Autoplan's tricks was that, in order to deal with the very rudimentary power of the computers available at that time, the software had the ability to leave out anything other than the detail necessary for the task in hand.

Following page:
Self-builder design kit,
working electronic system,
John and Julia Frazer, consultants, with John Potter, research assistant, for architect Walter Segal 1982.

So, this idea of subdividable tasks is crucial. The way that the model is subdividable can directly affect how you keep control of the model. What you could do is allow some of this linearity of connections to be isolated at one level and adjusted, but inside the model. The model could then be put back together and the designer look at the implications of the changes, stretched all away from the doorknob to the region of the planet. I'm talking about Buckminster Fuller's omni-directional halo approach. Our initial model started with the planet and with a nervous system for the planet. In such a system you can go all the way from the planet down to the doorknob, which is always a kind of metaphorical example, but you obviously don't model every doorknob on the planet in order to run the model. However, the way in which you model the doorknob might well have a huge effect on the way you plan the bigger model in its totality.

AM What is a learning city for you?

JF I think all cities learn already. We have previously discussed intentionality. One might say one vernacular city, a little Italian hill town, is not designed since there's no intentionality. The reality is that there was a sort of urge to build a city in a particular way and, as it went on, it kind of self-organized. I think there is indeed intentionality in that process, in the sense of having a collective consciousness in self organization. One can see such city models as self-organizing systems, and in a way all we need to do is to tap into that ability of a city to self-organise.

If we observe the human body, we can actually detect the waste and leftovers of cellular activity. We are just a pile of dead cells. Isn't that what a city is? A skin made by the cellular activity of all the people in it can tell us everything about this city. There is a reciprocity between form and behaviour. Form influencing behaviour, behaviour influencing form and, whatever operation one performs in such a system, it has to tap into that reciprocity, linking and getting inside it, being part of it. The learning city is just an extension of that.
Another crucial operation is the one of linking cities together. My former student, Cristiano Ceccato made a project called "talking cities". Cristiano was working with me on the Groningen project and his idea was to boost the ability of cities to learn from each other. Using a series of computer screens, each with a different city, Ceccato was running the Groningen model on all of them in an effort of trying to modify this model in order to fit each city and then for them to talk to each other. Cities could exchange information about how to organise each other, and perhaps New York could learn from a bicycle city like Amsterdam. Within this idea there could be some lateral learning, and I think that is an important aspect when we deal with the idea of Learning Cities. Rather than focusing on just one intelligent city, we should consider a network of Learning Cities around the globe – interconnected cities talking to each other, exchanging information among them and eventually talking and exchanging information with the environment, such as the forests or rural areas, consolidating a deep understanding of that interaction.

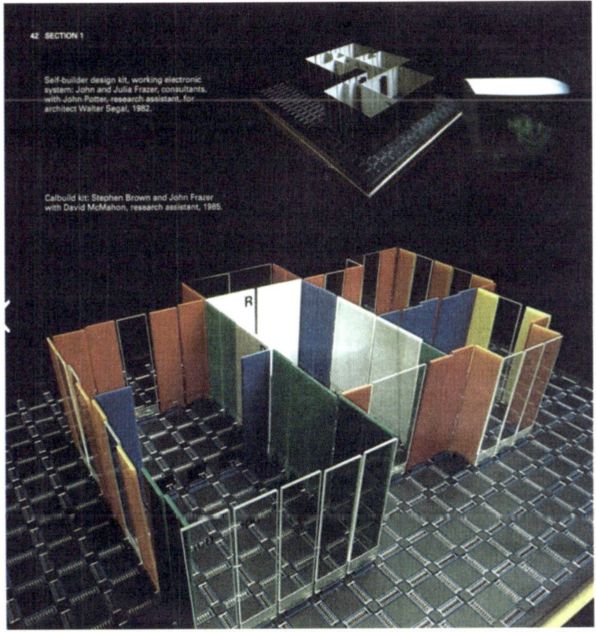

It is crucial to remember Buckminster Fuller's "World Game" in this context a world game sort of updated to a massive computational level, far beyond the computation we've got at the moment. Although we can't do that yet, we need to think about doing it. It is important that some people think ahead and imagine the implications. That's my idea of computing without computers: just imagine you've got these technologies and see what the implications would be before you go to all the trouble to write all that complex code. You need to envision what you want, the interface you need, the software required, but, above all, you need to answer the following question: What are you going to do with it as an architect?

Social Realism in the Age of Simulation

Jose Sanchez

The work of social realist artists such as Diego Rivera, Jose Clemente Orozco, or David Alfaro Siqueiros between the 1920s and 1930s made a conscious attempt to reconnect with the public by the practice of a form of figurative realism, bringing attention to the exploitation of anonymous workers. This movement was instigated by the political turmoil of the time, dominated by an economic depression, racial conflict, and the rise of fascist regimes[1]. The artist's gaze was turned towards the worker and the labor practices that structured the economic system. The portrayal of exploitation was coupled with a depiction of the heroism of the working class in the form of endurance and resilience, and ultimately with a sense of optimism for social revolutions. Amid the current political turmoil, with the rise of economic inequality as studied by Thomas Piketty[2] and the rise of new forms of behavior manipulation with social media platforms as argued by Shoshana Zuboff,[3] it has become imperative to turn our gaze again towards the labor practices that enable and perpetuate social inequality. In architecture, the software tools used by architects every day have been 'sanitized' of areas that are not productive to the discipline. Under the banner of the 'division of labor',[4] architects have been able to indulge in geometry and abstraction or be content with the engagement of politics through aesthetics.[5]

Previous page:
Common'hood screenshot.
Community management and
means of production.

Previous double page: Common'hood. Screenshot of opening scene. Eviction and dispossession.

Today, the majority of computational models preferred by architects consider labor as an externality, focusing on tools for computational geometry and representation. This has been achieved by design, mirroring the requirements of clients and contractors who see architecture as a speculative investment. There is no value spread 'trickling down' the supply chain, as the supply chain is invisible to designers.

Outside the realm of architecture software developed with intrinsic biases, it is possible to develop a discourse of design and conceptualization of tools that integrate historic externalities such as ecological dependencies, cultural heritage, or labor practices into novel design environments. Revisiting social realism today does not only mean turning our gaze toward the narrative of workers in the form of figurative representation; it also means allowing for the design of environments that are unable to produce models that are blind to social and ecological variables. The inclusion of the worker should be seen as a necessary reintegration of labor and human conditions into simulated models of production for their contribution to value production.[6]

Social organizations that are able to define local forms of value should be understood as sympoietic actors in the production of architecture. Sympoiesis, as discussed by Donna Haraway, places emphasis on the idea that nothing is truly autopoietic or self-organizing; rather, there is always a form of co-production, or 'making with'.[7] In architecture, case studies such as cooperative organizations or community land trusts are mechanisms of co-production that carve out resilience from market forces. How might it be possible to generate design frameworks or technological platforms that facilitate the production and maintenance of such organizations? The role of platforms should be scrutinized as potential mechanisms of value extraction, where the term 'participation' is a way to outsource the production of knowledge or a publicity stunt to support a public 'buy-in'. Participation only becomes meaningful if it is engaged as a form of co-production, with the legal frameworks to ensure the ownership and attributions of value to those producing it. It is in this context that participation is formally defined and capable of establishing codependence with the expertise of architects. However, such codependence is not possible unless architects are able to define new bridges between the discipline and the public.

The video game research conducted as part of the Plethora Project aims to design public interfaces for advancing a collective idea of architecture, one that is intrinsically mediated by scarcity and integrates cultural narratives in the process of creation. Video game interfaces are understood as software with an explicit bias, one that is carried by a narrative. In the tradition of social realism, the narrative presented is a literal reading of the consequences of a neoliberal economy, populated by foreclosures, poverty, displacement, and homelessness. The design environment is no longer a neutral container but is charged by an awareness of cultural narratives that have become far too common in our current economy. Still, the projects remain purposefully optimistic, attempting to construct a shared vision of economic autonomy through cooperative enterprises and mutual aid networks. The co-production of the commons as a design agenda should be understood as a collective enterprise, one that will need tools for the coordination and emergence of collective subjectivities.

The project Common'hood is an architectural design platform for the coordination and peer-to-peer propagation of self-provided architecture. The game rejects the narrative of abundance perpetuated by contemporary design software, which offers an infinite supply of primitives and operations for design. Abundance is conceptualized as a 'common' only achieved if a large population of designers decides to contribute to the production of a common pool of architectural knowledge. Common'hood uses 'blueprints' as a form of knowledge propagation. Blueprints in the game are data structures that group and store a series of player actions. The software does not store geometry but rather human decisions in space, allowing the game to establish a peer-to-peer protocol for knowledge transfer.

The game has been structured as the interaction between different datasets: resources, technologies (machines), agents (workers), know-how, moods, and environments. Each of these datasets establishes a codependence with other datasets, making it possible to model scenarios that alter a designer's perspective. Unlike 'God-Games', where the player is able to dictate all workers' actions or materialize resources, or 'Tycoon' games that aim to demonstrate a player's ability

Common'hood screenshot. Community management and means of production.

to amass wealth through strategic decision making, Common'hood seeks to bring players onto a flat ontological plane, where their actions in the game can be understood as symmetrical with those of simulated agents. This perspective forces players to 'request' help and design production plans that must incorporate an equitable distribution of wealth if they are to succeed. The game is designed to offer players the opportunity to define their own objectives or metrics of progress, placing emphasis on the possibility of the emergence of communities of players who might share similar value systems. An example of this might be the emergence of communities of players specialized in farming practices or 'tiny-houses' as areas of interest that are already present in DIY cultures.

Common'hood also subscribes to the thesis behind discrete architecture,[8] in which the organization or patterning of standardized materials is seen as more critical than the customization of parts. Discrete design reconsiders serial repetition, allowing the differentiation of form to be achieved through combinatorics.[9] The discrete movement also seeks to distance itself from the tradition of modularity as a homogenizing strategy towards standardization and instead focus on the compatibility and linkages between otherwise incompatible geometries. The movement also sees the necessity of conceptualizing a distributed and diverse economy, rejecting practices of vertical integration that seek to monopolize markets.[10]

Moving away from the fluid tectonics of parametrics, which attempts to dissolve parts into larger impenetrable wholes, parts are central to the discourse of the discrete as they are thought to offer a 'combinatorial surplus,' a positive externality that allows for the knowledge embedded in tectonics to potentially migrate and find new architectural contexts. Similarly, Common'hood expands on the infrastructure that supports discrete design and rejects the idea that discrete architecture is just a post-parametric style of pixelation and big data. The challenge for the discrete movement is, in fact, to go beyond the technical knowledge of discrete aggregation utilizing Grasshopper platforms such as WASP[11] and double down on the possibility of an architectural movement focused on the participatory capabilities of form, and the novel forms of coordination and cooperation, using the tectonics of the building as a common language.

Previous page: Common'hood screenshot. Self-sufficiency and autonomy in the occupation of an abandoned structure.

Common'hood screenshot. Online interface for sharing designs in the form of blueprints.

While a project such as Common'hood started as an independent research initiative, the project will not succeed unless it is able to open up channels for 'user occupation.' Beyond just participating as a user of the game, the project aims to grow towards a true form of co-production. An opportunity in this respect can be seen through

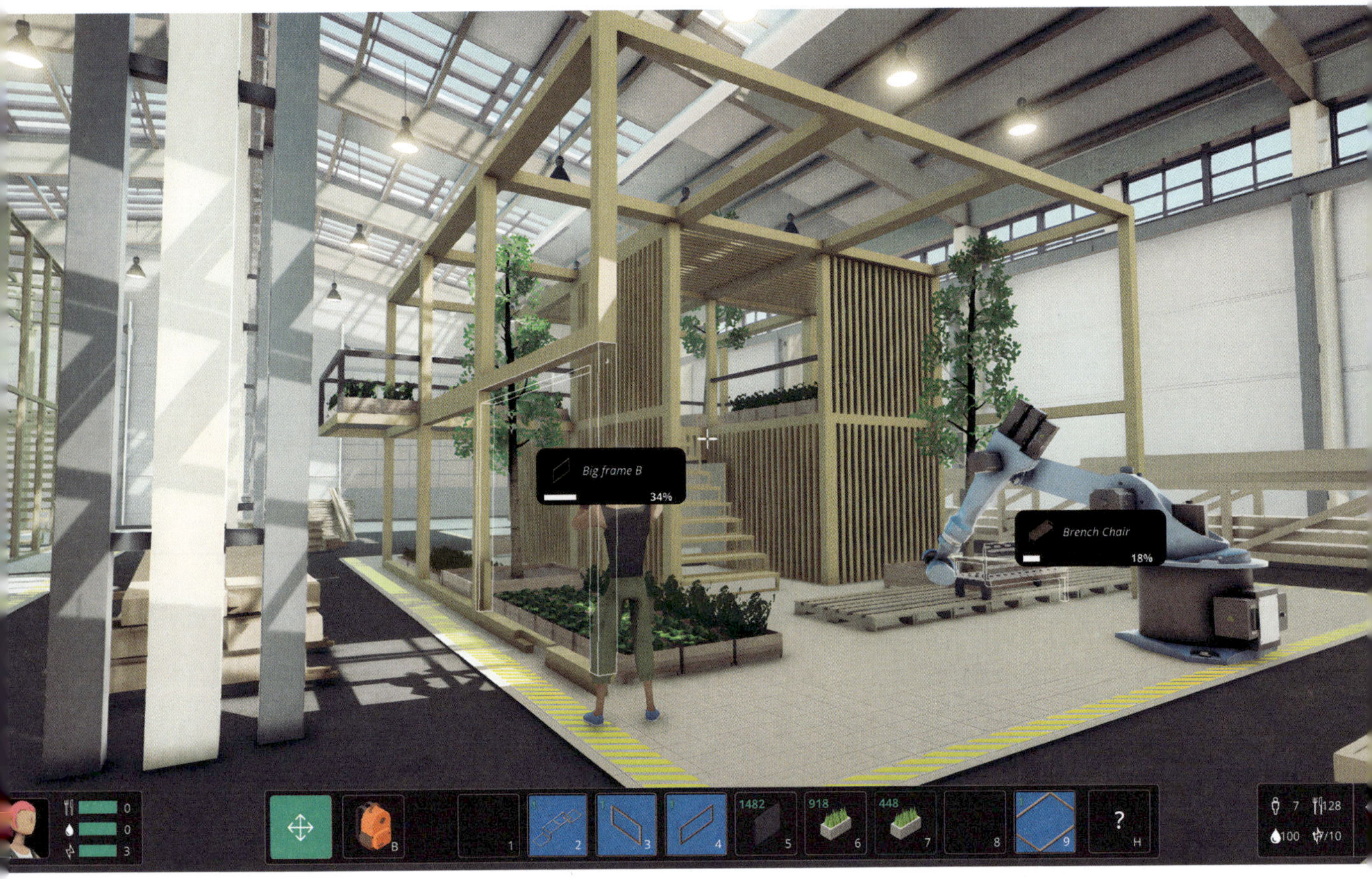

the practice of 'modding', where players or independent developers are able to expand the game beyond the original foundation. Here again, the question of fair compensation of labor should lead the implementation, in order to prevent the free labor of hobbyists from becoming a source of capital extraction. With these questions in mind, Common'hood attempts to explore forms of player coordination, enabling tools for sharing and establishing a dialog with the architects producing the platform.

The production of form within a simulated environment such as Common'hood, just like any medium of representation, will have some distance from actual materialization. Nevertheless, the project is on a trajectory to support the propagation of real-world designs, offering catalogs of design recipes that can range from ideas for urban farming to housing. The accuracy and effectiveness of the content produced within the platform are inevitably outside the complete control of the architects and will only be dictated by the emergence of meaning and appropriation within the online communities.

Top previous page: Common'hood screenshot. Player's creations utilizing the blueprint system.

Bottom previous page: Common'hood screenshot. Design utilizing a large number of blueprints, combining simulated human labor and robotic automation.

References

1. Rochfort, D. (1998). *Mexican Muralists: Orozco, Rivera, Siqueiros.* Chronicle Books.

2. Piketty, T. (2014). Capital in the Twenty-First Century. Belknap Press: An Imprint of Harvard University Press.

3. Zuboff, S. (2019). *The Age of Surveillance Capitalism: The Fight for a Human Future at the New Frontier of Power.* PublicAffairs.

4. Riach, J. (2014). Zaha Hadid defends Qatar World Cup role following migrant worker deaths. Retrieved September 16, 2020, from https://www.theguardian.com/world/2014/feb/25/zaha-hadid-qatar-world-cup-migrant-worker-deaths

5. Gage, M. F. (2019). *Aesthetics Equals Politics.* MIT Press.

6. Mazzucato, M. (2018). *The Value of Everything: Making and Taking in the Global Economy.* PublicAffairs.

7. Haraway, D. J. (2016). *Staying with the Trouble: Making Kin in the Chthulucene.* Duke University Press Books.

8. Sanchez, J. (2020). *Architecture for the Commons: Participatory Systems in the Age of Platforms.* Routledge.

9. Sanchez, J. (2014). Polyomino – Reconsidering Serial Repetition in Combinatorics. Riverside Press.

10. Sanchez, J. (2020). Architecture for the Commons: Participatory Systems in the Age of Platforms. Routledge.

11. Rossi, A. (2019). WASP. Retrieved September 16, 2020, from https://www.food4rhino.com/app/wasp.

HUAWEI
Mobility Program
Car Park
Bike Parking

Superbarrio
Gamification tools for data-driven participatory urban design

Marco Ingrassia, Areti Markopoulou
and Chiara Farinea

Participatory design strategies of the urban environment have been implemented since the 1960s with multiple benefits, including addressing the citizens' needs and desires,[1,2] educating citizens on the impact of alternative design solutions and creating a consensus,[3] educate on diversity and foster community-making through the confrontation and synthesis of diverse positions and identities,[4] and activating the citizen agency and behavioral change.[5] The traditional approach to spatial participatory design is based on procedural logic, with a combination of one-to-one activities and community gatherings, aimed at developing final design solutions that are later implemented and delivered to the citizens, who are considered final users.

In order to inform decision-making in a "rational" and systematic way, spatial participatory design has been based mainly on the collection of extensive quantitative data through closed-question surveys or polls, i.e., preferences regarding demanded functions or the selection of alternative design solutions. On the contrary, the collection of qualitative data, capable to report individual positions without superimposed methodological framings, has been limited by the time-extensive collection process - through design proposals, open question surveys, interviews, mental maps - and the difficulty to discretize and interpret data to inform decision making.

Previous page:
Figure 1: Superbarrio video-game interface for Barcelona.

In the last decades, the emergence of a systemic and ecological vision has questioned the traditional cartesian epistemology based on a rational *res cogitans* that interprets, and rules on, a static reality. With Bateson, reality is revealed as an evolutionary, complex, and unstable system, based on stochastic non-linear processes, and knowledge becomes distributed, collective, relational, and embedded in the reality itself.[6]

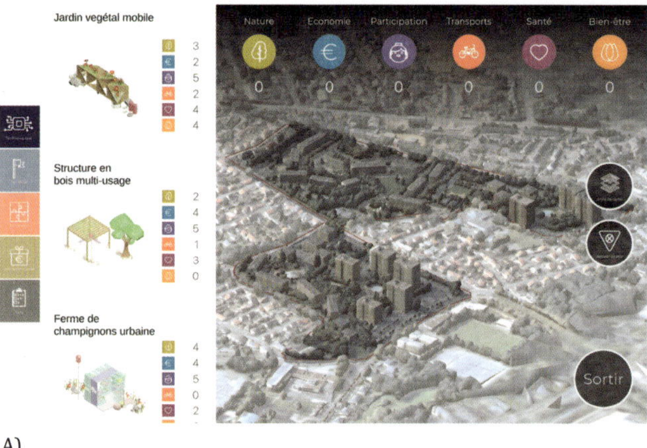

A)

B)

Figure 2: Superbarrio video-game interface for the cities of A) Nantes and B) Barcelona.

Within this vision, participatory spatial design methods are required to develop new approaches to the "collective intelligence" of society, developing solutions that support evolutionary and collective processes, continuous participation, and transformation, instead of static and final design solutions. Furthermore, if "collective intelligence" , defined by Surowiecki as Wisdom of the Crowd],[7] is based on the dynamic, unstable, and transformative relation of its multiple nodes, then participatory design must engage with individual visions and proposals and, as a consequence, should rely on proper systems to collect and interpret *qualitative data.*

The emergence of information and communication technologies of our digital era has enabled crowdsourcing methods and collective knowledge -i.e., Wikipedia, crowd-funding, crowd-mapping, crowd-sensing - as well as collective decision-making tools like e-democracy platforms. At present, algorithms and artificial intelligence (AI) support the collection, interpretation, and interaction with quantified data, fostering *relational analysis* and widening data sets through big-data analytics.

However, when dealing with spatial participatory design, specific disciplinary challenges emerge, demanding innovative solutions and lateral thinking. First, spatial participatory design demands dedicated interfaces, such as 3D environments, that can merge technical features and information with sensitive and emotional aspects related to the experience of the built environment. Additionally, participatory design qualitative approaches have been traditionally limited to a small audience representing large communities. Since design solutions have an impact on the society as a whole, the challenge lies in developing enhanced processes and tools that expand the engagement of the audience and educate citizens on both the impact and requirements of design solutions.

To address the challenges of spatial participatory design processes, virtual gamification and serious games strategies combined with data science, can be explored as a tool to harvest the potential of the evolutionary, relational, and dynamic collective intelligence of society. Presenting and assessing the video-game platform Superbarrio, developed by a multidisciplinary team of the Advanced Architecture Group of IAAC, and implemented in the city of Nantes, this work individuates key principles, methods, strengths, and limitations of tech-based and gamified participatory design of the built environment.

Gamification, Serious games and Participatory Spatial Design

The concept of Serious game emerged in the 1970s, thanks to seminal thinkers like Clark Abt and Dick Duke, to describe game environments structured to address real life issues.[8,9] They identified the potential of games to develop analysis, support decision-making, provide information and influence a user's behavior. Since then, serious games were implemented in different contexts, from scenario-simulation to decision-making processes. In the 2010s, Ekim Tan proved the efficacy of serious games in urban planning, developing participatory processes with physical game-items and tokens, to be played during community gathering.[10] Applying game mechanics such as challenges, role-playing and scores, similar processes are able to enhance decision-making, facilitate understanding of urban issues, and strengthen social relations between participants. However, critical limitations of the conventional participatory process persist, including a limited audience, and the focus on final design solutions.

On the other hand, the combination of game mechanics with information and communication technologies, beyond conventional videogames, is currently pervasive. *Gamification* strategies are implemented in all kinds of non-game environments - including websites, social networks, and learning management systems - to facilitate audience engagement and participation, foster dialogue and promote specific behaviors.

The combination of both gamification strategies and serious game approaches, with the potential of digital interfaces, has a broad potential in the field of spatial design. A pioneer project, referred to as Block-by-Block, was developed by UN Habitat to foster participatory design in local communities, through community gatherings and collective play

Figure 3: Snapshots of the Superbarrio video-game interface.

sessions.[11] Block-by-Block uses Minecraft[12] to represent the urban space in a 3D environment, and co-develop alternative design proposals that are later voted for and debated by community members. The digital interface acts as an enabler, boosting design capabilities of non-specialist users, but can only be used with a limited audience, as it is conceived as a tool to support in-person dialogue and debate.

Block'hood allows players to design a hypothetical urban district from scratch by placing different functional elements, each one acting as an input and/or output of a metabolic process.[13] Continuously challenged to maintain ecological equilibrium, players learn to interact with the systemic and evolutionary features of urban environments. The game promotes a design approach that does not include static final design, but rather a processual and dynamic logic.

Superbarrio

Within this research context, the Superbarrio video game was conceived as a tool to support spatial participatory design processes and is focused on the public space to achieve the following results: (i) engage a broad and varied audience, (ii) collect and interpret qualitative and quantitative data, (iii) co-design informed spatial solutions, and (iv) support a continuous and evolutionary process of co-implementation and co-monitoring.

The ongoing case study presented was developed in the framework of the H2020 URBiNAT Project. URBiNAT focuses on the regeneration and integration of deprived social housing urban developments through a catalogue of Nature-Based Solutions (NBS), in order to ensure sustainability and social cohesion. The main objective is to co-create new urban, social, and nature-based relations throughout different neighborhoods with the citizens.

Based on a holistic approach, URBiNAT considers the full physical, mental, and social well-being of the citizens, and aims to co-create a healthy corridor with them as an innovative and flexible NBS, which will integrate a large number of micro NBS that emerge from a community-driven design process.

This co-creation process was organized in four stages: co-diagnostic, co-design, co-implementation, and co-monitoring. Throughout these phases, citizens were invited to participate and to contribute with their own experience in several activities, workshops, and public events. Superbarrio has been developed as the main enabler of the second stage, focused on co-design processes through ideation and validation of urban plans, and supporting collective implementation and monitoring. Superbarrio is a video game for tablets that allows players to visualize and navigate their neighborhood in a 3D environment. Superbarrio was carefully restituted through a combination of satellite images and textures in order to facilitate recognition of urban spaces and maintain the sensitive and aesthetic features of the built environment experience (Figure 2 and 3).

Figure 4: Catalogue of the different urban public space modules co-created with the communities of Barcelona, Nantes and Sofia.

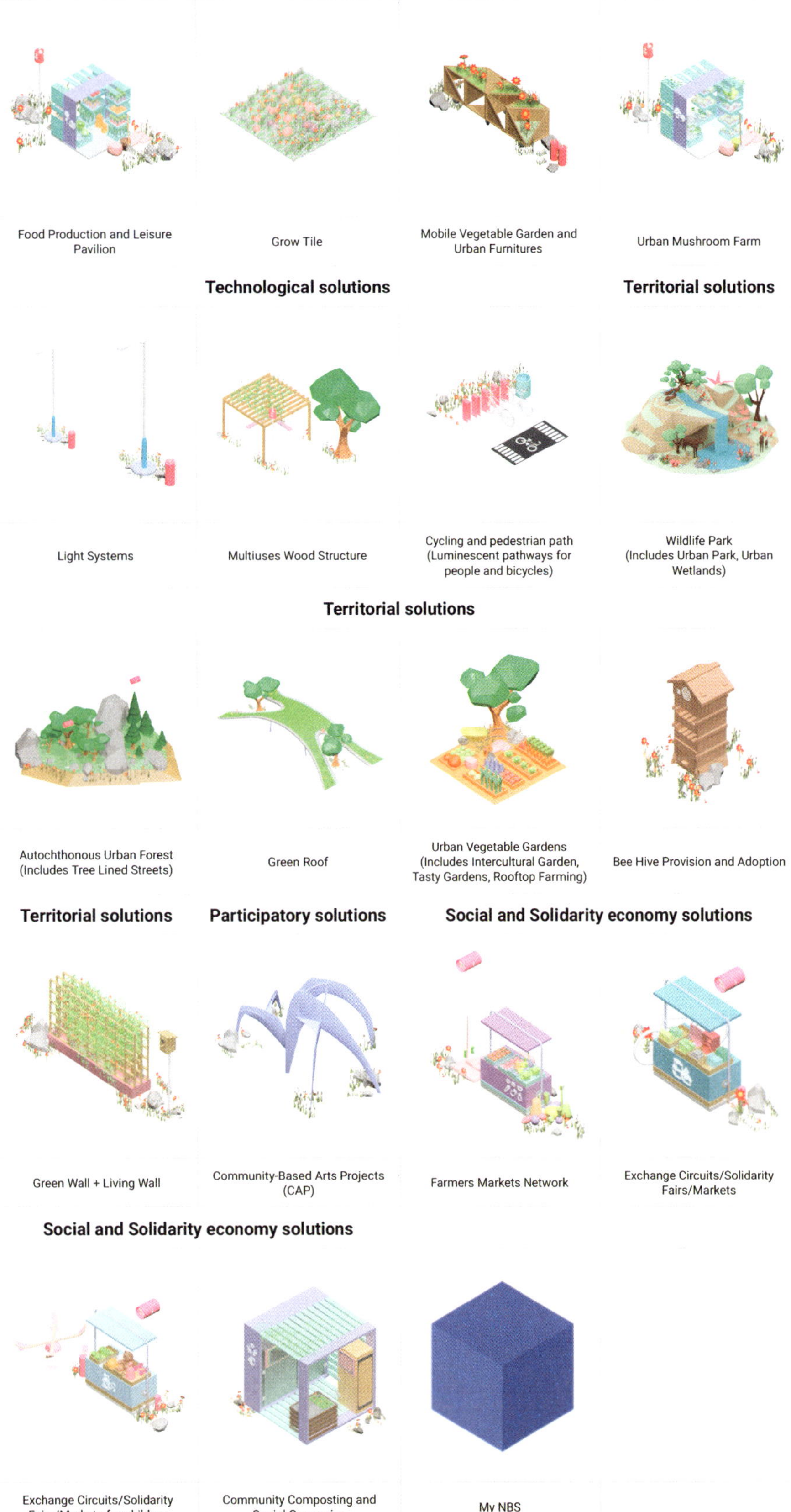

After players log in, enter their personal data (age, gender, domicile), and watch a short tutorial, they are challenged to develop a design proposal for the public space by positioning 3D modules that represent diverse NBS including Food Production and Leisure Pavilions, Cycling and pedestrian paths, Wildlife Parks, Green Roofs, Urban Vegetable Gardens, and Farmers Markets (belonging to different categories) such as Technological, Territorial, Participatory, Social and Solidarity economy. In order to avoid limitations related to methodological framing or biases in the catalogue proposal, and also to collect qualitative data from citizens, a customizable 3D module, called my-NBS, that players can personalize with a name and a function, is included (Figure 4). Finally, the entire public space of the district is the game field, including squares, streets, roofs, façades, and parks, without limitations.

Throughout a metric system and score mechanics, the game engine informs and educates players about the impact of design proposals and the values of a livable district, promoting informed decision-making: each module impacts on indicators of *nature, economy, participation, mobility, health, and wellbeing,* and the score increases proportionally to the number of modules deployed and to the overall balance of indicators.

Superbarrio is a multiplayer game that enables a collective process of co-design due to the data visualization engine. In fact, each design proposal is collected in real time on a cloud server, creating a geolocalized database concerning players' desires, needs and solutions. With this system, superbarrio can collect qualitative data in the form of free spatial design solutions and the locations of major interests - which can be interpreted with relational analysis methods. The gaming engine can additionally collect quantitative data regarding the number of modules selected or the preferred typology of modules, and which data are combined with players' demographic profiles (age, gender, address) (Figure 5).

Superbarrio is a video game that can be downloaded from the Google Play store at no cost, and it can be played in any location, individually or in a group as a collective game. Similarly, the decision-making process can take place in-person or during online gatherings, sharing the results of data analytics and promoting debate among citizens.

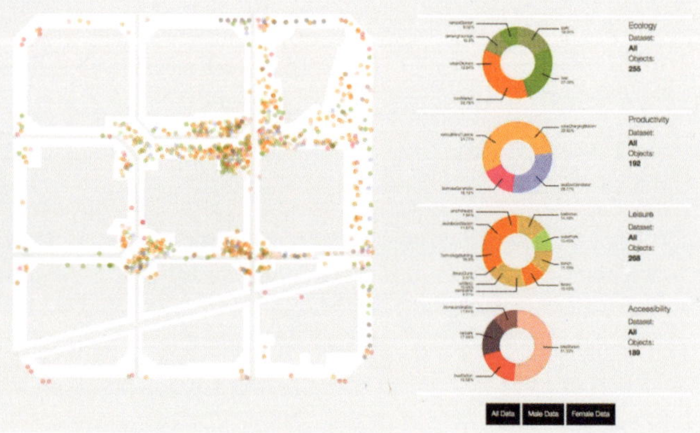

Figure 5: Geolocated data analytics of the preferences of urban modules selected by players.

In the first test of the interface, the game session and the subsequent interaction, took place during a community gathering in the Nantes Médiathèques. More than fifty citizens, whose ages ranged from 10 to 65 years old, participated. This test allowed us to evaluate it under the four above mentioned aspects. First, it proved to be successful at engaging a broad and varied audience of over 50 players with simple means like tablets. Second, it enabled the collection of qualitative and quantitative data regarding the citizen's desires and proposals, building a dataset that develops with each new player log-in. This data is examined by an analytics engine and is interpreted in various ways with relational analysis methodology. Locations of major interest, for instance, can be determined according to the demographic data of the players, or it is possible to visualize which modules are related to a specific age group, understanding relational logics in the wide spectrum of players' preferences and desires. Third, all players developed meaningful proposals for a livable and inclusive neighborhood, guided by the game mechanics and scores. Last, the game does not offer a final design solution, but a combination of possibilities and proposals which informs the decision-making process and is open to future developments.

Future developments include the creation of a data analytics engine embedded in the tool, combined with a social communication "forum" system, with the aim to promote interaction between citizens. As an alternative in cases where low-cost solutions are a priority, the tool could be combined with existing open-source e-democracy platforms, reassuring the creation of a spatial decision-making system.

Digital tools combined with gamification and serious games strategies propose promising solutions to develop spatial participatory design to designers and decision-makers that engage with the collective intelligence of communities. Despite some limitations and challenges, co-design game engines such as Superbarrio allow engagement with a reality conceived as an unstable and evolutionary process, promoting qualitative interaction and data collection with citizens and communities.

References :

1. Jacobs, J. *The Death and Life of Great American Cities.*; Random House: New York, 1961.

2. Davidoff, P. Advocacy And Pluralism In Planning. *J. Am. Inst. Plan. J. Am. Inst. Plan.* 1965, *31* (4), 331–338.

3. Friedmann, J. *Retracking America: A Theory of Transactive Planning;* Anchor Press/Doubleday: Garden City [N.Y., 1973.

4. Kent, F. *How to Turn a Place around: A Handbook for Creating Successful Public Spaces.*; Project for Public Spaces: New York, 2000.

5. Forester, J.; Cornell University; Program in Urban and Regional Studies; Cornell University; Department of City and Regional Planning. *What Are Planners up against?: Planning in the Face of Power*; Dept. of City and Regional Planning in conjunction with the Program in Urban and Regional Studies, Cornell University: Ithaca, N.Y., 1979.

6. Bateson, G. *Steps to an Ecology of Mind*, 1st ed.; Chandler: San Francisco, 1972.

7. Surowiecki, J. *The Wisdom of Crowds;* Anchor Books: New York, 2011.

8. Abt, C. C. *Serious Games;* Viking Press: New York, 1970.

9. Duke, R. D. *Gaming: The Future's Language;* Sage Publications; New York: [London] : Distributed by Wiley: Beverly Hills, 1974.

10. Tan, E. *Play the City Games Informing the Urban Development;* Jap Sam Books: Heijningen, 2017.

11. Westerberg, P.,; Von Heland F.: Using Minecraft for Youth Participation in Urban Design and Governance, 2015.

12. Minecraft is a video game, where players explore a blocky, procedurally generated 3D world with virtually infinite terrain and may discover and extract raw materials, craft tools and items, and build structures, earthworks, and simple machines.

13. Sanchez, J. Block'hood, Developing an Architectural Simulation Video Game | ECAADE 2015. In *Proceedings of the 33rd eCAADe Conference;* Vienna University of Technology; Vol. 1.

JOGOO RD
HIGHEST MATATU TRAFFIC IN NAIROBI

KENYATTA AVE ROUND ABOUT
HIGHEST TRAFFIC VOLUME IN NAIROBI

MOMBASA RD
HIGHEST PRIVATE VEHICLE TRAFFIC IN NAI

LAVINGTON ESTATE
AVERAGE 1 BUILDINGS PER ACRE
HIGH INCOME NEIGHBORHOOD

GIKOMBA MARKET
LARGEST SECOND HAND CLOTHES MARKET IN NAIROBI

KIBERIA
AVERAGE 32 BUILDINGS PER ACRE
LARGEST INFORMAL SETTLEMENT IN NAIROBI

MUKURU FUATA NYAYO
AVERAGE 67 BUILDINGS PER ACRE
HIGHEST DENSITY INFORMAL SETTLEMENT

Figure 4: The first openly available data set for Nairobi developed by Sarah Williams while Co-Director of the Spatial Information Design Lab at Columbia University. Image created by Sarah Williams.

Data Action

Sarah Williams

We have the sixteenth-century philosopher Sir Francis Bacon to thank for the familiar idiom "knowledge is power," and one of the fundamental ways we gain knowledge by is collecting data.

When it comes to cities and their systems, data collection has traditionally been designed by those with the resources to collect the information, and thus has largely been the activity of governments, corporations, and institutions. Now anyone can collect data with a little training because innovations in digital technology are turning everything from mobile phones to dog collars into data collection devices.

Often referred to as participatory sensing projects, or crowdsourcing,[1] these citizen-based efforts in data collection fill gaps in knowledge by equipping people with the ability to collect raw data that was previously unattainable and then to process that data so it can be visualized, analyzed, or otherwise transformed. But perhaps more importantly these projects help build communities that together gather the evidence to both fight for and understand their rights. Participatory sensing projects also teach data literacy and give communities control over their narrative. Beyond creating the data itself, they are Data Action tools that provide a critical way of addressing power imbalances.

Previous page:
Figure 1: The first openly available data set for Nairobi, developed by Sarah William while Co-director of the Spatial Information Design Lab at Columbia University. Image created by Sarah Williams.

In the last decade leveraging big data has become big business, and tech companies want a piece of the action. But as analysis and collection of data about cities are further commoditized, we run the risk of excluding communities on the margins because their data is missing or not reflected in the analytics that corporations develop. In the introduction I mention the International Data Corporation (IDC) estimate, that in 2025 the world will create and replicate 175ZB of data: that astonishing amount represents more than a tenfold increase from the amount of data created in 2015.[2] And it's even more mind-boggling to consider that a single zettabyte is roughly equal to 250 billion DVDs. Private companies own the majority of this data, and it is largely inaccessible. The only way for some communities to counter prevailing narratives and work for change is by *building their own data* where governments and institutions have failed to do so.

Participatory Data Collection: The Act Itself Is the Tool

One method we can use to build our own data sets is to collect data with the participation of broader, interested, self-selected communities. An emphasis on such participatory and collaborative planning processes emerged in the mid-1980s; it emphasized using community data collection as a way to counter the data collected, controlled, and presented—and especially ignored—by governments and institutions.[3] This ideological shift, often referred to as participatory action research (PAR), has its roots in the theory of critical pedagogy that Paulo Freire outlined in his 1968 book *Pedagogy of the Oppressed.*[4] Fundamental to Freire's theory was the idea that education could help liberate the oppressed because they could more actively engage in a conversation with those in power.[5] Freire believed that poor and exploited peoples must construct their own narratives by collecting data on their own reality, and thus be co-creators of knowledge.[6] For others the movement toward more community driven planning processes was a backlash to government analytics projects from the 1950s, 1960s and early 1970s, which set policy agendas that often left those on the margins underrepresented, causing large social divides in the development of cities.[7] Whatever the reason for the shift, planners began to develop community-led data projects that have been referred to using numerous and varied terms, including counter-mapping, community mapping, participatory mapping, critical cartography, ethno-mapping, participatory GIS, Volunteered Geographic Information (VGI).[8]

Participatory sensing is the mostly widely used term to describe community involvement in data collection; it first appeared in an article by Jeffrey A. Burke and colleagues, where the authors describe the term as using "deployed mobile devices to form interactive, participatory sensor networks that enable public and professional users to gather, analyze and share local knowledge."[9] Many early participatory sensing projects made use of data in mobile phones, such as GPS data for location; others focused on using platforms available through mobile devices to send information amassed from sensors, which were placed elsewhere, back to centralized databases.[10] One project created a platform based on SMS (short-message service, or text messaging) to send air quality data from Environmental Protection Agency (EPA) sensors to users who texted requests for it; the responses provided real-time information on air quality.[11] Another project originating from Nanyang Technological University in Singapore created a system for Android phones that used signals transmitted between smartphones and cell phone towers to geolocate users and buses; it allowed users to submit and query bus arrival times based on their identified locations.[12] For the most part, participatory sensing projects aim to maximize the capabilities of mobile devices, reaching beyond their primary uses for voice and text communication to also collect data.[13]

What's interesting about these participatory data collection methods is that accuracy does not always matter. The data purist may find the lack of accuracy unthinkable, but because participatory sensing projects are often used to inform and teach citizens about an issue, the act of collecting the data becomes the primary learning tool.

Any inaccuracies unearthed in the process are another opportunity to teach participants to be skeptical of any data they are presented with in the future. For the designer of participatory processes, planning the project to engage a diverse range of stakeholders and then maintaining their cooperation are as important as the data collection itself.

More and more people can now use data analysis to advocate for government policy or reform because sensor networks have become ubiquitous. Today, mobile phones come embedded with an array of sensors—from GPS, cameras, microphones, accelerometers, and more. Social media apps also help facilitate data collection projects through the sheer scale of their reach. Facebook, Twitter, and Foursquare reach vast numbers of people whose opinions can be harvested by place and time. Although there is and ought to be much concern about how this data is used by governments and private corporations, these ubiquitous data recorders can just as easily be leveraged by the public to answer questions important to society. When using data for action, the people affected by the data must be aware of the project and should also be able to critique the results. The public, like anyone else, collects data from its perspective and can intentionally or unintentionally use that data unjustly. It is essential that novice data collectors hold themselves to the ethical standards established by Data Action.

The impulse to volunteer information captured by mobile sensors is the basis for the term *volunteered geographic information* (VGI), first introduced in Michael Goodchild's seminal piece, in which he describes VGI as "a special case of the more general Web phenomenon of user-generated content."[14] VGI has largely been used to describe geographic data that is contributed through the web or mobile technologies. Though the term VGI seems largely relegated to the work of academic geographers, it was developed to highlight that a community of people exists who are interested in telling us *what* they are doing and *where* they are doing it, and if we can tap into that community we can use it to understand new social-spatial phenomenon.

Crowdsourced Data: Why Governments Need It

We expect governments to have the data they need to make informed decisions—whether or not they steward it well—but that's not always the case. Crowdsourcing techniques can help governments to generate that data. An exemplary project of this sort is Safecast. It grew out of a desire to map radiation levels after the Fukushima-Daiichi nuclear disaster in Japan in 2011 and is now a global project working to empower people with the use of data. The Fukushima-Daiichi nuclear power plant suffered major damage from an earthquake (rated as magnitude 9.0) and a subsequent tsunami. Several reactors on site were permanently damaged, and all have since been decommissioned. While the government was monitoring radiation in and around the site, its sensors were not sufficiently spread out geographically, which made it difficult to know to what extent and to what degree communities near the plant were affected. According to several reports, the power plant operators and several governmental organizations, including the Japanese Atomic Energy Agency, failed to share information with the public.[15]

The Safecast team developed *bGeigie sensors*, short for "Bento Geiger Counter," a name they were given because the sensors looked like Japanese lunch boxes.[16] These sensors, developed soon after the disaster, comprised existing technologies including a Geiger sensor and GPS attached to an SD card device to save the data. The team also added the means for people to upload data from the sensor to a collective database. Ultimately, the team developed a more streamlined sensor, which could be bought as a DIY kit from the KitHub website.[17] Rather than going to test the sites themselves, the Safecast team decided to employ *crowdsourcing* techniques to collect data from all over Japan.

Crowdsourcing is a term that describes a spectrum of initiatives involving (sometimes) massive numbers of people participating in task-based problem solving. Jeff Howe codified the term's more contemporary meaning in a 2006 article in *Wired* titled "The Rise of Crowdsourcing," using the term to describe the strategic appropriation of specialized labor markets to "create content, solve problems, even do corporate R&D."[18] Howe tied crowdsourcing to Amazon's Mechanical Turk program, a "Web-based marketplace that helps companies find people to perform tasks computers are generally lousy at," such as identifying images, sifting through interpretive information in documents, creating annotations, and more.[19] This is where historical and contemporary treatments of the term "crowdsourcing" diverge: modern crowdsourcing privileges human intervention over computational algorithms, and relies on the dialectic relationship between humans and technology. Although the term "crowdsourcing" was coined for application to corporations, many public participation science research projects have employed elements of crowdsourcing methodologies in order to annotate or collect

Figure 2: Participants of Safecast. Safecast and Marc Rollins, "Safecast Blog Image Compilations" n,d., https://blog.safecast.org/.

large amounts of data that could not otherwise be annotated with a smaller number of researchers addressing the problem.

Crowdsourcing is controversial. One of the criticisms levelled at the crowdsourcing method of data collection involves the same criticism of participatory methods: data inaccuracy. Some methods of crowdsourcing are extremely exploitative: at sites such as Amazon's Mechanical Turk, CrowdFlower, Clickworker, or Toluna, for example, workers are often paid well below minimum wage—exploiting labor pools at home and abroad. [20] Data Action does not support using exploitative crowdsourcing.

In many ways the popularity of crowdsourcing was driven by technology that allowed easy access to vast groups of people. The increased availability of smartphones beginning in 2007 with the release of the first iPhone and Android HTC device catalyzed widespread personal, mobile access to the internet. Preceding this was the launch of two major social media networks, Facebook (2004) and Twitter (2006), which would eventually become venues for communicating and sourcing information and data. Yet these sites often only reach part of the crowd because their user base does not represent the wider population. While reaching the entire universe of people is often not the point of data collection projects, getting enough data to provide evidence for a claim is, and crowdsourcing can therefore be an effective technique for collecting data meant to generate civic change. Crowdsourcing projects appear to work best when the groups involved have a stake in collecting the data. Whether it is an

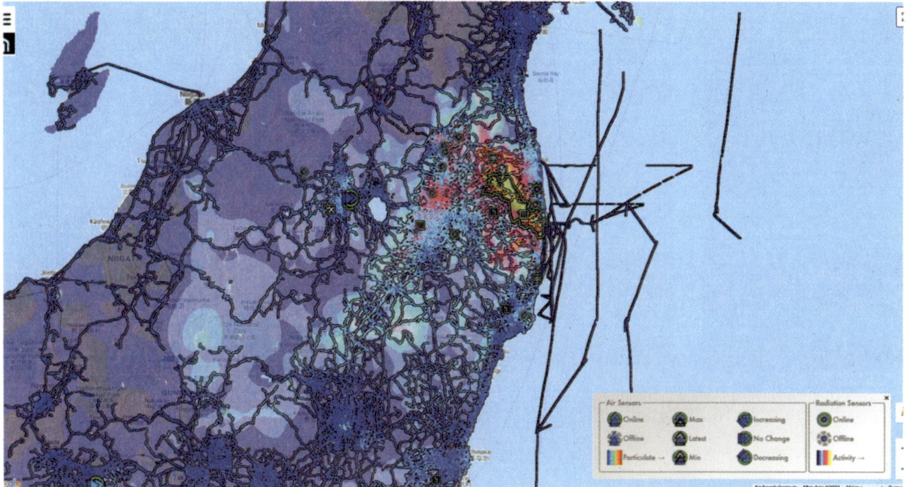

Figure 3: This map shows radiation in Japan detected by Safecast devices. Source: Safecast, "Safecast Tile Map." 2021, http://safecast.org/tilemap/: Google, "Google Maps Tiles," n,d., via Safecast.org.

interest in helping during a disaster event or concerns for environmental conditions in their neighborhood—personal connections help generate better data.

The Safecast team originally thought to sell the bGeigie fully assembled, but realized that people seemed more invested in the project and contributed data more regularly when they received the kit and had to build it with their own hands. Co-creation of the sensor made them feel like co-owners of the project itself.[21] Perhaps the greatest successes of the Safecast team are the education workshops and programming they perform to teach people to use Build It! Data Is Never Raw , It's Collected 75 the devices, but also about the dangers of radiation, how sensors measure, and how to physically make this electronic equipment (Figure 2). The project was about much more than collecting data, it was also creating a community around building that data. Data Action is not just about data analytics; the process helps build the action needed to create change.

Ultimately, a map of radiation levels throughout all of Japan was created (Figure 3) that Safecast insists operates outside the politics of nuclear power. They claim that they are neither proponents of nuclear power nor against it, which according to them means the data is more trustworthy as they have no motivation to discredit or exalt the data they generate. There have been questions as to the relative accuracy of the bGeigie devices, but while Safecast acknowledges that the reading may not be precise, they say the purpose of the devices is not precision but a relative understanding of risk, which can help the government take action should there be an environmental threat in the community. Having a completely crowdsourced database for radiation levels in Japan is itself an accomplishment. Gathering complete data in a crowdsourcing project is often difficult, because it is challenging to obtain participants across all geographies or socioeconomic groups. Automated sensing projects—those in which machines do most of the work without direct human monitoring—often track subtle differences

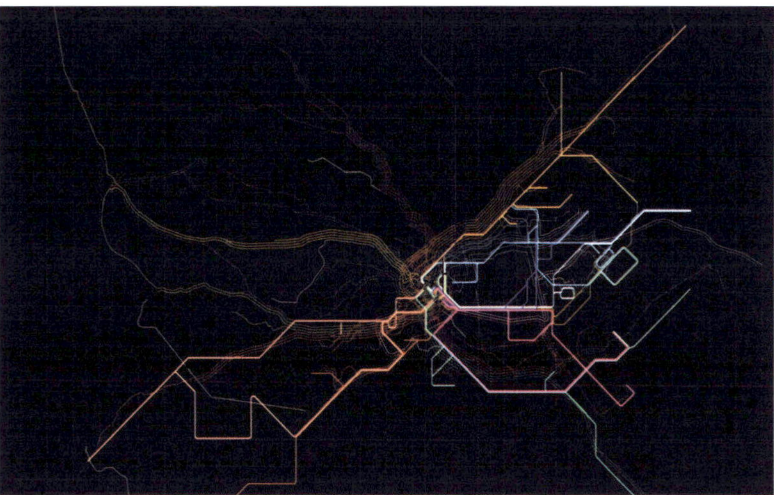

Figure 4: Process map for the development of the Digital Matatus System map. Source: Sarah Williams, Civic Data Design Lab.

in the environment. The Rainforest Connection is a standout example: it uses upcycled mobile phones to monitor deforestation rates, eliminating the need for a constant human presence in the rainforest to collect data. The sensors respond to spikes in noise levels that could indicate the presence of chainsaws, bulldozers, or other tools used to cut down trees. In Brazil, where dozens of environmental activists die in a given year defending environmental policies surrounding deforestation,[22] deploying a mobile phone in lieu of a person can save human lives.

Recently many sensing projects have attempted to capture data about informal infrastructure services (such as transit or trash collection) that are not officially provided by local government but are essential to daily life in many rapidly developing cities in the Global South.[23] This is work that has influenced me personally, as I mapped and shared data on Nairobi's informal transit system of minibuses (called *matatus*). The Digital Matatus project, as the work came to be known, had many of the elements important for making data work for policy change. Not only was an original and essential data set developed, it was done in collaboration with the stakeholders and then freely distributed.

The majority of people in the world depend on semiformal transit systems for mobility. From Nairobi to the Philippines, these private systems operate in areas where the government has provided no alternatives, and there is usually no published data on routes or schedules, which if available could be extremely helpful for transportation-planning efforts in these cities. In some cases, a private company may have the data but does not release the information. The Digital Matatus project used cell phones to collect route and schedule data and, with a team of students from the University of Nairobi, was able to generate a comprehensive map of the *matatu* system. In other words, from a simple tool that almost everyone in Nairobi holds, we were able to generate a database searchable in Google Transit, allowing anyone in Nairobi to map out their transit routes, essentially putting information that now we may take for granted in New York City, into the hands of people in Nairobi for the first time.

The data developed for Nairobi was essential for developing the counter-narrative of the *matatu* system, which was often perceived as a disorganized mess with hundreds of operators. The data showed that the *matatu* owners in fact planned their routes and stops and collaborated among each other to enforce those routes. The data helped multilateral agencies understand that the *matatu* system was well organized, and they could work to develop collaborative projects to ensure safety and improve the quality of transport in Nairobi. In collaboration with the World Bank, the Nairobi city and county government used the data to plan for a Bus Rapid Transit (BRT) system on the most traveled routes.

"For the First Time, We Can See Our Power"

One of the most powerful moments of the Digital Matatus project occurred when we were able to successfully share the data and maps we created with all our partners (from goverment officials to matatu

Figure 5: Hackathon at the University of Nairobi with the local technology community.

drivers) and the public of Nairobi. When the team presented the stylized maps to the matatu drivers and owners they ere excited—for the first time they could see the comprehensive system they had created. The matatu owners are the de facto planners of the city's transportation system—and they instinctively began to use the map to plan new routes for Nairobi's future. The Digital Matatus map also opened the eyes of government officials. Until they saw this map of matatu routes they were uninterested or perhaps didn't understand the need for our data collection project. Once visualized, the map

Figure 6: The maps went viral on social mediaand the internet, and were printed in thelocal newspaper. This image shows the mapcentered on a page of Nairobi's newspaperThe Star. Source: Photo by Sarah Williams.[26]

became a powerful tool for their politics. The Ministry of Transport held a press conference releasing our visualization as the official matatu map of the city.[24] This happened because the government trusted the data we had created, and did so in large measure because we had kept officials informed about how the maps developed; all along the way, they trusted the data. The press conference helped create a discussion among the government, the transportation community, and the public about the future of the matatus system. Participants questioned the government about how it would respond to necessary service changes. After the press event, the downloadable maps went viral on social media. Large copies were printed in local newspapers allowing anyone to make use of the data we had collected and the map we had designed to visualize that data. Our team also held a hackathon at the University of Nairobi to teach the local technology community about the GTFS data format and the opensource software that extends its use (Figure 5). Our hackathon spawned two mobile applications using the collected data before the paper map was officially released. One of these programs, Ma3Route, became one of the most-used transit applications in Nairobi.[25] Users of Ma3Route share realtime data about the matatu system, noting changes to the routes, traffic accidents, and traffic congestion. In due course, it won Kenya's Vision 2030 ICT Innovation Award in April 2014.

The Institute for Transportation and Development Policy (ITDP) and consultants at UN Habitat also used Digital Matatus data as the basis of the planning of Bus Rapid Transit (BRT) Service Plans for the city. Nairobi city planners used the data to develop a map of the BRT system that looked like a copy of our map. The city planners were smart to borrow the visual language of our map to earn support for the BRT project because the Digital Matatus map had become an icon in the city (Figure7).

Digital Matatus: Co-creation Is Powerful

Following double page: Figure 7: UN Habitat Map that copied the style of the Digital Matatus Map for a proposed BRT system.

The early work accomplished by KIPPRA paved the way for our now legendary Digital Matatus project because we created a trusting relationship between our research team and Nairobi's transport community. The work of digitizing the matatu routes encompassed many of the methods that I argue are important when employing data for action. Our team built a data set and developed open-source technology to create and edit the data. We shared the data openly by posting it online in a standardized format (to help extend its use beyond our Digital Matatus project) and by creating visualizations.

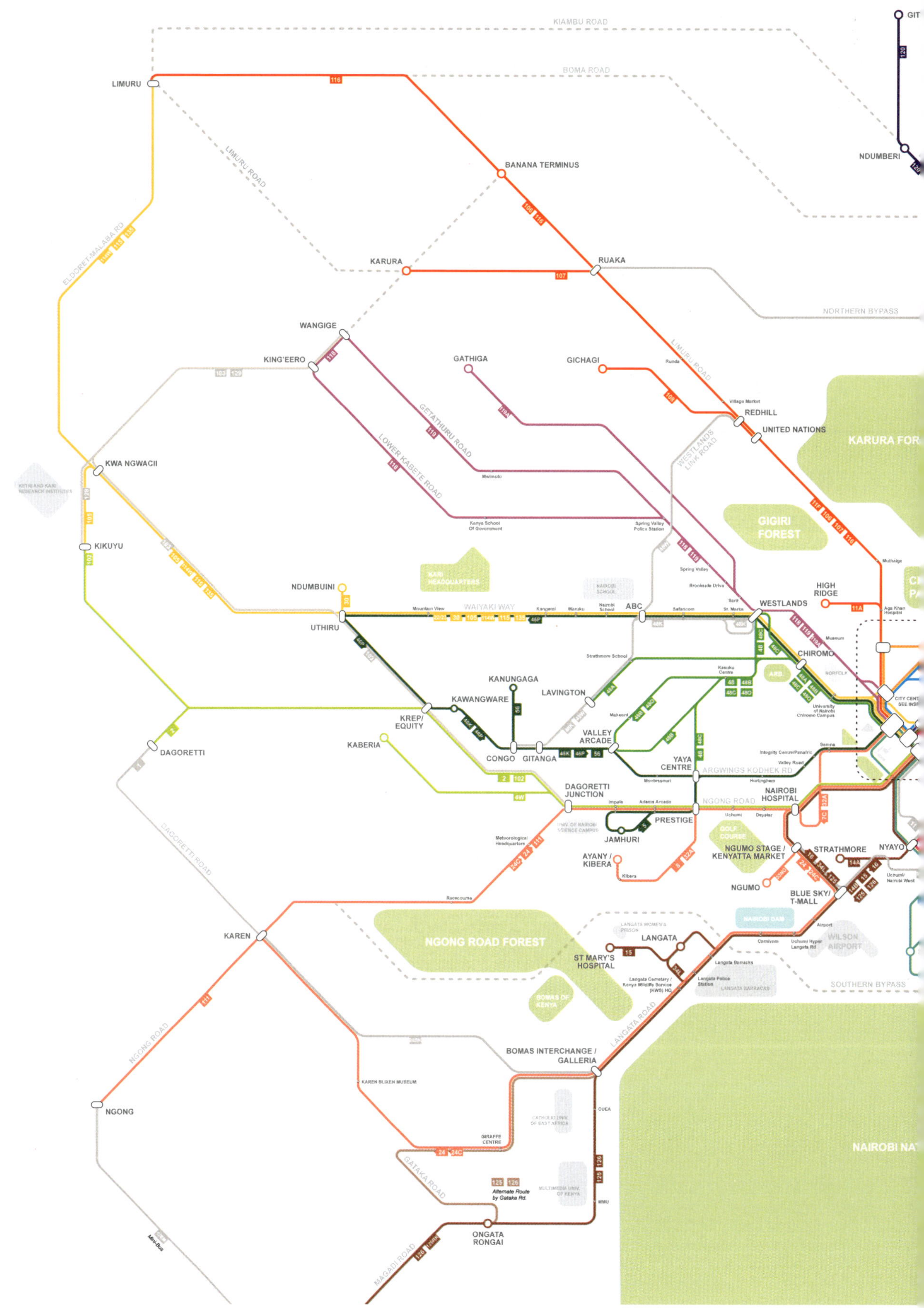
KIAMBU ROAD
BOMA ROAD
LIMURU
LIMURU ROAD
BANANA TERMINUS
ELDORET-MALABA RD
KARURA
RUAKA
NORTHERN BYPASS
NDUMBERI
WANGIGE
KING'EERO
GATHIGA
GICHAGI
REDHILL
UNITED NATIONS
KARURA FOR
GETATHURU ROAD
LOWER KABETE ROAD
WESTLANDS LINK ROAD
KWA NGWACII
KIKUYU
GIGIRI FOREST
KARI HEADQUARTERS
NDUMBUINI
UTHIRU
WAIYAKI WAY
ABC
WESTLANDS
HIGH RIDGE
CHIROMO
KANUNGAGA
KAWANGWARE
LAVINGTON
KREP/ EQUITY
VALLEY ARCADE
KABERIA
DAGORETTI
CONGO
GITANGA
YAYA CENTRE
ARGWINGS KODHEK RD
DAGORETTI JUNCTION
NGONG ROAD
NAIROBI HOSPITAL
PRESTIGE
JAMHURI
AYANY / KIBERA
NGUMO STAGE / KENYATTA MARKET
STRATHMORE
NYAYO
NGUMO
BLUE SKY/ T-MALL
DAGORETTI ROAD
KAREN
NGONG ROAD FOREST
LANGATA
ST MARY'S HOSPITAL
WILSON AIRPORT
SOUTHERN BYPASS
BOMAS OF KENYA
NGONG ROAD
LANGATA ROAD
BOMAS INTERCHANGE / GALLERIA
NGONG
GATAKA ROAD
Alternate Route by Gataka Rd.
ONGATA RONGAI
MAGADI ROAD
NAIROBI NA

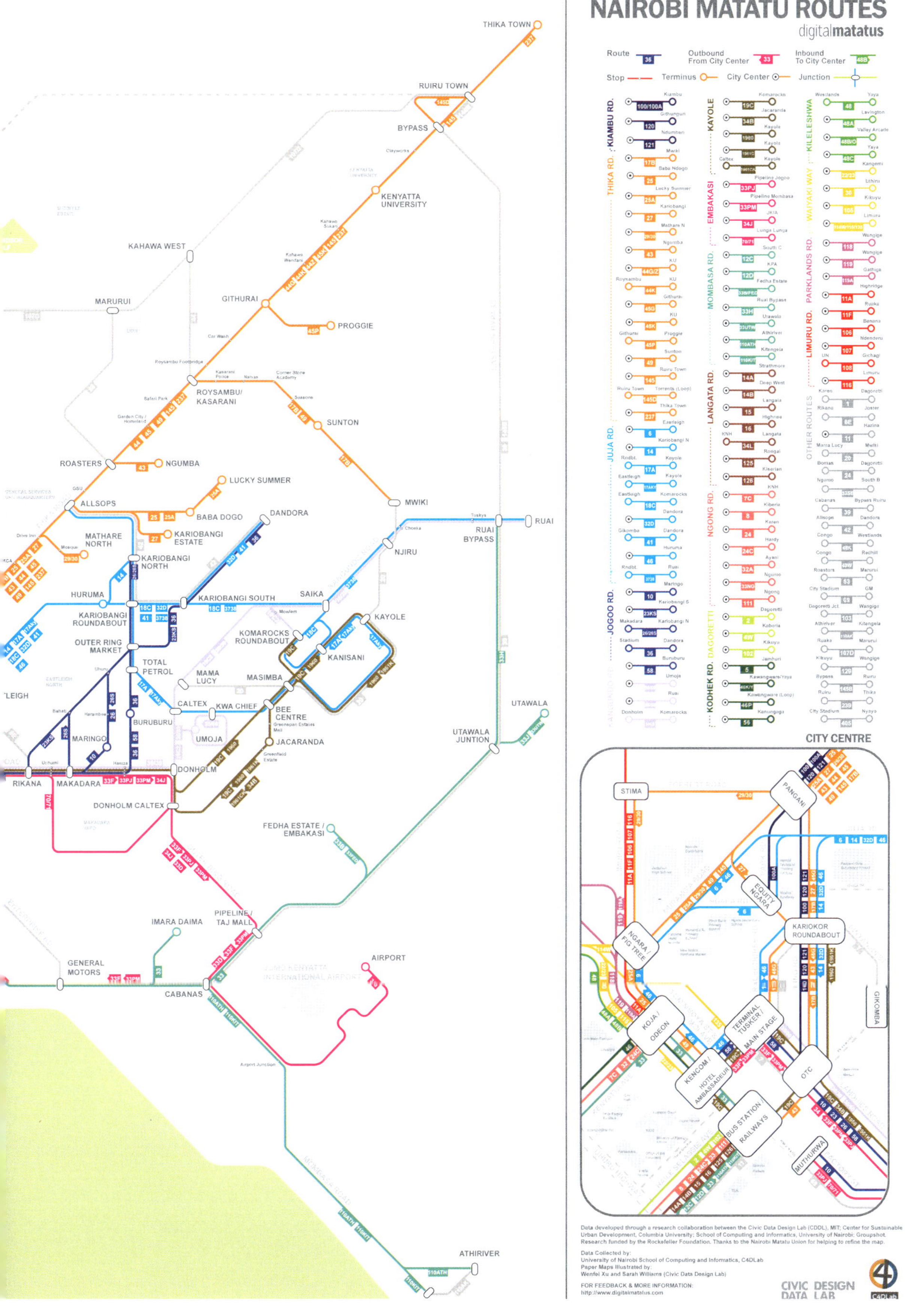

NAIROBI MATATU ROUTES
digitalmatatus
Route
Outbound From City Center
Inbound To City Center
Stop
Terminus
City Center
Junction
THIKA RD. / KIAMBU RD.
JUJA RD.
JOGOO RD.
KAYOLE
EMBAKASI
MOMBASA RD.
LANGATA RD.
NGONG RD.
KODHEK RD.
DAGORETTI
WAIYAKI WAY / KILELESHWA
LIMURU RD. / PARKLANDS RD.
OTHER ROUTES
THIKA TOWN
RUIRU TOWN
BYPASS
KENYATTA UNIVERSITY
KAHAWA WEST
MARURUI
GITHURAI
PROGGIE
ROYSAMBU/ KASARANI
SUNTON
ROASTERS
NGUMBA
LUCKY SUMMER
ALLSOPS
BABA DOGO
DANDORA
MWIKI
MATHARE NORTH
KARIOBANGI ESTATE
KARIOBANGI NORTH
RUAI
RUAI BYPASS
NJIRU
HURUMA
KARIOBANGI SOUTH
SAIKA
KARIOBANGI ROUNDABOUT
KAYOLE
KOMAROCKS ROUNDABOUT
OUTER RING MARKET
KANISANI
TOTAL PETROL
MAMA LUCY
MASIMBA
CALTEX
KWA CHIEF
BEE CENTRE
BURUBURU
UMOJA
JACARANDA
MARINGO
UTAWALA
UTAWALA JUNTION
DONHOLM
RIKANA
MAKADARA
DONHOLM CALTEX
FEDHA ESTATE / EMBAKASI
PIPELINE / TAJ MALL
IMARA DAIMA
GENERAL MOTORS
CABANAS
AIRPORT
ATHIRIVER
CITY CENTRE
STIMA
PANGANI
EQUITY NGARA
NGARA / FIG TREE
KARIOKOR ROUNDABOUT
GIKOMBA
KOJA / ODEON
TERMINAL TUSKER / MAIN STAGE
KENCOM / HOTEL AMBASSADEUR
OTC
BUS STATION RAILWAYS
MUTHURWA
Data developed through a research collaboration between the Civic Data Design Lab (CDDL), MIT; Center for Sustainable Urban Development, Columbia University; School of Computing and Informatics, University of Nairobi; Groupshot. Research funded by the Rockefeller Foundation. Thanks to the Nairobi Matatu Union for helping to refine the map.
Data Collected by:
University of Nairobi School of Computing and Informatics, C4DLab
Paper Maps Illustrated by:
Wenfei Xu and Sarah Williams (Civic Data Design Lab)
FOR FEEDBACK & MORE INFORMATION:
http://www.digitalmatatus.com
CIVIC DESIGN DATA LAB
C4DLab

In time, transportation actors in Nairobi used the data to help change some of their city's policies. Sharing data, both as visualizations and in a standardized data format, did indeed extend the life of our transport work in Nairobi and build trust. It allowed others to use the data for their own policy change, create a community around the data, and provide an essential resource to the public. The Digital Matatus project shows that data visualizations are powerful vehicles for generating debate and presenting evidence for planning strategies. The stylized transit maps we developed allowed the government to engage in conversations with the public. Nairobi's matatu operators used the map to identify and develop new routes for the system. Perhaps more importantly, the citizens of Nairobi now have essential information for navigating their city.

Digital Matatus has inspired cities all over the world from Cairo to Bogotá—twenty-six cities in total at the time of this writing in 2019. This network led us to launch a Global Resource Center for the Development of Informal Transit Data with headquarters in Mexico City and Addis Ababa in 2018. The center provides open-source tools, trainings, links to other cities that have done this work, as well as assistance with policy impact and integration. Ultimately the Digital Matatus project has given life to a new form of collecting data on informal systems, one that is collaborative, open, and transparent.

Maps Are a Powerful Medium—They Persuade

Maps are associated with truths and can be powerfully persuasive; however, their presentation of the data can be intentionally or unintentionally misleading, and some people are therefore wary of using them. It can be easily argued that we rarely pay enough attention to the sources on the maps we read, let alone critique their accuracy or the data they are based on. Indeed, as we've seen, the very act of developing data visualizations involves a bias since designers must choose what to simplify and what to abstract to make their maps. Therefore, more critique is warranted.

Critical cartographers including the likes of Brian Harley, Denis Wood, John Pickles, Michael Curry, Jeremy W. Crampton, Sarah Elwood, Annette Kim, and Matthew Edney argue that maps are inherently political; that what is added to and left off a map illustrates or points to social constructs.[27] For example, cartographers often leave out poor areas or slums, alleyways, and much more to display a pristine representation of place that serves their purpose. Studying the symbols on a map can reveal systems of power and control. Critical cartographers ask us to interrogate the political meaning behind maps. Being political doesn't necessarily make the construct of a map harmful—quite the opposite. The politics of maps can be used for good, too.

Following double page: Figure 8: The maps went viral on social media and the internet, and were printed in the local newspaper. This image shows the map centered on a page of Nairobi's newspaper The Star. Source: Photo by Sarah Williams.

References

1. The term "citizen" here should be understood broadly: "citizen data" might in fact be collected by noncitizens, resident aliens, and undocumented immigrants in addition to citizens proper, any of whom may become involved in an effort to deploy their data findings to improve the lot of their communities.

2. Reinsel, Gantz, and Rydning, "The Digitization of the World From Edge to Core," accessed January 25, 2019, https://www.seagate.com/files/www-content/our-story/trends/files/idc -seagate-dataage-whitepaper.pdf.

3. Robert Chambers, "Participatory Mapping and Geographic Information Systems: Whose Map? Who Is Empowered and Who Disempowered? Who Gains and Who Loses?," *Electronic Journal of Information Systems in Developing Countries* 25, no. 1 (2006): 1–11; Wen Lin, "Counter-cartographies," *Introducing Human Geographies*, 2013, 215.

4. Paulo Freire, *Pedagogy of the Oppressed* (New York: Bloomsbury Publishing USA, 2018).

5. Lin, "Counter-cartographies."

6. Robert Chambers, "The Origins and Practice of Participatory Rural Appraisal," *World Devel opment* 22, no. 7 (July 1, 1994): 953–969, https://doi.org/10.1016/0305-750X(94)90141-4.

7. Raymond A. Mohl, "Stop the Road: Freeway Revolts in American Cities," *Journal of Urban History* 30, no. 5 (2004): 674–706.

8. For more information on the various terms see: J. Brian Harley, "Maps, Knowledge, and Power," *Geographic Thought: A Praxis Perspective*, 2009, 129–148; Jeremy W. Crampton and John Krygier, "An Introduction to Critical Cartography," *ACME: An International E-Journal for Critical Geographies* 4, no. 1 (2006): 11–33; Sarah Elwood, "Critical Issues in Participatory GIS: Deconstructions, Reconstructions, and New Research Directions," *Transactions in GIS* 10, no. 5 (2006): 693–708; and Daniel Sui, Sarah Elwood, and Michael Goodchild, *Crowdsourcing Geographic Knowledge: Volunteered Geographic Information (VGI) in Theory and Practice* (New York: Springer Science & Business Media, 2012).

9. Jeffrey A. Burke, Deborah Estrin, Mark Hansen et al., "Participatory Sensing," UCLA Center for Embedded Network Sensing, 2006, https://escholarship.org/uc/item/19h777qd.

10. Deborah Estrin et al., "Participatory Sensing: Applications and Architecture [Internet Predictions]," *IEEE Internet Computing* 14, no. 1 (2010): 12–42.

11. Eric Paulos, Richard J. Honicky, and Elizabeth Goodman, "Sensing Atmosphere," *Human Computer Interaction Institute*, 2007, 203.

12. Pengfei Zhou, Yuanqing Zheng, and Mo Li, "How Long to Wait?: Predicting Bus Arrival Time with Mobile Phone Based Participatory Sensing," in *Proceedings of the 10th International Conference on Mobile Systems, Applications, and Services* (ACM, 2012), 379–392.

13. Sasank Reddy, Deborah Estrin, and Mani Srivastava, "Recruitment Framework for Participatory Sensing Data Collections," in *International Conference on Pervasive Computing* (New York: Springer, 2010), 138–155.

14. Michael F. Goodchild, "Citizens as Sensors: The World of Volunteered Geography," *Geo Journal 69*, no. 4 (2007): 211–221. 42. Azby Brown et al., "Safecast: Successful Citizen-Science for Radiation Measurement and Communication after Fukushima," Journal of Radiological Protection 36, no. 2 (2016): S82.

15. Azby Brown et al., "Safecast: Successful Citizen-Science for Radiation Measurement and Communication after Fukushima," *Journal of Radiological Protection* 36, no. 2 (2016): S82.

16. "First Safecast Mobile Recon," *Safecast* (blog), April 24, 2011, https://blog.safecast.org/2011/04/first-safecast/.

17. "Hands-On Projects for Curious Minds," n.d., KitHub homepage, https://kithub.cc/.

18. Jeff Howe, "The Rise of Crowdsourcing," *Wired*, June 1, 2006, https://www.wired.com/2006/06/crowds/.Notes 237

19. Ibid.

20. Alek Felstiner, "Working the Crowd: Employment and Labor Law in the Crowdsourcing Industry," *Berkeley Journal of Employment and Labor Law* 32 (2011): 143–204; Alana Semuels, "The Internet Is Enabling a New Kind of Poorly Paid Hell," *Atlantic*, January 23, 2018, https://www.theatlantic.com/business/archive/2018/01/amazon-mechanical-turk/551192/.

21. Brown et al., "Safecast."

22. Jonathan Watts, "Almost Four Environmental Defenders a Week Killed in 2017,"*Guardian*, February 2, 2018, https://www.theguardian.com/environment/2018/feb/02/almost-four-environmental-defenders-a-week-killed-in-2017.

23. Dietmar Offenhuber and Carlo Ratti, Waste Is Information: Infrastructure Legibility and Governance (Cambridge, MA: MIT Press, 2017).

24. Gilbert Koech and Chrispinus Wekesa, "Kenya: Nairobi Transit Map Launched," *Star*, January 29, 2014, https://allafrica.com/stories/201401290479.html.

25. @ma3route, "Ma3Route Is a Mobile/Web/SMS Platform That Crowd-Sources for Transport Data and Provides Users with Information on Traffic, Matatu Directions and Driving Reports," accessed August 1, 2019, http://www.ma3route.com/.

26. Gauff Consultants, *Nairobi / Proposed MRTS Commuter Rail Network*, 2014.

27. Jeremy W. Crampton, "Maps as Social Constructions: Power, Communication and Visualization," *Progress in Human Geography* 25, no. 2 (2001): 235–252.

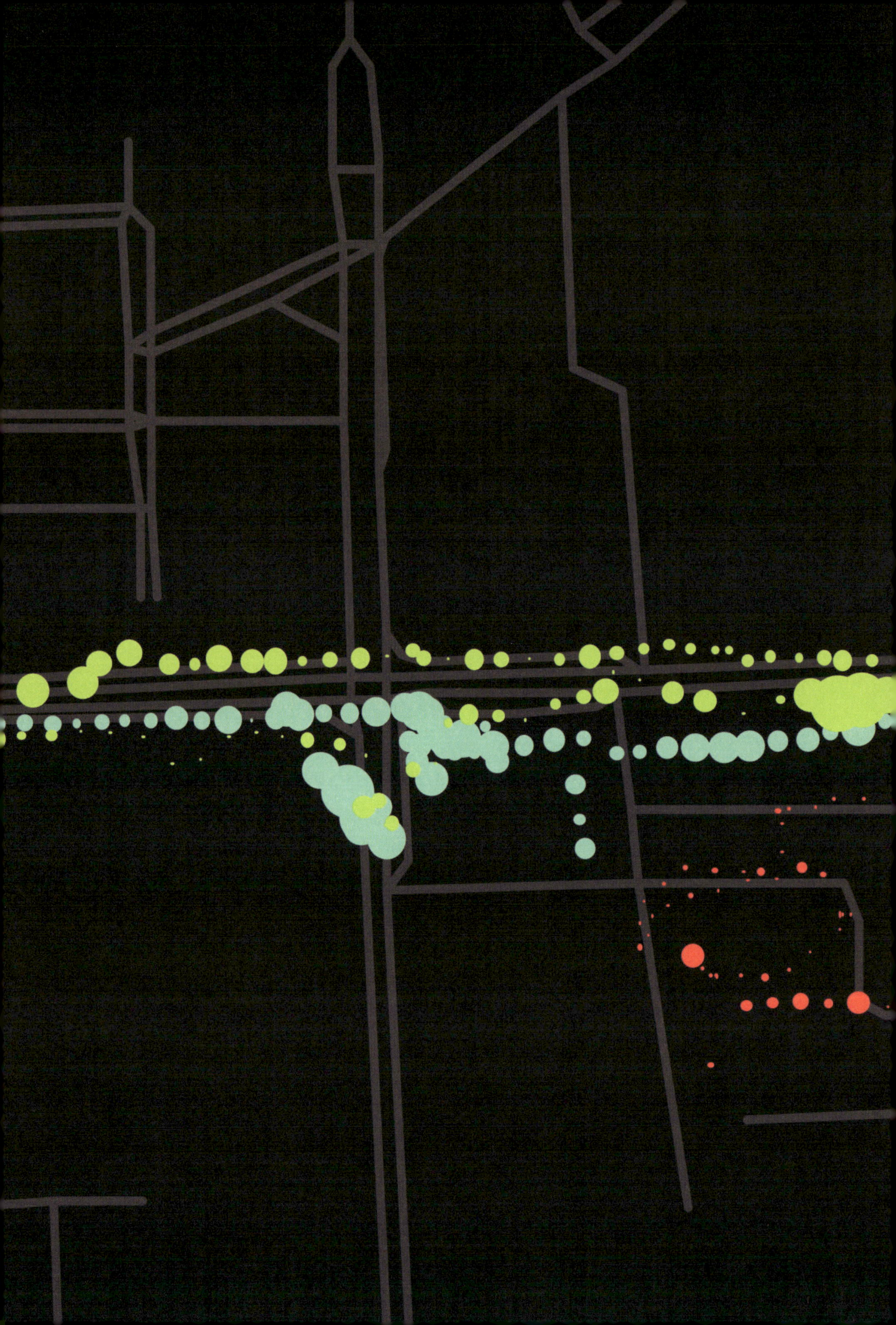

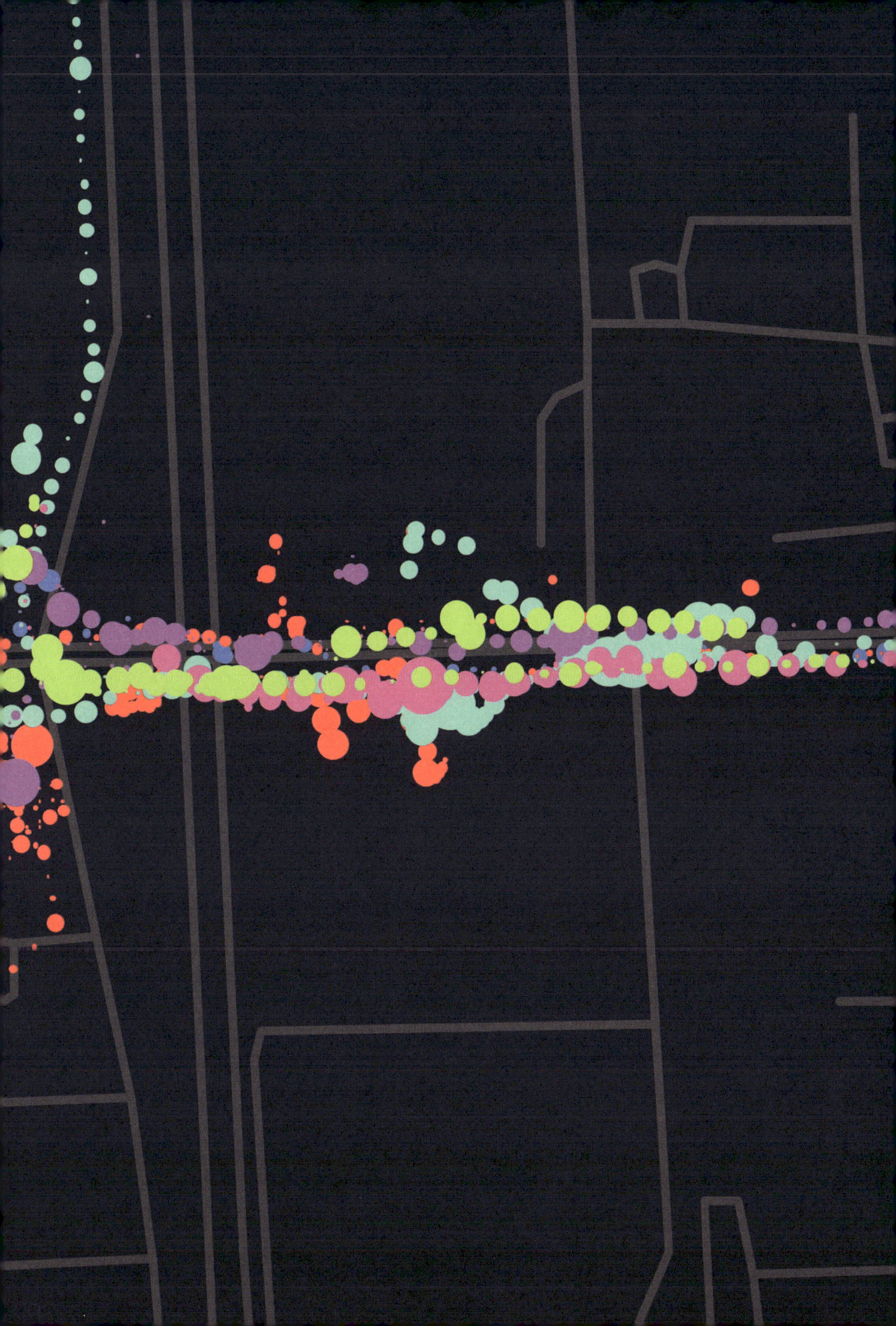

A City Like You and Me. Embracing Uncertainty in the Age of Precise Data

Rodrigo Delso & Javier Argota

Every second, millions of inorganic forms of intelligence move around invisible data-cities, under the threshold of human perceptibility, scavenging reality through billions of machinic eyes. These electric beings do not need to be believed in, like previous god-like human fictions, to change the materiality of physical cities. Every day, these artificial algorithms hunt inside gigantic data centers and networks of urban sensors to extract patterns, establish correlations, predict flows, and create a simulation of a metacity that determines, for example, how long you wait at a traffic light or the advertisement you see at the bus stop.

Simultaneously, billions of organic entities travel around heavily material cities, built largely with static matter, analog procedures and onsite workers. Instantaneous algorithms, moving living beings and immobile constructions coexist in a city whose shape, concept and elements have not changed qualitatively since the Industrial Revolution, rendering the digital turn nearly irrelevant in the evolution of material human habitats. Today, artificial intelligence is the version on steroids of Cerdà's vision from the 1800s: cities are infrastructures to move people efficiently from home to work.[1] This perspective conceives people as particles and human habitats as logistics platforms: more like airports or train stations than public spaces.

In the production of cities, everything takes place in the dilemma between permanence and mobility. Some entities, such as architecture and infrastructure, are thought of as extremely static so others can be mobile: people, cars, money, information, product, etc. For now, artificial intelligence seems only to affect the latter; the low-frequency city is out of its scope.[2] Beyond using high tech simply for instrumentalizing and augmenting the orthodox industrial city,

Previous page:
Neural city: deep learning algorithm that creates an atlas of connected databases available in the city of Madrid as of 2014.

urban agents need to articulate a new urban framework[3] with a real hybridization between human experts, inhabitants and computers.[4] We need a new model of collaboration that addresses the ignored complex relationships associated with environmental, cognitive, cultural, economic and social issues, and prioritizes systemic urban actions in an unfinished city, leaving room for alternatives and changes. Do we dare to imagine a post-car city? Do we really want to know how people live, or is it easier to design without knowing?

Following page:
617 trees (JARD, Cañadas, C., Sánchez, O., and Sost, R.): system of occupation for an empty urban public space based on a convolutional algorithm that allocates the evolving distribution of ecological conditions, citizen input and developers' spatial needs over time, using vegetation as the single available resource.

Frictions in the Ideology of Urban Data

Rehoboam is the name of the artificial brain that controls the human world in the TV show *Westworld*. Through the quantum processing of all imaginable data, Rehoboam can automatically create infinite simulations of the world in order to produce the desired materialization of reality through the control of labor, economics and mobility. Among the endless possible worlds, the machine decides that perfection is accomplished with the exact same urban and human reality we have today, just without any kind of friction. The AI's ideal city is the total synchronization of the current status quo with no traffic jams, protests, vacant lots or abandoned infrastructures.[5] Rehoboam's urban utopia-dystopia is not a singularity but the paradigm of how AI applications are imagined in cities. The lack of divergence and conformism around the design of human habitats takes form in the uninterrupted replication of the industrial models based on transport analytics and secular databases.

Still, cities are the most complex human creation.[6] The built environment is the result of contradictory, opposing and diverse agencies, goals and needs, accumulated over time in an intricate network of interests in constant friction. However, urban agents dismiss in their planning the broad network of dynamic social, cultural, environmental and cognitive factors and relationships taking place in the city. This omission is a political and ideological act that takes form in the selection, omission and collection of certain data.[7]

Today, almost all available urban data is related to logistics and economics, used to reinforce the utopia of a city in perfect motion synchronization. Moreover, data is mostly used as a tool for corroborating preconceived ideas and biases,[8] instead of a tool for discovery – disregarding the potential of data-driven models to establish unprecedented correlations and, therefore, see the world through an exponentially different lens with the ability to match the different scales of organic life.

01.02 PARCELARIO PLAN ESPECIAL: PLAN DE SOMBREAMIENTO
centro cívico
esc. jardinería
1:500
0 5 10 20 40 m

Empiricism and the Limits of Artificial Imagination

The positivist vision of endlessly feeding information into a universal machine solver, able to make sense of everything to answer anything, clashes with the contingency of the data and our existing technology. The results of such a machine are a direct consequence of the conditions set by the data and the well-bounded programming rules that depend on human dexterity. So, even the outcomes of the most obscure and deepest AI algorithm are defined within its programming; we are still far from the singularity.

Paradigms such as the city as a "wicked problem"[9] show the limitations of our machines for treating intractable realities,[10] in which uncertainty, unknowns and alternatives are fundamental components. Current AI machines can seek perfection in what is given (data, an analysis or a hypothesis), but not eccentricities in what is undetermined.

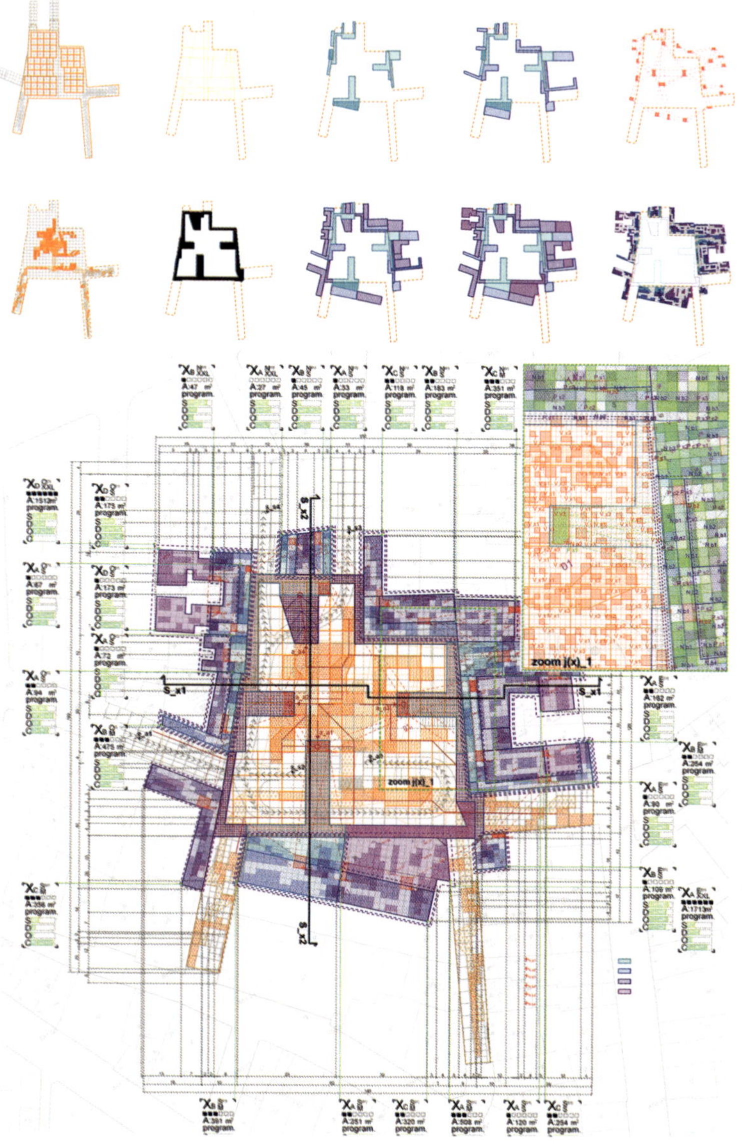

Algorithm (x) M_p06. (JARD, Cañadas, C., Sánchez, O., and Sost, R.): resulting overlapping patterns extracted by genetic algorithms from simulations of all possible design strategies in an urban square according to an atlas of myriad information that includes affects, energy, comfort, flexibility or available spaces of opportunity (rooftops, balconies, public areas and abandoned places).

Despite these limitations, data-driven machine learning algorithms are powerful tools for learning and thinking for every single urban agent. One of their main strengths is the ability to generate infinite alternatives to a question, helping to visualize the underlying logics and flows of our own reality created by conscious decision making and unconscious constructs. AI processing creates a network of available diagnoses for the urban agent, whose decision-making process can be aided by this 24/7 exploration of materialized alternatives.

Roles and Human Cognition

Cities are neural networks of infinite realities in continuous evolution and change. Machine learning algorithms are already capturing lots of these realities: class, gender, race, geolocation, emotional responses, social activities, sexual preferences, music trends or consumption preferences. In a context of increasing information, urban agents decide to ignore easily available or collectable information due to ideological biases, lack of interest or knowledge on how to design with it.[11]

The infinite capacity of artificial intelligence to create analytics and solutions to a given problem creates a sea of data that needs to be interpreted by human cognition. Between the extraction of the data and taking action in the urban environment, there is a huge unresolved abyss that needs to be addressed both by urban developers and citizens. New models of communication and interpretation of information are urgently needed but also new models of urban learning, negotiation and production.[12]

Urban agents need to make a direct effort to create systems and strategies in which data analytics has an active voice and there is space for that input to modify projects – for the algorithmic diagnosis to evolve within the material context. Machine intelligence can enable a richer understanding of urbanity, complementing human intelligence in hybrid design frameworks.[13] AI gives us access to the endless latent space of possibilities and scenarios of reality's bounding conditions and contradictions, otherwise unreachable through simple human cognition. In this context, experts become responsible for describing the design context in machine-human cooperation[14]: they are not prescriptors of shapes and topologies, but of conditions and scenarios[15] for informing urban operations. For that to happen, an expansion of their knowledge is required, not only in technical aspects but also conceptually, in a way that critically bridges the gap between analytics and actions in the built environment.

Real Time and Evolution in Urban Data Streams

Machine learning algorithms are able to digest continuous flows of data and measure the smallest variations in their content or context. The endless ingestion of inputs permits a new type of quantification

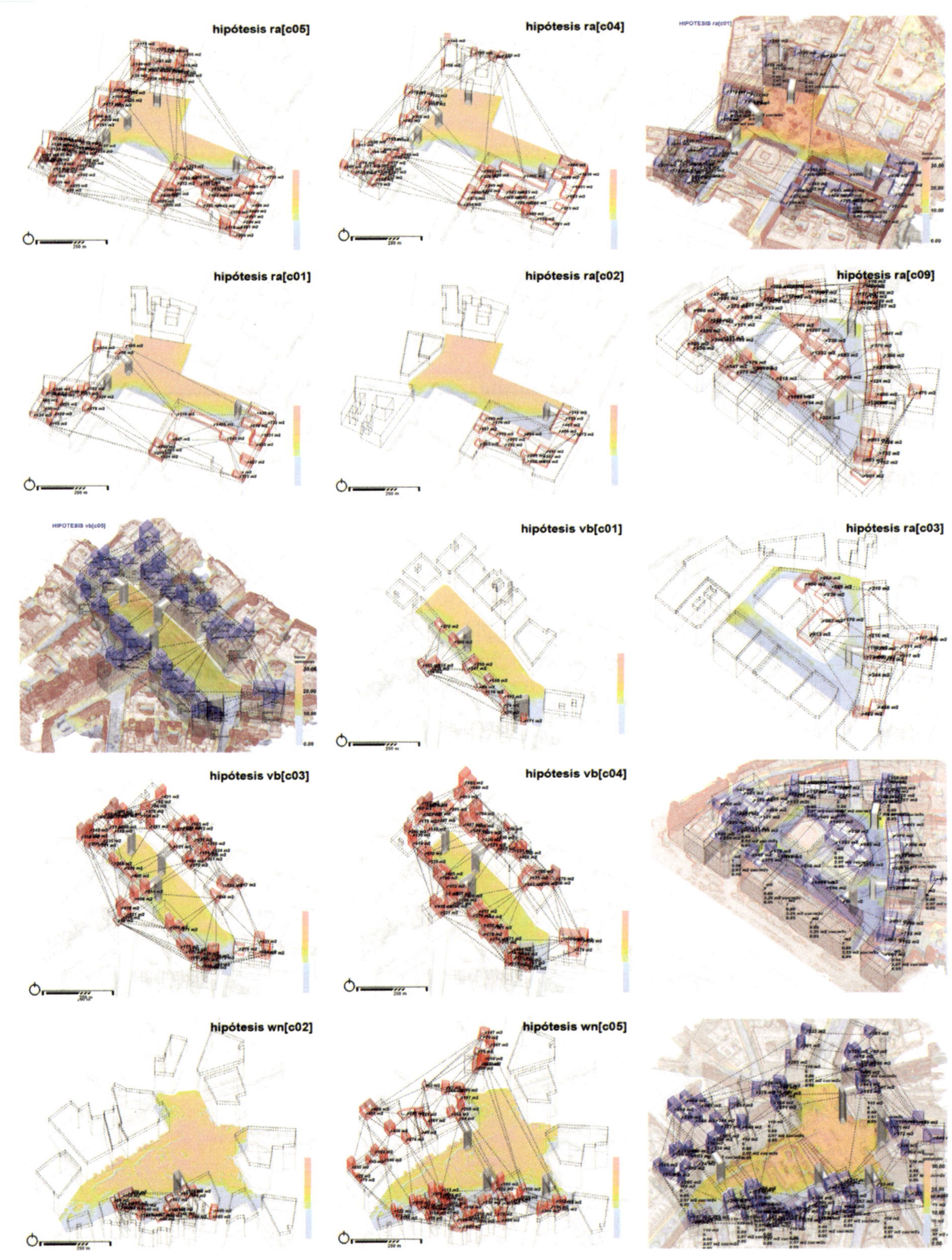

hipótesis ra[c05]
hipótesis ra[c04]
hipótesis ra[c01]
hipótesis ra[c02]
hipótesis ra[c09]
hipótesis vb[c01]
hipótesis ra[c03]
hipótesis vb[c03]
hipótesis vb[c04]
hipótesis wn[c02]
hipótesis wn[c05]

Previous page: Hyperplanning II (JARD, Cañadas, C., and Sost, R.): architectural system based on the correlation of different data sources through machine learning that creates multiple versions of occupation according to desired vectors (economic, gender, leisure, work, socialization, or collaboration).

based on transformative variations of data and its evolution over time, in real time; this not only extracts static conclusions but, more importantly, an operative continuous diagnosis of the shifting reality.[16] At the same time, current urban plans are built on top of static and inherently outdated data, rejecting an aspiring real-time urbanism informed by dynamic data. Live urban development could account for the different scenarios of human situations, reacting automatically to the changes happening in the environment and integrating the informed opinions and necessities of the different stakeholders.[17]

A real-time city risks being overly presentist, however, resolving only momentary necessities. It will need to actively deal with the future as something unpredictable and uncertain. Today, high-frequency trading algorithms follow the evolution of the market, analyzing both the main movements of the system as well as the minimal variations, previously known as noise. These machine-learning models follow disruptions and include errors as a crucial part of their learning processes in order to detect new trends. In the same way, contemporary urban planning needs to include uncertainty and noise as part of its strategy and stop seeing divergence as an enemy to the integrity of the manager's vision.

Post-humanist Crowd Analytics

In this real-time city run by ultra-fast algorithms, data is the most valuable asset. While it is constantly needed to fuel projects aimed at improving the quality of life of citizens and the performance of urban operations, today its access is restrictive and opaque. As a result, although the most technocratic visions of Smart Cities put citizens at the center,[18] they are despotic highly technological versions: citizens are supposedly the main beneficiaries of the improvements for which they generate data, but they have no control. This paternalistic vision of authority privileges the opportunistic concentration of power and knowledge among a limited number of urban agents, which hinders cooperative learning and discovery by citizens and other unprivileged stakeholders in the city.

Beyond learning, AI makes it possible to articulate the commoning and participatory processes of citizen information, whose coordination between contradictory and opposing agencies remains unclear to experts.[19] Massive self-generated data from citizens does not only entail ubiquitous constant collection but access, discovery, utilization and coordination by the inhabitants themselves. Hence the value and opportunity of using post-humanistic frameworks – in other words, computer intelligence – for the coordination of crowd analytics and large-scale human organizations in an actionable way. For that to happen, we need to create effective tools for facilitating conversation, evaluation and knowledge to inform participatory city-making.

Infostructuration (JARD, Cañadas, and Sost, R.): an information infrastructure for Paris suburbs that proposes a hybrid collection of data from sensors, servers, diverse devices and citizens' input about their surrounding environment (sensations elicited by a spot, sound comfortability, scoring or personal attachment) so designs can be adapted to real-time needs and problems.

The Unavoidable and Uncertain Mutant City

Today, we live in the nonstop city, in which crowds are envisioned as a fluid in permanent movement that cannot stand still, waste time or do nothing, whereas the material world around them is motionless, long-lasting and untouchable. Machine learning analytics continuously come up against the conflict of providing a dynamic real-time data stream to inform an environment that is incapable of learning and applying this knowledge because of its extremely static conceptualization, design and materiality. There is an urgent need to propose new models of planning, legislation or construction that can reconcile the innate mutability of organic forms with the artificial rigidity of architecture.

Simondon described organic forms as "metastable minds". For him, humans are never completely formed but always maintain a level of "transindividuality" that allows them to be able to change, maintaining a high level of indeterminacy.[20] Cities as the background for these mutant lives need to be able to match the rhythms of the present by being open-ended, both materially and strategically. However, the continuous adaptation to real-time events has the risk of reacting purely to the existing conditions of the present and eternally repeating the doxa: what everyone does or the majority already knows.

In that sense, the continuous diagnosis of data allows for the constant creation of urban hypotheses and, therefore, the re-articulation of aims and operations in a context of changeability that needs room to accommodate that mutation of reality. Cities need to leave gaps to adapt to present and future contingencies, creating a hybrid model of human-machine cooperation. Change is only possible when there is space or material for change; this could be accomplished by leaving a high degree of indeterminacy in urban plans or designing unfinished buildings with constructive systems that can grow but also diminish.

A truly mutant city is only possible through algorithms that expand human knowledge with new systems of aggregation, correlation and prediction, as opposed to simply adapting to the data being fed in by stakeholders. Simultaneously, humans need to evolve from using technology as a validation of personal ideas toward letting it become a mode of discovery of the "unknown". Machine-human cooperative systems can create cities, projects or public spaces that remain undone, unfinished, with multiple gaps, open-ended in order to leverage the complex urban agencies and let time, the biggest creator of successful cities, operate.

Maybe, the advancement of digital architectural thinking will not mean making more complex operations but rather simplifying urban strategies and evaluating them based on their systemic impact. Maybe, leaving a block empty in the center of London or infra-designing the next Times Square could be a more advanced digital architecture than the Taylorism of Google's Sidewalk labs.

Archcoded: parametrization and automatic AI generation of hypothetical architectures, from analytics to structural calculations, that can evolve over time responding to the different program needs of the moment.

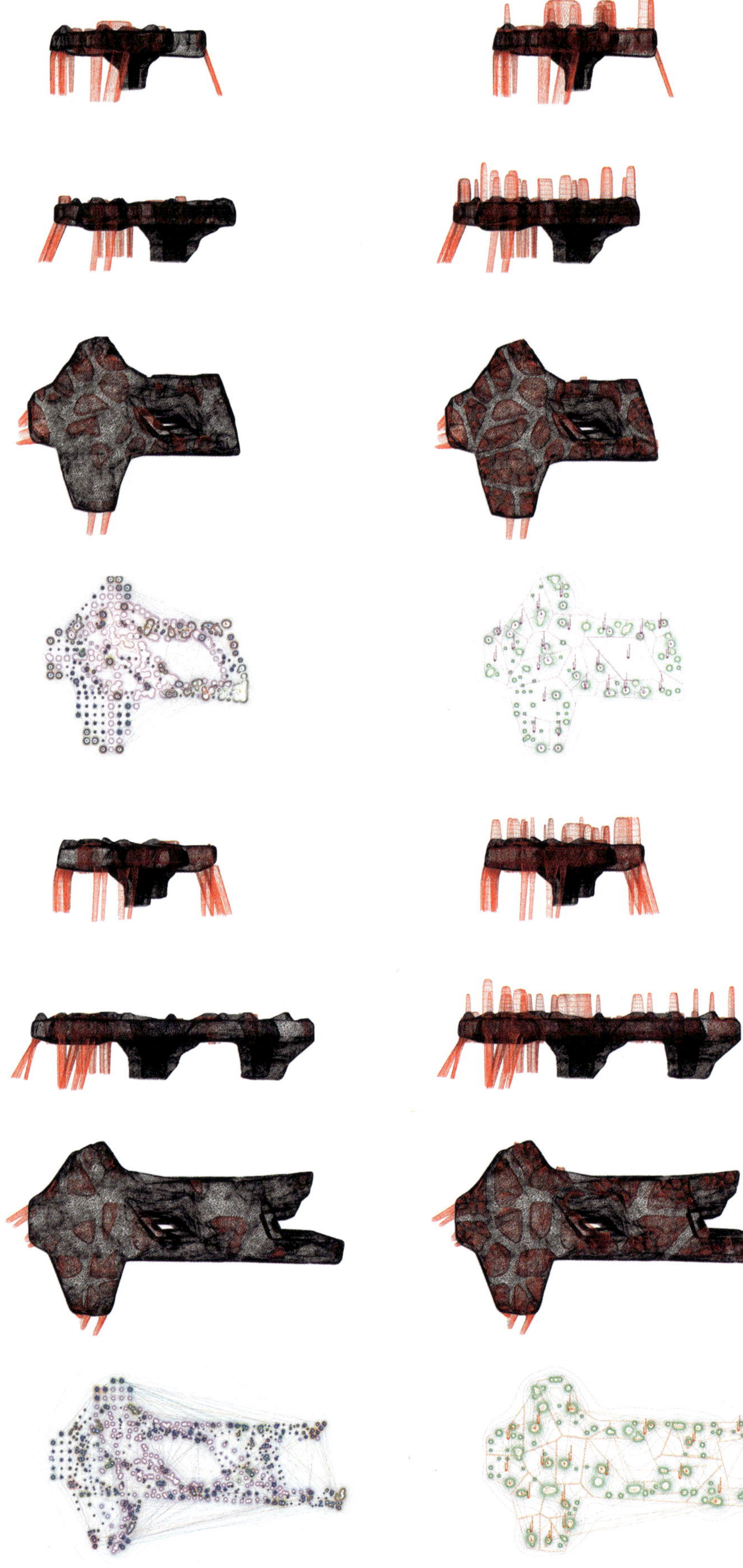

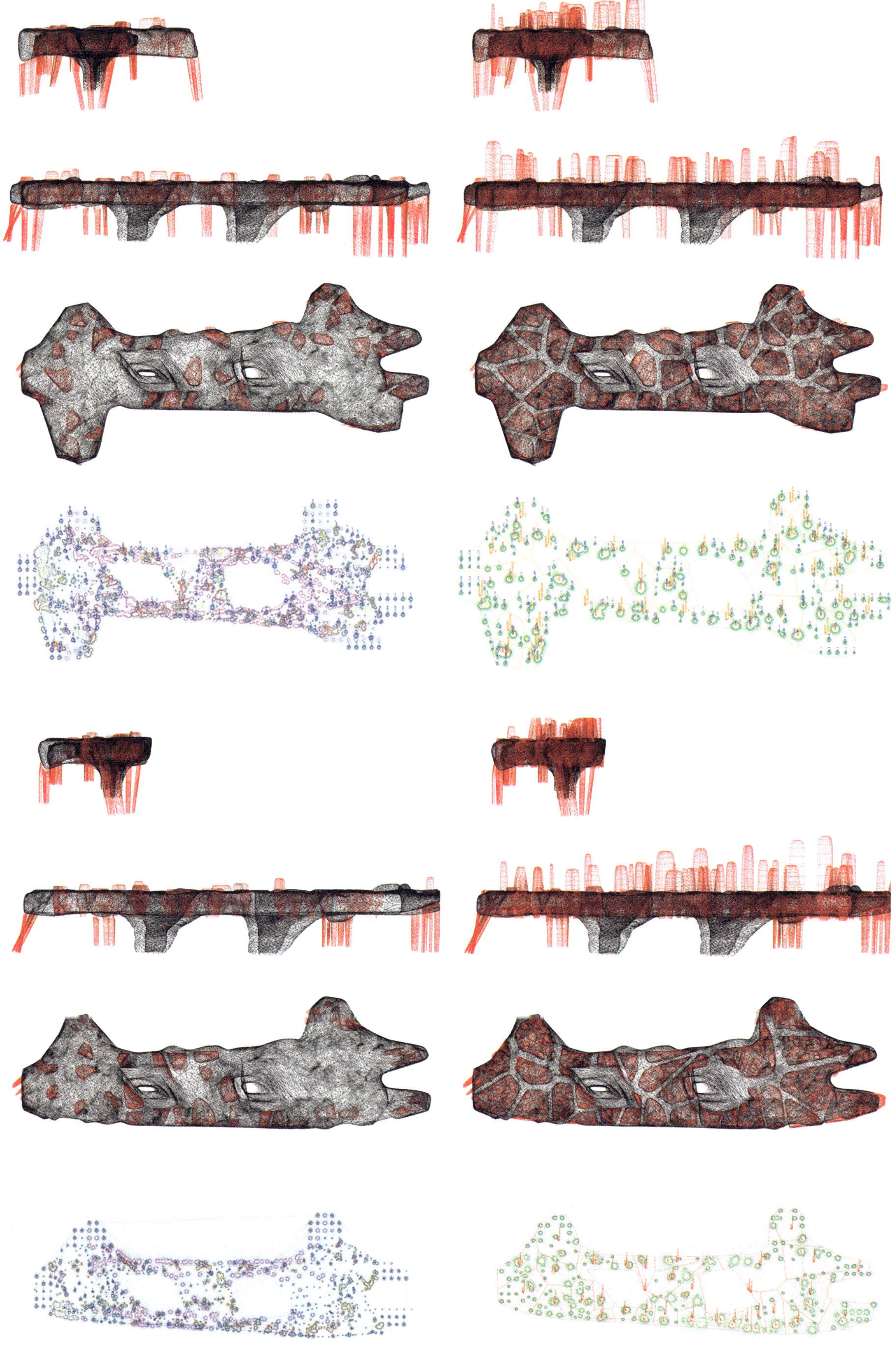

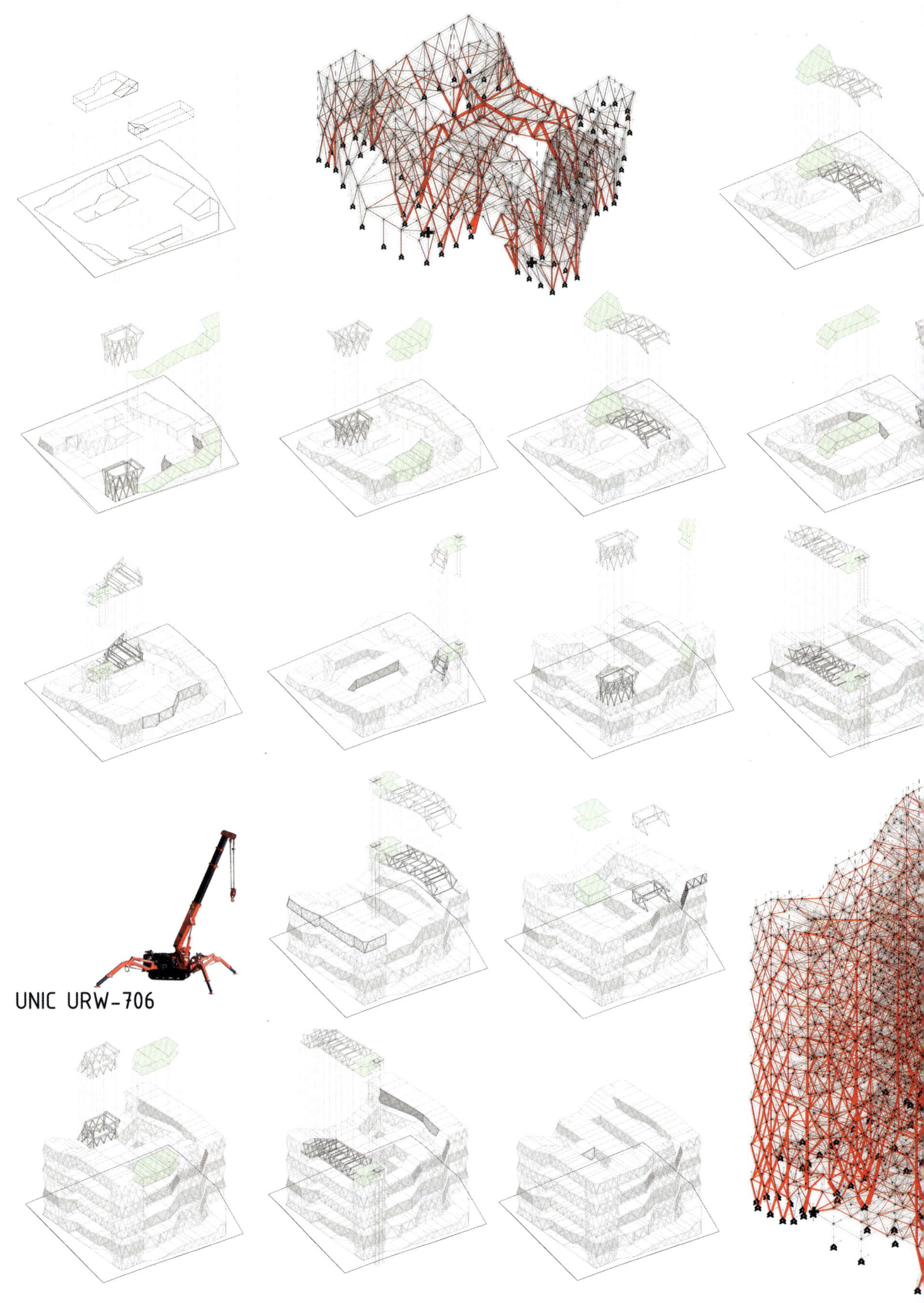
UNIC URW-706

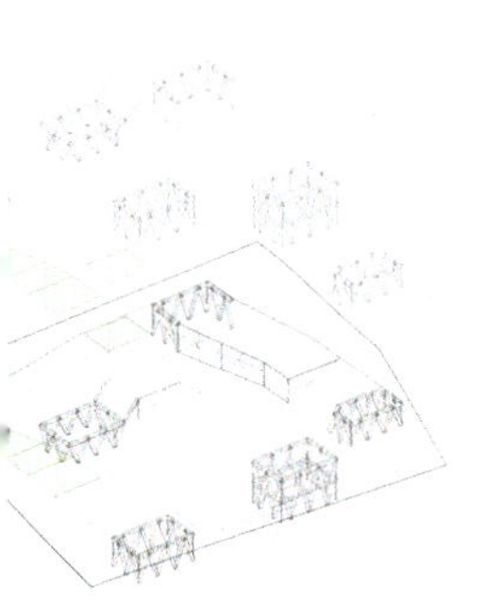

Previous page:
Time Micro-City:
construction solution based on the condition of an always unfinished architecture in which machines, humans and computers create a system that allows forpermanent growth and reduction of space.

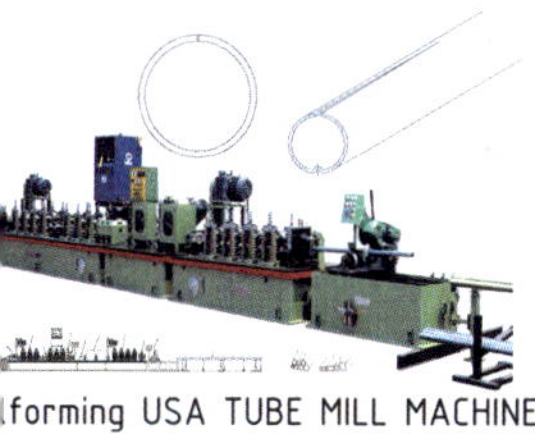

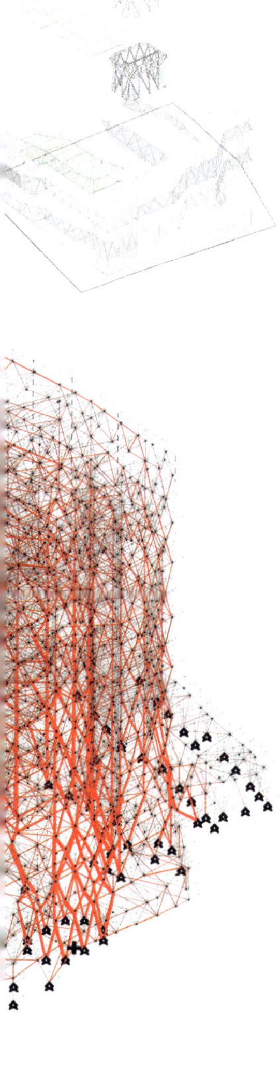

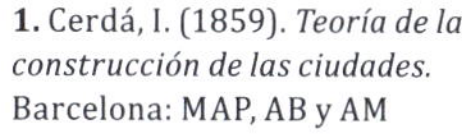

References

1. Cerdá, I. (1859). *Teoría de la construcción de las ciudades.* Barcelona: MAP, AB y AM

2. Batty, M. (2018). *Digital Twins.* Environment and Planning B: Urban Analytics and City Science 45 (5): 817–20. https://doi.org/10.1177/2399808318796416.

3. Cuthbert, A. R. (2006). *The Form of Cities:* Political Economy and Urban Design. The Form of Cities: Political Economy and Urban Design. 1st ed. Malden, MA; Oxford, UK; Victoria, Australia: Blackwell Publishing Ltd. https://doi.org/10.1002/9780470774915

4. Licklider, J. C. R. (1960). *Man-Computer Symbiosis.* IRE Transactions on Human Factors in Electronics HFE-1 (1): 4–11. https://doi.org/10.5100/jje.7.314.

5. Chamayou, G. (2014). *Patterns of Life: A very short history of schematic bodies.* The Funambulist Papers 57: 1-44.

6. Levi-Strauss, C. (1955). *Tristes Tropiques.* Terre Humaine. Paris: Plon.

7. Rancière, J. (2001). *Ten Theses on Politics.* Theory & Event, vol.5, no.3

8. Steyerl, H. (2016). *A Sea of Data: Apophenia and Pattern (Mis) Recognition.* E-flux, no.72

9. Rittel, H. W. J., and Webber, M. M. (1973). *Dilemmas in a General Theory of Planning.* Policy Sciences 4 (2): 155–69. https://doi.org/10.1007/BF01405730.

10. Bettencourt, L. M. A. (2014). *The Uses of Big Data in Cities.* Big Data, 2(1), 12–22. https://doi.org/10.1089/big.2013.0042

11. Hayles, K.N. (2014). Cognition Everywhere: *The Rise of the Cognitive Nonconscious and the Costs of Consciousness.* New Literary History, vol.45, no.2

12. Parisi, L. (2017). *Reprogramming Decisionism.* E-flux, no.85

13. Carpo. M. (2017). *The Second Digital Turn: Architecture in the Age of Intelligence.* Cambridge: MIT Press,

14. Nagy, D., et al. (2017). Project Discover: *An Application of Generative Design for Architectural Space Planning.* Simulation Series 49 (11): 49–56. https://doi.org/10.22360/simaud.2017.simaud.007.

15. Negroponte, N. (1975). *Soft Architecture Machine.* MIT Press.

16. Claypool, M. (2019). *Discrete automation.* E-flux, Becoming Digital.

17. Keller, S. (2017) *Automatic Architecture.* Chicago: The University of Chicago Press.

18. Picon, A. (2015). *Smart Cities: A Spatialised Intelligence.* Edited by Helen Castle, Miriam Murphy, and Calver Lezama. Digital Birmingham. 1st ed. Chichester: John Wiley & Sons Ltd. https://doi.org/10.1007/978-3-319-47361-1.

19. Ratti, C., & Claudel, M. (2015). *Open Source Architecture.* Thames & Hudson.

20. Simondon, G. (2015). *Individuation in the Light of the Notions of Form and Information.* Dordrecht: Springer.

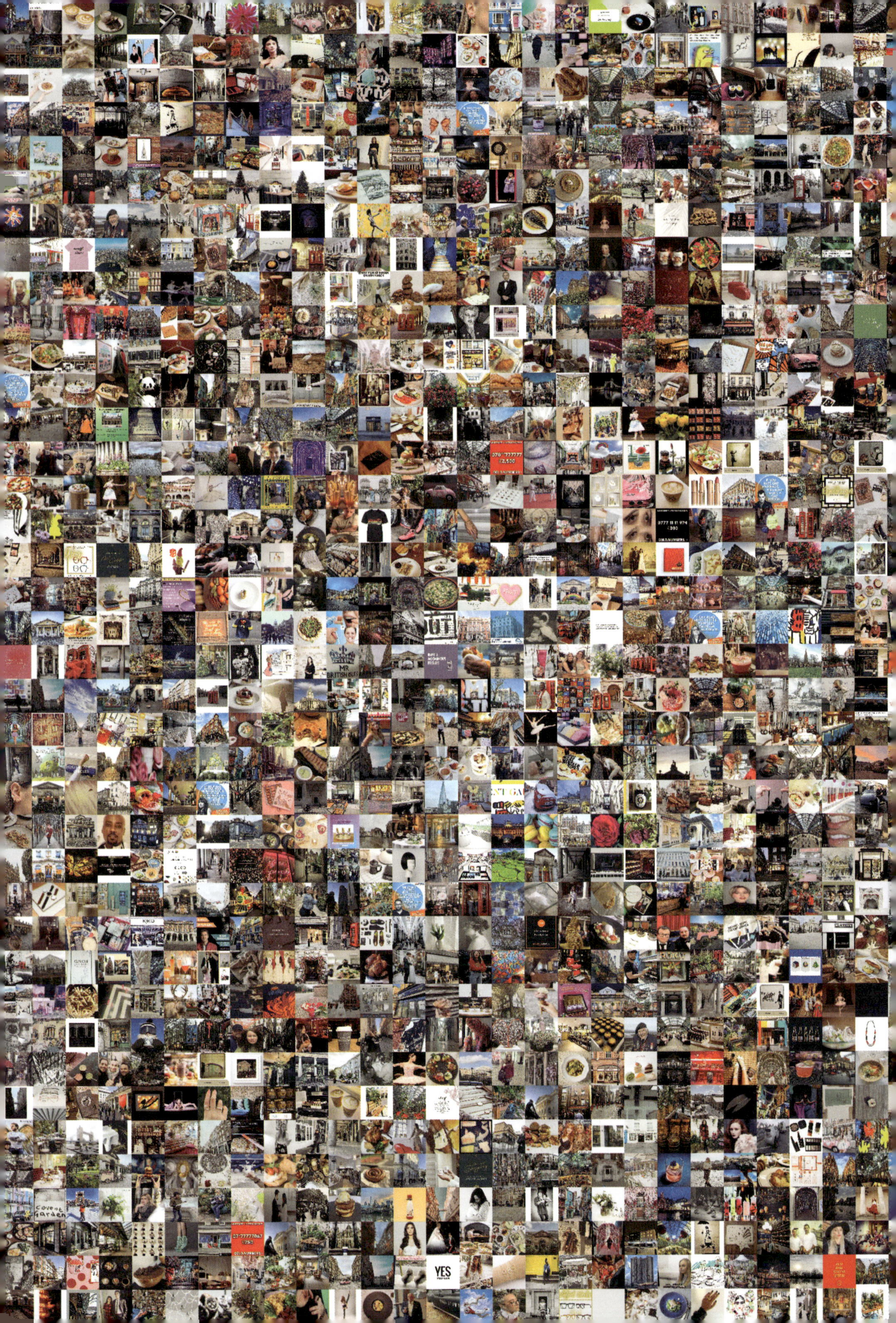

Relating human to machine
Symbiotic augmentation in architectural design

Aleksandra Sojka, Snoweria Zhang,
Deborah Churchill, Cobus Bothma,
Kohn Pedersen Fox

Cities house the communities we thrive in. Understanding the requirements and performance of future urban spaces is becoming more challenging for the modern architect or urbanist. How do we, as designers of urban environments, approach densification, development, and growth whilst creating places that meet their inhabitants' needs and desires, let alone the requirements for sustainability and wellbeing?

The influences in thriving cities are numerous and extend far beyond the drawing board, with many of the final functions and the use of spaces not in the control of the designer, operator, or local authorities. This is why our approach at Kohn Pedersen Fox (KPF) for designing thriving neighborhoods goes beyond the design of buildings and spaces to include frameworks allowing future growth, use, and adaptability. We need to ensure we can simulate and analyze our various computational design models as an integral part of the design experience for these frameworks.

Previous page:
Copyright Kohn
Pedersen Fox.

This leads to the designer seeking to augment the design process through multiple layers of design, technology, processes, and data. We develop and use these functions to simulate possible future scenarios and develop a scalable design approach to ensure the resilience and longevity of the completed neighborhood. The full design experience requires analytical and spatial design, various data layers, and simulation for immersive experiences of the future spaces.

Our main areas of informing the design experience thus include (but are not limited to):

Geometry - Parametric, computational, and generative design approaches to optimize design, use parameters and analysis-based clustering, and goal-driven design methodologies.

Analysis - Extensive environmental and build analysis to ensure we have the best sustainability results while maximizing the site benefit. This analytical process includes sustainable design approaches focused on carbon-neutral buildings.

Visualization - Our approach allows all designers to visualize their designs in real time and includes a collaborative process to communicate, review, and develop our designs through mixed reality experiences.

Data – Social - Capturing data through social platforms allows us to understand what attracts people to certain neighborhoods and leverage this dataset to affect future spaces and the direction people move through these urban spaces.

Data – Spatial - Static and live data allows us to use captured information as an overlay to understand the urban makeup, from demographics to typical transport patterns.

Simulation - Simulations allow the overlay of geometries, analysis, and various data sources with virtual AI agents populating, informing, and moving through the designed spaces, experienced through immersive visualization, to complete the design experience.

We have highlighted some of the development in the geometry, analysis, social data, and simulation categories of the design experience below to illustrate how we implement and develop urban understanding with design technologies.

Scout – An Inclusive, Interactive Platform for Design Review and Selection

Computation in architecture is frequently associated with animation. Greg Lynn's 1999 treatise on animation and form portrays the current practice of architecture as the wrestle between stasis and movement. Acknowledging that "architecture is the study of the inert", Lynn categorizes movement in architecture into two models: one of procession and one of superimposition. While procession uses the object of permanence – architecture itself – as a frame upon which visual or physical movement transpires, superimposition imagines a prequel for the building form and arrives at an alibi for the genesis of the shape. Words such as "shearing" and "rotating" signify the forces that drive architecture to its final, permanent form. Computational design practices today take on a third model, one that explores the meaningful possibility of space before a design decision emerges.

Such a process relies on the parametrization of the design constraints and several measures to evaluate each design option. Contrary to many evolutionary models that have dominated the computational imagination of the early aughts, which focus on deriving the optimal, we have built our computational design tool to enable the designer and the community to make informed decisions. This process is best manifested through Scout: a shared web platform that helps our global firm gain quick data-driven insights, present to clients, and engage with the community. Through Scout, designers and collaborators can easily explore and compare thousands of options, make more informed decisions, and enjoy the creative freedom of visualizing results in real time. By automating specific components of design, Scout frees focus for deeper development, innovation, and craft. It is software-independent, easily accessible, and packages complex design scenarios into one click. Whether for two minutes or two hours, different types of users can coexist and get quick takeaways or obtain deep insights.

Such insights can exist in conflict with one another. For instance, suppose that the designer, in addition to wanting to shower the ground plane with sunlight, also wants the proposed towers to have good views. A taller set of towers will likely produce better views because they can stand above surrounding obstructions, but they will likely cast longer shadows and reduce the amount of direct sunlight on the ground plane. This example highlights the fallacy that there is one "optimal" design option – a balance must be found between sometimes opposing objectives. As such, it is imperative for a design process to be evaluated along multiple axes and highlight the trade-offs of decisions.

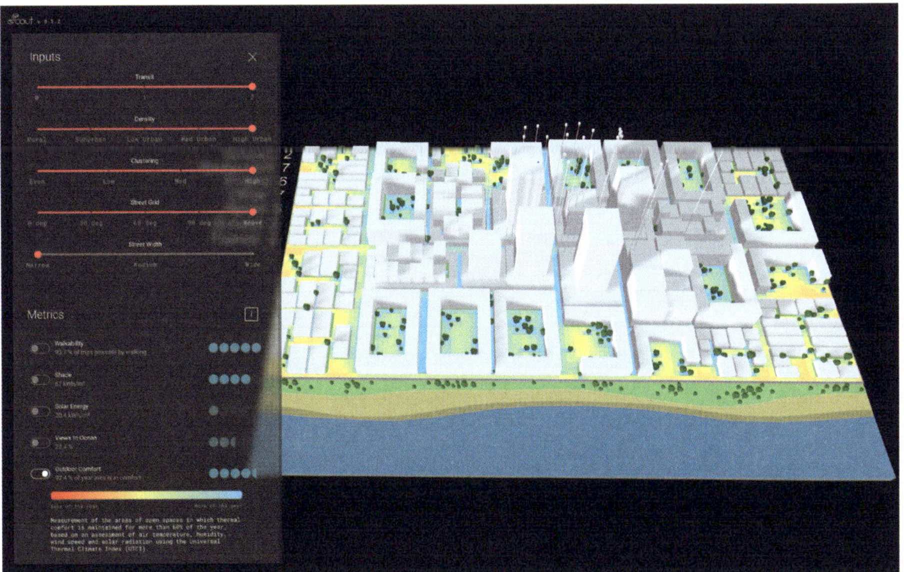

Copyright Kohn Pedersen Fox.

ML-CFD – Real-time Pedestrian Comfort through Machine Learning

Design decisions made in the early stages of a project do not just affect the performance of one building but directly impact the surrounding built environment: the urban microclimate, the urban systems, and the communities that live around it. When we design buildings, we also create the spaces in between and microclimates around them, which in turn have a significant impact on the quality and usability of those spaces.

While some building performance simulation tools are fast and easily integrated into design workflows, others – like computational fluid dynamics (CFD) for wind flow, energy modelling, and detailed daylight studies – are computationally extremely expensive and time-consuming. They require following special modelling guidelines, sometimes geometry simplifications, completely different software environments, and are not smoothly integrated in the architectural design workflow.

With the goal to create a fully integrated computational performance-driven design cycle, we looked at one of the most challenging problems: computational fluid dynamics for wind flow in external urban environments. One wind simulation can take from 8 to 16 hours, and during the design stage, typically, more than one simulation is needed. By using ML, can we make this process faster? Can we bring this down to a second? Can we provide this feedback in real time?

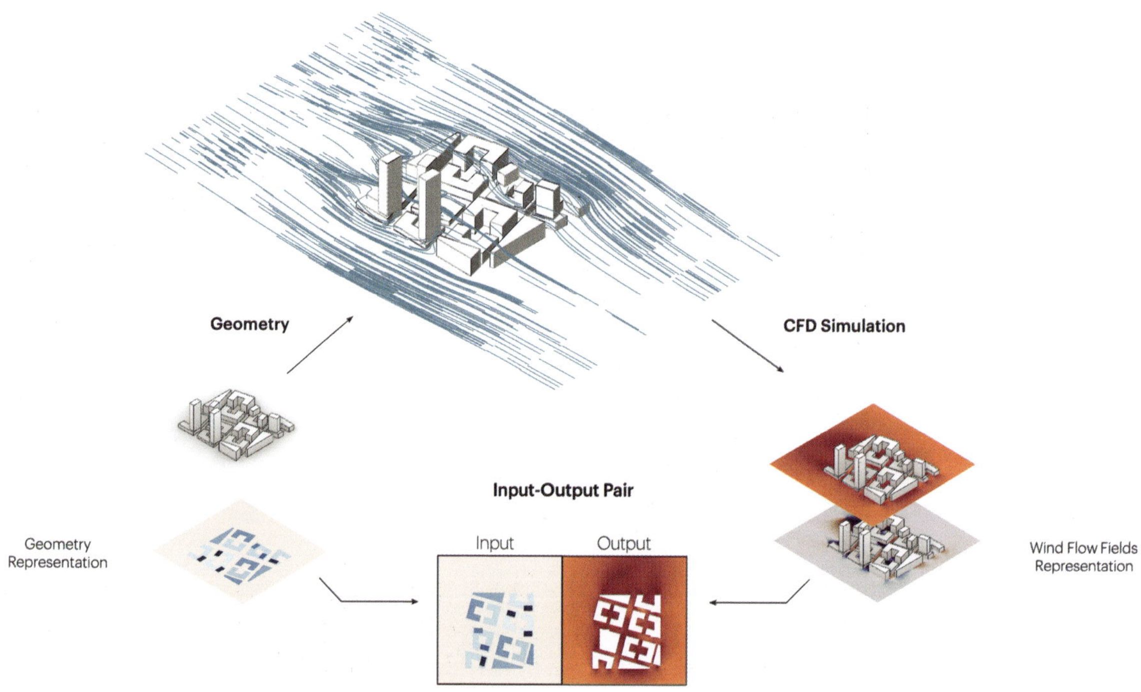

Copyright Kohn Pedersen Fox.

The first challenge was finding the right method of encoding a multivariate environmental simulation of the urban block into a two-dimensional representation that the training algorithm can consume, and later translating the model's output into a format that is helpful to the designer and the architectural software.

We started the process by generating a synthetic dataset based on CFD simulations of procedurally generated urban configurations. We were exploring different geometries and data encoding techniques to

Copyright Kohn Pedersen Fox.

cover a large representation of urban morphologies. The inputs were encoded as an image of a 2D height map representing 3D geometry. The outputs were represented by an image with the color-encoded wind speed values produced by CFD simulation.

The generated dataset of about 13,000 image pairs was used to train a conditional GAN model, a Pytorch implementation of Pix2Pix algorithm. While running experiments, we fine-tuned the model by adding additional layers to the neural network encoder, introducing different loss functions, performing data augmentation, adjusting batch sizes and learning rates. The testing set consisted of 15 unseen geometries, each one with several height variants, which gave us about 500 cases to test. For the model evaluation stage, we calculated the L1 loss for generated samples to see how far they were from the ground truth. We also performed perceptual validation since it is essential that the output images show clear and smooth wind flow tunnels since they should be readable to the designers.

This deep learning approach showed promising results, with prediction accuracies acceptable for the early design stages at a fraction of the corresponding simulation computational time.

The selected model was deployed into a dedicated web server and is accessible via API. We integrated the model inference into the typical architectural design process in Rhino + Grasshopper. The designer would model the geometry, assign the orientation and height of interest. The generation of the heightmap is automated and used to call an API endpoint through a Grasshopper plugin that returns an image result, which is further converted back to a mesh and a matrix of wind speed values. This integration brings insights that would typically take hours in seconds, all within the same design environment.

Copyright Kohn Pedersen Fox.

City Fingerprints – Using Machine Learning to Understand Urban Patterns through Social Media

As highlighted earlier, social media provides a rich source of data on our collective behavior. As urbanists, we can use it to discover city experiences and places where city dwellers and visitors tend to gravitate. Instagram, as a visually rich medium that is not as polarizing as other platforms, is a powerful vehicle for such discovery.

In the recent study, we used Instagram posts to analyze the social activity around Covent Garden, where our KPF London office is situated, using ML tools. The techniques described below can easily be applied to other geographies, although they are suited best for city/ neighborhood scale analysis.

We started by programmatically collecting a sizable corpus of about 10,000 Instagram posts tagged with the hashtag #CoventGarden using the official Instagram API. Only the image, hashtags and text were used in the analysis. All information about the users was stripped to protect the privacy of the authors.

We built data enrichment pipelines and used cloud-hosted cognitive services to detect the sentiment of the content of the posts (99% turned out to be positive or neutral) and to apply multiple labels to the images. The labelling enrichment allowed us to better understand the content and the scene depicted in the image. We used that textual corpus to execute a high-level categorization of the posts.

By performing topic modelling with an LDA algorithm, we learned that the posts fluctuate around the following topics: food/meal (Topic 1), city/urban/architecture (Topic 2, the most interesting to our case study), advertisement/text (Topic 3), plant/flower/bloom (Topic 4, a surprising finding in the urban environment), apparel/clothing/accessory (Topic 5).

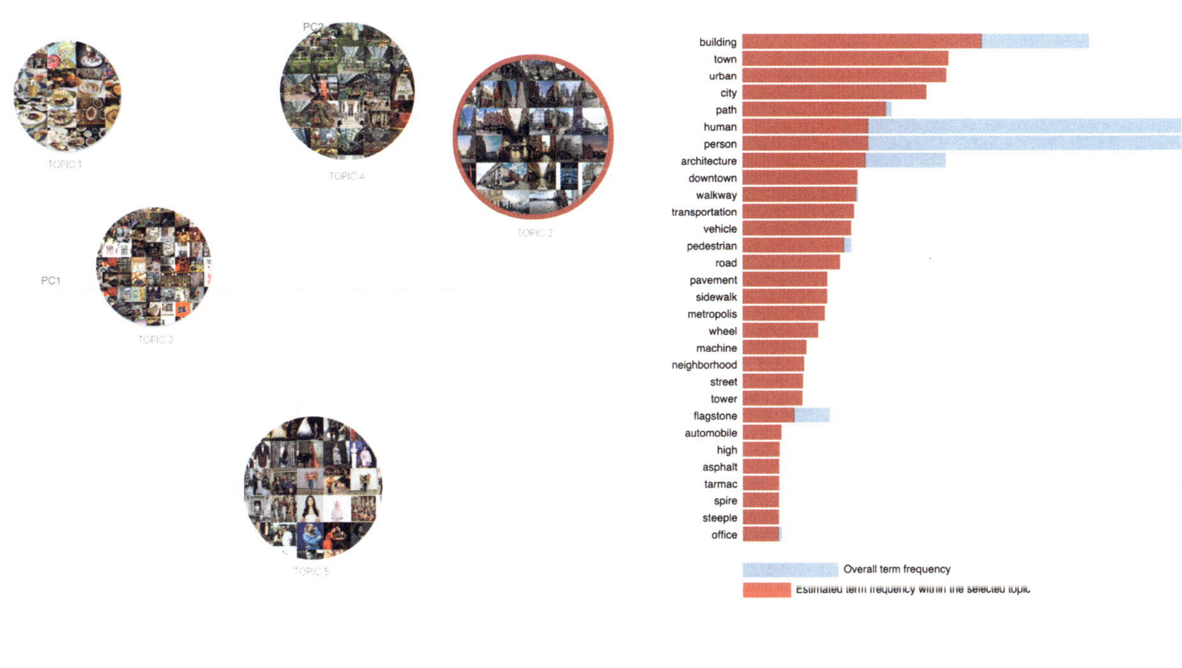

TOPIC 1 TOPIC 2 TOPIC 3 TOPIC 4 TOPIC 5

This preliminary analysis allowed us to refine the dataset to the topics that are relevant to our study. We could easily eliminate any advertisement posts from the dataset.

The next step was visual analysis. The goal was to discover the clusters of images that would allow us to map the places the Instagram audience gravitates towards. We used a pre-trained neural network to extract feature vectors from the collected images (resulting in 2048 features per image). Feature vectors are numerical representations that are still true to the original image content but, at the same time, can be consumed by ML models.

We did not want to partition the image data into clusters, but instead, we wanted to find the groups of somewhat similar images. We decided to use HDBSCAN, a clustering algorithm that can detect dense regions in the dataset and is aware of the noise. We pre-processed the dataset again with UMAP, a dimensionality reduction technique well suited for image data, and reduced the dataset features from over 2000 to 50 features and then scaled it before feeding it to the model. The model discovered several clusters of various sizes and density.

What we learned is that people are attracted to specific spaces and objects.

Copyright Kohn Pedersen Fox.

What would make us stop by, cross the street and take the photo? Space with interesting lighting effects, intimate colonnades, work of art, colorful facades and winding street, flower arrangements, beautiful landscaping, rustic storefronts, restaurants rich with greenery. We need to be aware that the landmarks will definitely resurface as their own clusters, but the user can quickly eliminate those by concentrating only on small high-density clusters by fine-tuning model hyper-parameters. We can use those discoverers as an inspiration or point of reference for the urban design.

Agent Simulation – Collaborative AI

Copyright Kohn Pedersen Fox.

Urban planning operates on an assumption of agreement, especially at the edge where differences meet. However, this is not always the case. How do you resolve differences when stakeholders disagree? In unequal power gradients, spatial negotiation is key. However, the burden of negotiation frequently falls on the less powerful. As such, it is possible to imagine a future design paradigm that relies on multivalent collaboration, where AI acts in the spatial negotiator's role.

As it is closely tied to access to housing and public space, the production of an urban artefact highlights the importance of recognizing such power disparities. In a playful thought experiment, we sought to reserve space for AI to assume the negotiator's role, which bridges the interstitial space that is often fraught. Using a tool similar to Scout, the human participates in generating urban designs with desired characteristics in an asynchronous fashion. As the process develops, an AI agent continuously learns from the extant materials and generates new spatial boundaries. This model can not only allow for a less contentious human-human collaboration, it also introduces the notion of human-AI collaboration and offers a paradigm that accommodates divergent needs and voices.

The legacy of Modernism is strong and can still be seen in most buildings that are designed today. This is not surprising. However, what is surprising is that the notion of an inventive architecture cannot break the mould either. As such, it would be interesting to use AI as an explorative and speculative tool, especially around the notion of collaboration. Here manifested as machinery, the mystic public acts to bridge the interstitial space that is often so fraught. It can generate the playful, seek the just, and manifest the imaginative.

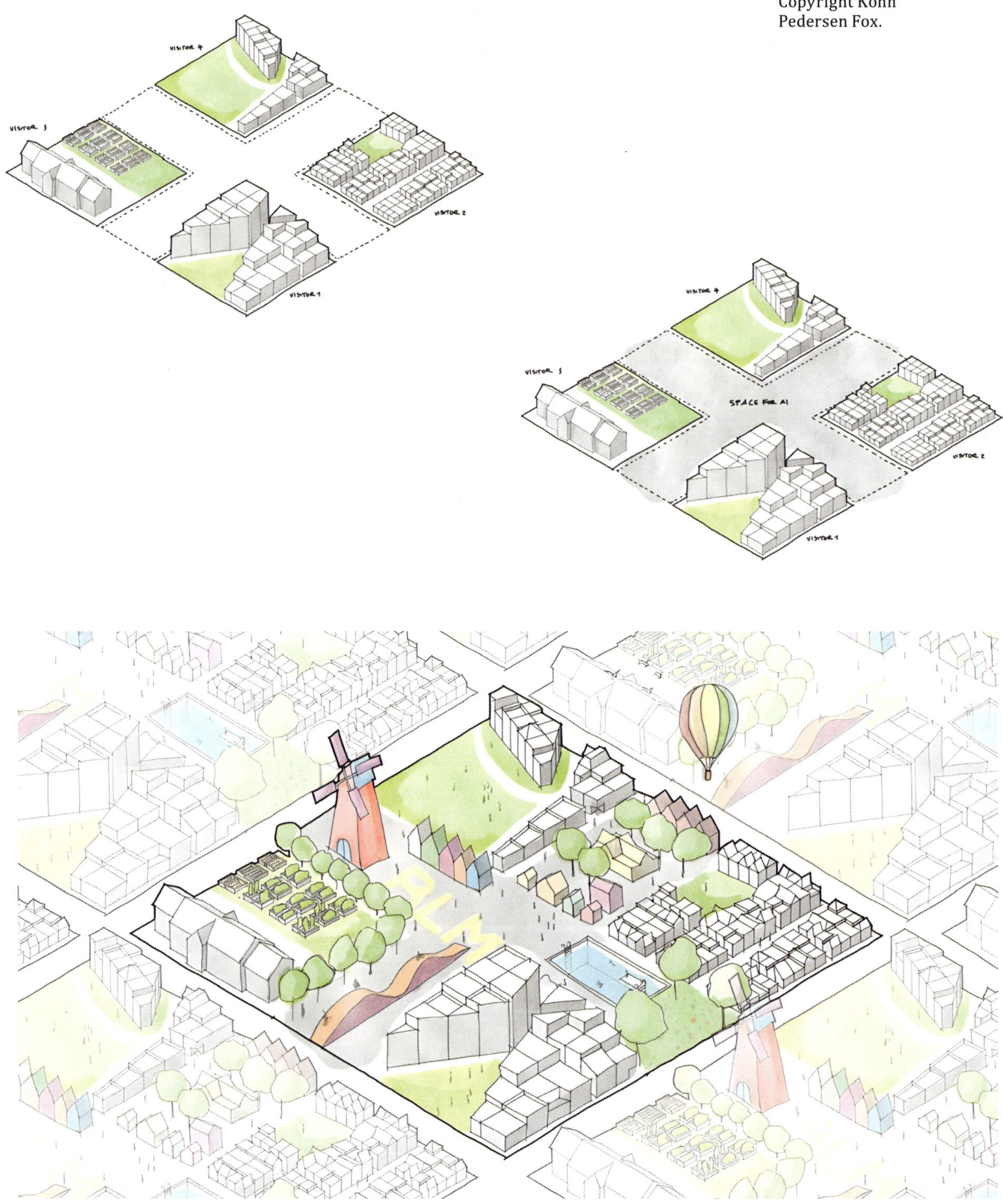

Copyright Kohn Pedersen Fox.

Copyright Kohn Pedersen Fox.

Conclusion

We have illustrated only four functions in a large and complex approach to the urban design experience. Our continual drive is to offer more layers of data and information to the designer, through an immersive simulated environment, which incorporates geometric, data, and visual information – available in real time. The renewed design process cycle of designer creating, machine computing, designer evaluating and reacting/continuing in the design process is a possible symbiotic way of expanding on the overall design experience: designing, understanding, and simulating future urban designed spaces.

Urban and city-scale design demands many influencing factors, and there is currently no straightforward approach to consuming this allin-one design/developing environment. However, the focus on design and the augmentation of the design experience through computational functions beyond spatial/geometric design is an important field to develop further to respond to the requirements for our developing cities. Hopefully, the possible future result will be a combination of the virtual and physical simulated environment allowing designers and future occupants to experience and influence the pre-build design and maybe even the possibility of some of the digital design remaining as personalized spaces post-occupancy.

Learning Cities, Shared Co-Cities, Empathic Cities

Manuel Gausa

Learning Cities: Towards a New Vocabulary

The digital revolution has not only brought about fundamental transformations in our technological tools and our operating systems, but ongoing changes that affect key aspects of our intellectual, cultural, and ethical relationships with our living environments, our habitats and our own relational spaces. These dynamics no doubt require a new kind of innovative and hybrid vocabulary.

As we will see in this text, these transformations range from new interactions with augmented matter – *(Hyper)matters* – and increasingly overlapping, complex, diverse and diversified processes – *(Multi)processes* – to a new social demand for involvement between networked citizens and citizenships responding to responsible and responsive interactions in and with our environments *(Citi-zens & City-sens).*

Also, a new perception of the aesthetic factor opens up – no longer as more or less predetermined, fixed and canonical category/ies but as a polyhedral condition, increasingly related to intelligent (artificial or natural) phenomena of option/decision and self-generation *(AST-ethics)* that summon up new visions of *fluid scenarios* fluctuating between being strategically oriented and contingently and co-decided, adapted and adaptable *("Scena-rios", in Spanish).*

Previous page: "Umbrellas Manifestation" in Honk Kong, 2017. Self-organized mobilization with networked cells. http://mimamamememe.com/manifestaciones-moviles-revolucion-paraguas/.

We are talking about a new individual and collective, shared intelligence augmented by the new digital/informational potentials between agents and media *(Inter-diligence)* but also of a new *actant* drive to act, which is both operational and operative, more holistically qualitative – defined through actions *(and operations)* that are strategic and tactical at the same time *(Oper-actions)*. In and between all these phenomena underlies the notion of Learning Cities, which is the subject of this text.

UNESCO defines a Learning City as an urban context that effectively mobilizes its resources and its knowledge in multiple sectors, revitalizing the notion of permeable exchanging communities and extending the use of modern networking technologies for qualitative goals (https://uil.unesco.org/lifelong-learning/learning-cities).

The emergence of the concept of Learning Cities Networks (LCN) promotes immersive interactive policies that can increment sharing experiences intended to favor innovative responses to current serious urban issues. Evidently, the outcomes of these new co-active (reactive, responsive, but also co-generative and self-decisional) processes (both social and material) mark the new key-items in the advanced urban logic capable of mobilizing shared and interactive proposals at multidimensional levels.

In fact, the concept of Learning Cities (or Cities of and for Learning) encourages the drive not only to think but to act beyond the walls of established conventions and structures, increasingly understanding the n-City as a multiple ecosystem (a system of systems) of vast opportunities, resources and potentials to be developed through circular and informational feedback, which can ask (and respond) better to current needs, concerns, interests, expectations and ambitions.

(Hyper)matters &(Multi)processes

The second decade of the 21st century has promoted the notion of Learning Cities through the exponential development of new technologies that have multiplied the potential for interaction between spaces, contexts, environments and societies (medium, media, means and mediators... uses, users and usages).

This has brought about a new phase of increasingly ubiquitous and augmented capabilities, embedded in a new material-virtual dimension called upon to define the "expanded" and immersive" condition of our contemporary *(hyper)reality* that tends to assume – in an accelerated way – its own hybrid definition, material and immaterial, physical and virtual, systemic and specific.[1]

The exponential development of algorithmic programs and digital devices (robotics, apps, drones, multi-interfaces) associated with more sophisticated three-dimensional processes of simulation, representation and fabrication – of recording, modeling, designing and producing – has contributed decisively to the improvement of a possible association between space, architecture, artificial intelligence and automata agents.

In this context, the evolution of mobile telephony – from the first generation 1G to the recent 5G – has ended up favoring not only a decisive portability linked with new interactive capabilities but the decisive importance of informational processing actions generated in real time *(Real-Time-Data)* and the potential of a new type of interconnected *co-coded surrounding*, dynamically distributed – collector and processor of information – destined to expand and amplify the interaction(s) "in" and "with" the habitat and the environment; evidencing, then, a new framework for operational-relational – or creative-vindictive – direct networked exchanges, with new social, economical, environmental and cultural – but above all productive and co-productive – goals, that have been addressed in recent publications.[2,3,4,5]

Chris Sugrue (2017): *Delicate Boundaries.* Action of virtual microbes happening from the screen to the agent's body at the moment he extends his arm, contacting with synthetic surface.

Whereas at the end of the first decade of the 21st century the generalized concept of *Smart-Cities* seemed to be an unescapable urban topic, today a new concept, that of the *(Co)Learning City* is emerging with force, combining the previous "smart" capacities with new proactive and co-generative (bottom-up) challenges.

The increasingly parametric (and parameterizable) dimension of these new evolutionary urban definitions, in which the very notion of information tended to be understood, more and more, as a data-indicator – economic, functional, environmental, etc. – progressively tended to interpret the *nCity* itself not only as a great multi-organism – an urban-territorial system of systems – but as a big reactive, sensitive and sensorized environment: an *"increasingly (inter)mediated and interactive medium".*[6, 7, 8.]

The research conducted in this moment of exploration – at the end of the second decade of the 21st century – tended, in fact, to delve more and more into the new capacities associated with the accelerated encounter between materiality and digitality (bio-technology, bio-materials, nano-technology, artificial intelligence, robotics, new interfaces, etc.); between Matter (reactive) and Environment (reactivated); but also, between Environment (activated and actuated) and Agents (activators and actuators), subject to progressively co-generated (spatial) actions (co-produced, co-participated, co-decided, co-generated, co-activated) associated with new urban (and not only urban) collective processes.

Agents & Matters suggest new points of interest that reinforce the capacity to interact with multiple socio-environmental and informational conditions, not only optimizing them but taking note of the different associated and derived behaviors, in potential feedback that can "learn" about the results and proceedings themselves; transforming them into new urban *opera(c)tive* and *performa(c)tive* processes that are capable of better reprogramming the initial formulations (and conditions).

This potential would be more significant today (if possible), when the capacity for interaction between the new processor-devices can also gradually be integrated into our bodies (tuned prostheses, digital tattoos, embedded chips, etc.) expressing this new "expanded" culture of our social, living and relationship spaces, more and more obvious in their mutable and mutant definitions: we are talking, of course, about a progressive digital development of artificial intelligence but also about the eventual (Inter)action between new Material and Collective *understanding-conducts.*

Metter Ramsgard Thomsen, "The role of the news technologies", in *IaaC Bits,* no. 1 (2014), 2.

Following page: *Networked Crow,* photomontage (Adrià Goula photographer, photomontage by Manuel Gausa).

Augmented Matters (new reactive and/or responsive capacities) but also Common Behaviors (new "co-active" behaviors) can be combined more and more into factors of interactivity and diversity: factors supported by multi-agency processes of exchange and relationships, of reactiveness and reactivity, of pervasiveness and ubiquity (informational simultaneity) rooted in synergistic mediations but also in new symbiotic operations.

The exploration of these new "responsive" and "adaptive" capacities for a "(hyper)matter" (digital Matter or Intelligent Matter) with augmented informational processing and elaborating capacities defines new *eco-* and *endo-* translations into spatial forms and/or formulations.

These material potentials can, at the same time, be combined today with the exploration of a new co-productive city or *Co-City* (co-generated and co-generative, co-responsive and co-responsible, co-participated and co-participative, co-decided and co-decisional).
A new type of networked "collective intelligence" (more hyper-connected and hyper-connective, more "in common" and intercommunicated, more empathic and/or eco-empathetic) directly associated with a new system of bottom-up and (self)oriented interchanges progressively incremented in their interrelated capabilities and applications (decidedly synergistic in/with a milieu and in/with a reality that has been augmented in its e-Co-technological and e-Co-relational possibilities) favors not only *hyper-connections (information, networks and fields)* but also *hyper-convections (energy, spaces and fluids)* called on to address this new *"co(ll/nn) ective"* condition, in/between social and environmental spaces and behaviors.[9, 10, 11, 12, 1.]

Citi-zens & City-sens

The explorations focused in this possible new techno-material, Explorations focused on this possible new techno-material, techno-social and techno-environmental *(pro)active (inter)activity* permeate recent research, propitiating new approaches to the contemporary *multi-city* as a more sensitive and processual environment in which Citizens and *City-Sens, City-layers and City-fields, City-agents* and *City-agencements* (new social collectivities and connectivities and new interactive communities and conductivities) can be combined in this new networked "shared logic" (in common and in community), which is decidedly co-Actant.[13]

When we talk about Learning Cities, we are talking, more specifically, about a new "mediation logic" materialized in a new type of capabilities and spatialities intended to favor new strategic bottom-up responses that are fast, immediate and exchanged in real time. Processes that are attentive to the mediating and mobilizing synergic vocation of a new type of *OSBURT* (Open Source, Bottom-up, Real-Time) activism – which is sometimes more upsetting, informal, fresh and unencumbered, and other times more vindictive. This activism is capable of combining a super-technology of connectivity and exchange (data, messages and experiences, but also solicitations and mobilizations) with a desire for more direct and spontaneous action, which is not necessarily hyper-technological but definitely interactive and interactivated by the new networked systems themselves.[14]

The goal of these dynamics is to propose new multi-functional and multi-level active – "co-active" – scenarios, coming from the operational assessment of new *inform(ation)al* models that are more open, dynamic, co-participated and innovated. We're talking about the force of new tools, related to the increase of new responsive

Coloco (2016). Courbevoie, Jardins Mobiles (photo Estelle Pardon).

and progressively autonomous (but strategically oriented) spatial and systemic physical devices able to facilitate the interpretation, conjugation, parametrization and orientation of our environments (through digital sensing/sensors, responsive matters/manners, flexible interfaces/interlaces, processing robotics/biotics, etc.).

But we're also talking about the increase in a more *immaterial and in-mediated* collective inter-activism implicit in the culture of our times, not so much for its technological vocation but for its willingness to infiltrate new inputs in the system and/to re-inform it (resetting it, sometimes radically, provocatively or mischievously – that is, reactivating it in a qualitative and engaged way): a new social *e-Co-mediation* in which the technological and the phenomenological are combined with the *actio-logical* (with a new logic of action); the sophisticated with the spontaneous; the processor with the mobilizing, the artificial with the natural, promoting (beyond aesthetic prejudices or stylistic filters) the obtainment and/or optimization not only of what is "simply necessary" but also of the "qualitatively indispensable"; from a clearly committed mediating (involved and receptive) vocation, without linguistic pretensions or more or less aesthetic or conventional prejudices (Gausa, Vivaldi, 2021). In fact, many of the collective proposal lectures that occur today (from "field experiences" to "experimental mediations") tend to prioritize the efficient management and re-elaboration of information (in all senses: data, indicators, programs, conditions) and its immediate formal resolution/translation into possible (optimized) synthesized scenarios.

Barcelona Las Ramblas. Study of the different spontaneous fluxes and density of crow dynamic movements in the lineal *net-set* of Las Ramblas. Interactions and self-oriented movements defined by different conditions and solicitations and environmental factors. Las Ramblas fluxes in a synthetic ratio-sequence time diagram and diagram of crows (by Barry Le Va and Stan Allen).(Fount: Actar Arquitectura, Multi-Rambles, 2010).

The emergence of this new type of social and environmental mediation linked to the direct action of an architecture of the instantaneous, of the urgent, of the *unpostponable* (of the interactive and of the activist) has been focused primarily, in recent times, on the social reconquest of a public space interpreted as a great relational and active topo-interface, open to simultaneity, multiplicity and mutability: to what is variable, unforeseen, indeterminate but above all plural, co-relational, co-experiential, convivial.[15, 16, 17.]

This direct, precise, immediate, "instantaneous" idea of the public or para-public sphere (where the old systemic definition of the "element" suddenly gives way to a new epistemic condition of the "elementary" or "elemental") continues to rely, today, on the abilities of craft and design (and, in this sense, it does not necessarily require sophisticated technological tools and apparatus, but interconnected networks of complicities) to formulate direct and efficient answers; shared search processes (co-produced and co-generated through plural and informational exchanges) capable of encouraging a space definitively associated with the assumption of a new eco-medium and a new eco-mediation: a social space called on to exponentially expand the potential for exchange between situations and solicitations; but also to eventually express this increasing ability to synthesize conditions

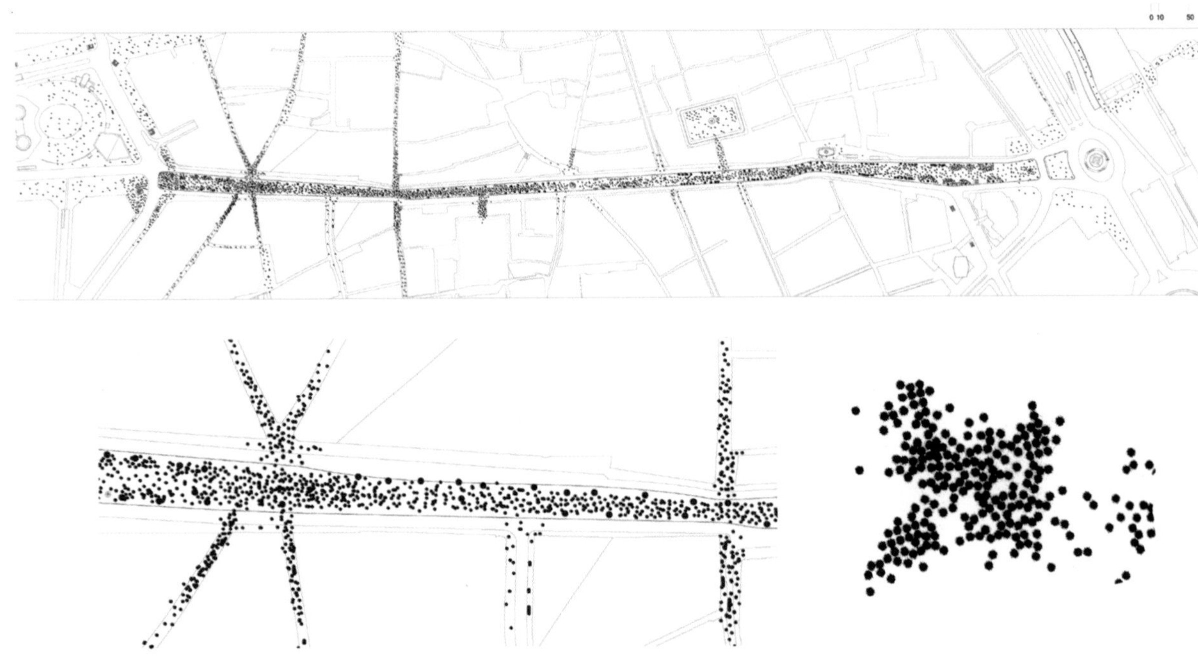

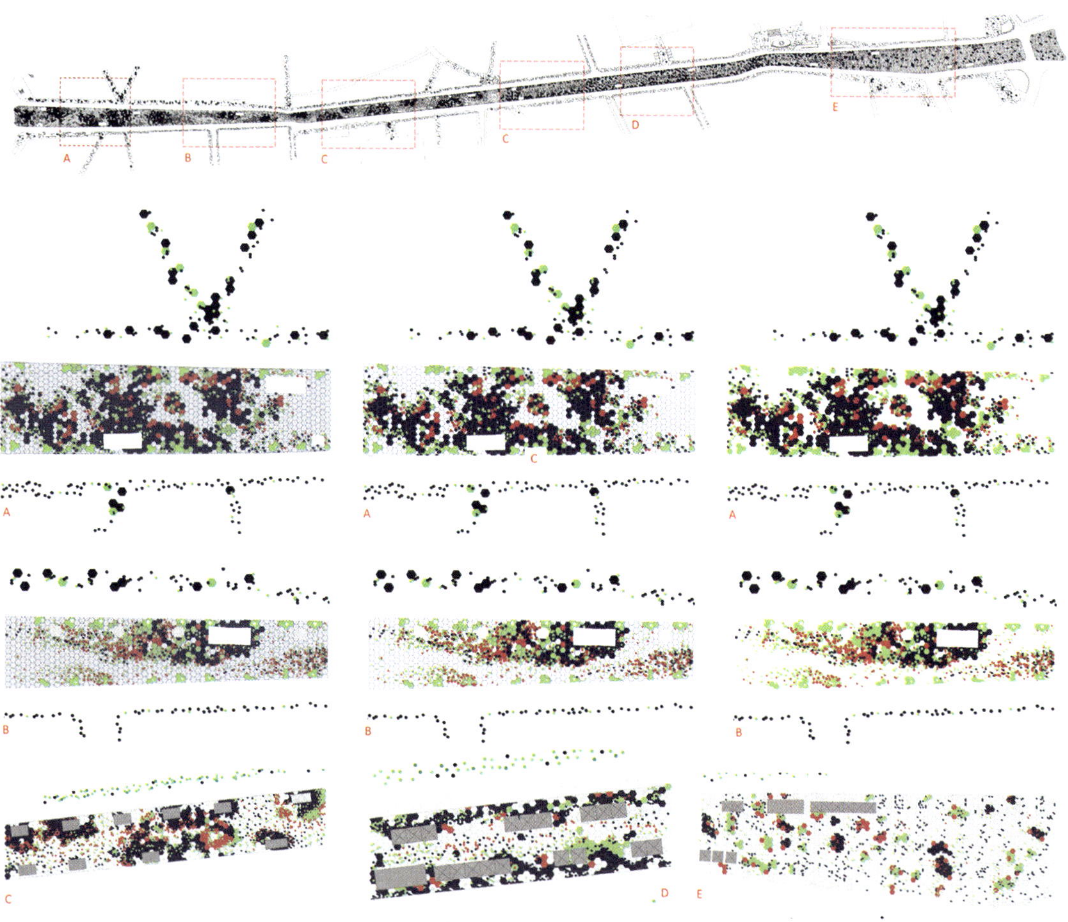

Barcelona Las Ramblas. Study of the different spontaneous fluxes and density of dynamic and evolving movements in the lineal *net-set* of Las Ramblas. Interactions and self-oriented movements defined by different conditions and solicitations as environmental factors. Las Ramblas fluxes and different movement patterns second localizations (Fount: Actar Arquitectura, Multi-Rambles, 2010).

and information(s) (in the form of precise parameters, indicators or algorithms that are recordable, retraceable and re-editable in formats and trajectories adapted to variable contexts and times) in our relational environments, translating them into more qualitative and innovative shared scenarios.

The contemporary emergence (and complementary appearance) of these new types of material capacities and immaterial sensitivities, connected to the force of attack *(force de frappe)* of a common qualitative interaction (and/or over-action) where "doing" and "learning" end up defining two mesh-concepts – is marking the interest of the new generations, involved with this collective responsible and responsive sensitivity.

Self-generation, self-organization, co-production and co-participation, multi-solicitations and multi-interventions tend to be combined in new *opera(c)tions (media(c)tions and installa(c)tions)* that are more or less sophisticated or economic, temporary or ephemeral (in ways and means), with the ability to resolve new living and relational spaces for urban reactivation and collective reaffirmation.

Many of these new urban operations can be understood, in some specific, radical or deficient contexts, as *Guerrilla Boardings,* without technological or formal pretensions, without rhetoric or spectacular performances, but with a strong sense of commitment and of engagement – able (from the "elemental") to offer networked mobilized proposals conceived beyond conventions, with imagination and intensity.

The decisive combination "information + interaction" – fundamental and foundational to our digital time – is completed with the new (and more complex) equation "information + interaction + integration + implication" (conjugated in social, material and spatially rich performing terms), aiming to take advantage of creative, imaginative and innovative resources and possibilities, expressing this assimilation (innovative, diverse, unprejudiced, synthetic and synergic) between "data" and "mandates", typical of our informational times.

The will to propose innovative, variable and adaptable proactive responses continues, through the concept of Learning Cities, to demand the exploration of processes linked to new emerging knowledges and operational logics directly evolved from the first 90s digital era intuitions combined with the new accelerated analytical and synthetic technological capacities: spatial logics that are socially involved and environmentally responsible, because they are progressively responsive and vocationally interactive at all levels. Contemporary complexity requires not only new tools but new logics: the old approaches based on a "imposed structural and formal control" for corrective or regenerative spatial responses, are replaced today – as we have pointed out – by new "synergic infrastructural and strategic inductions" addressed through preventive proactive, adaptable and evolving actions able to combine ancient *"scenarios of emergency"* (conflictive areas) with new *"emergency scenarios"* (areas of opportunity).

It is not only a question of more efficient strategic and adaptable dispositions, rules of the game, or adapted and variable open logics but of a new kind of dynamic *self-critical-analytical-operational* valences that, more and more, will be embedded in the new urban devices and behaviours themselves.[18]

AST-ethics & Scena-rios

In the framework of Learning Cities, the evocative lyric of the old designed "figuration" or the gestural and "iconic" strength of the objectual event seem to give way, today, to the optimized management and efficient elaboration of a reality (potentially improved and/or re-activated) that is tackled immediately, in real time (with precise data and concrete facts, for possible scenarios... positive and/or proactive) giving priority – beyond predetermined aesthetics – to a new *AST-ethics* of action, as stimulating and innovative expressions, translated onto the qualification/manipulation of matter, context, environment and inhabited space (Gausa, Vivaldi, 2021) --1-- : the *AST-ethics* neologism, similar in substance and semiotics to the term aesthetics, alludes to an overcoming of the "idealized" or "predetermined" aesthetic form by a mixture – also aesthetic but more indeterminate and directly reactive – between processed learning factors (AST, Advanced Skills Teaching) and ethical vocations (ethics).

It appears evident that in this new active, reactive and interactive logic (material and mental), a direct, elementary, expressive and adaptable urban architecture of the strategically and qualitatively operative/operational responds better to a new type of strange order of our holistic environments (non-lineal, non-predetermined

Social Cluster and Communities, NB-KAAU Symposium, Genoa 2016.

or deterministic). An Urban Architecture that is more responsive, variable, flexible, dynamic (and unprejudiced) in its manifestations.

In this new informational age, adaptative (open) strategies prevail over static (predetermined) aesthetics, but not necessarily over *AST-ethical* visions: over creative imaginaries and over the ability to project "shared scenarios" – unexpected (and generally "hybrid") – understood as possible multiple and consequentially variable and systematic "horizons of action": not already symbolic or totemic but strategic; conductors and inductors (and catalysts, at the same time) of better co-generative common habitats.

From an architecture understood as a ritual-typological figuration, we have shifted, throughout the 20th century, toward an architecture understood as a functional machine (a mechanical artifact and iconic object at the same time) and now, well into the 21st century, to an architecture conceived as a *(multi)relational* environment (an

In-Between Realities Towards a Socially Sustainable Urban Strategy for Beirut City (IAAC MAA02 2014-2015, Researcher: Rasa Sukkari).

interface space, a multi-layer system, and an interactive scenario all at once), which is synthetic and systematic (global) and unique and non-transferable (local) at the same time.

A new idea of design as an "operative system" – capable of processing the information received and transforming it into evolving and variable or "mutating" scenarios, according to general and specific demands – has emerged as paradigmatic.

The challenge of contemporary design, today, lies in exploring this operative and informational potential, combining analytic recognitions, strategic decisions and synthetic data-formulations.

Therefore, terms like "idea" or "concept" combined with others like "representation" or "expression" seem to continue to be necessary to drive or guide our *"work-in-process scenarios"*. And, in this sense, the capacity to combine reactive information(s) and expressive vision(s) continues to be one of the great challenges, today, when it comes to promoting these new shared horizons that are "narrative and performative, at the same time". *City–Senses* and *sens(c)ivilities.* Responsive contexts and responsible societies. Processing attention and creative innovation. Precise *DATAS* & holistic *VISIONS.*[18, 19, 20.]

Today, the combination *"information + vision"* (processing capacity and projective capacity, prospective, strategic and relational) lacks suitable reference areas and ambitious programs of inter-disciplinary innovative exchanges, and the old notion of urban morphology is therefore beginning to find itself in serious trouble when it comes to continuing to encourage univocal or coherent visions (figurative or votive-type compositions) in the face of a new genre of evolutionary self- or co- activated scenarios (generated beyond traditional figurative sceneries or *scenographies*). Scenarios that are not only more ambivalent but more multivalent (or decidedly polyvalent).

In this framework of action, it seems difficult to continue thinking that the future of urban design will continue to refer to a single type of aesthetic scenography that is more or less ideal, unitary or totalistic, correct and complete, meticulously delineated and designed. The evolution of our cities will go through programming, processing, projecting or simulating "bundles" of *AST-ethical* scenes-scenarios (co-cognitive, expressive, performative and qualitative scenarios), interpretable as virtual, differential, and oriented "fields of forces" open to differential equations of choice/decision, co-activated, co-regulated and (statistically and algorithmically) co-defined between technicians, creators (mediators) and a new type of inter-connected and inter-activated users.
Where will urban form or design belong in this new framework of action? Where will the traditional notion of morphology fit in?

In that shift from the re-formulator to the co-formulator (to the mediator, to flexibly, to the variable and adaptable) Learning Cities open up a new type of *scena-ríos* (*ríos,* in Spanish, understood as movements of fluctuant energies), dynamic trajectories that are malleable and adaptable: vectorized and bifurcated at the same time into bundles of diverse possibilities in which the very variation of the (re)active (the environmental and the temporal, the incident and the incidental) leaves behind any absolute idea of a substantive logic of form, driving it towards a new type of multiplicity inherent in its own (and new) responsive (and responsible) interpretation – at a time when architects/urban planners have moved away from the old role of prescriber/designer toward that of prospector/inductor: dynamics that prefer to summon, therefore, "varied forms associated with the same set of open and consequent logics" *(logomorphies)* rather than "regulated logics linked to the same type of closed and coherent forms" (morphologies).

Inter-diligence & Oper-actions

Unlike in the 1990s, when emerging digital computational development still seemed tied to the research of theoretical and spatial models that were tested or simulated in the virtual world and then constructed in the physical, "real" world, today Learning Cities

WARM AIR
rises
THE BODY
ascends
temperature : 20°C
temperature : 10°C

understand that the development of new information technologies and their translation into an efficient, multidimensional – and often nano-dimensional – *sensorization* combines virtuality and reality in new *performative* scenarios (networked, in nets and sets, knitted and knotted), offering an immense range of possibilities *on-going* in the realm of combining *materiality*, *informationality* and new *interactivity*.[21]

Like our own individual neuronal intelligence as humans, a new collective and artificial intelligence realized through networked statistical parameters (majorities determined in real time) and natural and para-natural or pseudo-natural interconnected agents will be able to recognize, link, react, adapt, structure and change our habitats and environments to "perform" collectively, spatial, urban and political actions, "empathic" and "experiential"; and here the word interactivity – more than interaction – will increasingly take over (Markopoulou, 2014).[10]

In this dynamic action, these common actions and investigations favor temporary or ephemeral "coagulations" ("clusterings" of consensus) formed and quickly undone, because they respond not so much to basilar or ideological sedimentations but to a regrouping of "involved and organized" individual complicities (*impliquées et agencées*, to use Deleuzian terms for a new type of organization more open and interconnected): "partners" of exploration, navigation and action, dynamically destined to "ungroup and/or to recompose in the next movement", sharing, doing and learning through innovative operations and experiences (Deleuze, Guattari, 1990).[22]

If the notion of homogeneous mass no longer exists (except episodically), it is therefore true that a certain collective *actant* capacity, individually and collectively involved, *engagée*[23] a new individual and collective intelligence at the same time, common and hyper-interactive, generated thanks to the exponential technologies of network exchange – can be called on to share and act, thanks also, of course, to the progressive capacity for interconnection and digital interaction.

The progress in "transmission/communication" exchanges has always made it possible to facilitate socio-cultural, instrumental, spatial and mental revolutions, and today this axiom is evident.

A new type of "*individual/collective, interconnected/integrated, intelligence*" (co-active and corrective at the same time, able to combine *doing* and *learning processes*) is what should permit, increasingly, a model of dynamic equilibrium based on mutually supportive feedback and an interactive collaboration – and integration – of different multiplied (multi-layer and multi-level) fields. We can talk of a new kind of common and shared intelligence that, for its implicit disposed and dispositional condition but also for its diligent will to action and proactivity, starts to approximate to a virtual inter-diligence.

Previous page: *ATMOSPHERA* (IAAC MAA02, 2015-2016. Researcher: Asya Guney).

The fundamental principle is that these new reactive and holistic *opera(c)tions* resolve their own needs by optimizing their contextual (local) conditions, demanding from the (global) network those inputs, forces and/or services needed to generate operational answers or responses, calling for a new interactive sharing exchange (with all the synonyms that we can imagine: solidarity, relationship, interchange, interconnection, inter-linkage, reciprocity, conjugation, combination, etc., that have been always paradigms of an empathic reason and sensibility).

Study and reasoning are often confronted with strangely universal impositions, axioms or plots that are not always well defined, in a surprisingly assumed global control, structurally multiplied by mediums and means that continually reiterate messages associated with "accepted" and "guaranteed" conditions.

It seems that this potential for a progressively creative and learning/knowing bottom-up citizenship tends to be more and more contrasted with the old top-down conventional systems (professional, academic, economic, cultural, etc.) that are apparently still standing; the actual capacity of an exponential and expanded *evaluative-knowledge* (analytical, interpretative, critic) seems – too – mostly installed in a hedonism of *zapping/surfing,* of mere indifferent navigation or of spectacle/spectacular distractions; or in the simple absorption of information (messages, news, statistics) that are *manipulated, faked* and/or *banalized*, etc. rather than the real interactive interpretation of them.[20] Although the resistance of all the current powers aims to turn the new technologies into sources of distracting and enslaving forms of imposition, our societies probably will return to the balance between individual freedom, collective well-being and – also – the need for creativity and knowledge progress to survive, expanding this potential "collective – *learning/knowing/doing* – intelligence" (not of masses but of collective diversities) called upon to produce changing and ex-changing scenarios, responsible and responsive in all senses, also – and especially – in spatial terms, according to the ability to influence through statistically oriented applications and variable algorithms in a new kind of co-decisional processes where individuals and collectives are able to express themselves freely and jointly, expressing the elementary confrontation between conservative resistance and new innovative shifts.

The combination between *learning synergies* and *empathiCities* (in ecological, social, creative and economical-productive terms) seems to be indispensable and inevitable in the future.

In this sense, if the first cities were, rightly, social mechanisms and systems made to facilitate exchanges (and defense) over short, dense, compact distances, today the distances of exchanges have freed and expanded these organisms (being distant and close at the same time), paradoxically combining the physical and the virtual in simultaneous multi-level, multi-scalar and multi-network interactions.

Whereas the industrial era of the 20th century favored a paradigm shift in the city and architecture based on the development of new protocols – new technologies and new materials – for construction and production (mechanical and functional developments, synonymous with "dignified" and "massive" progress but net consumers of resources and gross producers of urban waste), the information age of the 21st century seems poised to enact a new paradigm shift based on the development of new "infra"-, "intra-", "inter-", "trans", "info-", "socio"- and "eco"- structures – that are both material and immaterial, networked and site-worked – through more responsive and performative potentials for social and environmental interaction and co-production (critical and propositional, relational and plural, experimental and experiential, personal and common). At the same time, this informational condition, progressively variable and uncertain, must be combined with the ability to create "horizons of certainty", shared criteria of action, visions and forward-looking strategies capable of orienting (driving and inducing) new urban developments, combining advanced technology with new relational models, spatial and social strategies that are innovative and sustainable at the same time: capable of combining "sensing" and "sensitive", sensorial, sensual and "sensorized" logic processes.

Stimulating improvements and shared imaginaries: understanding architecture and cities no longer as functional "machines for the dignity of living" but as new "environmental habitats... for the pleasure of living and co-living".

References

1. Gausa, M., Vivaldi, J. 2021. The Threefold logic of Advanced Architecture. New York: Actar Publishers.

2. Komninos, N. 2008. *Intelligent Cities and Globalization of Innovation Networks.* London: Routledge.

3. Rifkin J. 2011. *The Third Industrial Revolution: How lateral power is transforming energy, the economy and the world.* Lewiston: Griffin.

4. Rifkin J. 2014. *The Zero Marginal Cost Society: The Internet of Things, the Collaborative Commons, and the Eclipse of Capitalism.* London: Palgrave Macmillan.

5. Ratti, C., Claudel, M. 2016. The City of Tomorrow: Sensors, Networks, Hackers, and the Future of Urban Life. New Haven: Yale University Press.

6. Gausa, M. 2012. City Sense: Territorializing Information. En VV.AA., *City Sense, 4th Advanced Architecture Contest,* (6-13). Barcelona: IAAC, Actar.

7. Offenhuber, D., Ratti, C. 2014. *Decoding the City Urbanism in the Age of Big Data.* Basel: Birkhauser.

8. Ratti, C., Claudel, M. 2016. *The City of Tomorrow: Sensors, Networks, Hackers, and the Future of Urban Life.* New Haven: Yale University Press.

9. Gehl, J. 2010. *Cities for People.* Washington D.C.: Island Press.

10. Markopoulou, A. 2014. In(Form) ation-Architecture of Data & Code. In Magazine *IaaC Bits* (Barcelona) 1.

11. Leach, N. 2014. Adaptation. In Magazine IaaC Bits (Barcelona), 1, 1-2.

12. D'Arienzo, R., Younès, C. 2018. *Synergies Urbaines.* Paris: Métiss Press.

13. Latour, B. 2007. *Reassembling the Social: An Introduction to Actor-Network-Theory.* Oxford: Clarendon.

14. Leach, N. 2014. Adaptation. In Magazine IaaC Bits (Barcelona), 1, 1-2.

15. Acosta, P. 2016. Learning from the Bottom Up. In AA.VV. *Slum Upgrading and Housing in Latin America. Rosario-Buenos Aires:* Banco Interamericano de Desarrollo.

16. Amann, A., Delso, R. 2016. The conflict of Urban Synchronicity and its heterotemporalities. In agazine Parse Journal, 4, 92-107.

17. Vera, F., Larach, C. 2017. *Dialogos Impostergables. XX Bienal de Arquitectura y Urbanismo de Chile.* Santiago de Chile: Metales Pesados.

18. Gausa, M. 2018. *Open(ing), Space-Time-Information & Advanced Architecture 1900-2000. The Beginning of Advanced Architecture.* New York: Actar Publishers.

19. Ricci, M. 2019. *Habitat 5.0. L'architettura nel Lungo Presente.* Lausane: Skira.

20. Gausa, M. 2020. *Resili(g)ence/ Intelligent Cities, Resilient Landscapes.* New York: Actar Publishers.

21. Ramsgard Thomsen, M. (2014). The role of the news technologies. In magazine IAAC Bits n. 1.2.

22. Deleuze, G., Guattari, F. 1990. *Mille Plateaux. Capitalisme et Schizophrénie.* Paris: Les éditions de Minuit.

23. Hessel, S. 2011. Engagez-vous!. Paris: Éditions de l'Aube.

Following page:
IAAC MaCT, Alzette 2.0. S.Subramani, L.Saadi, M.Galdys,
I.Reyes, 2020.

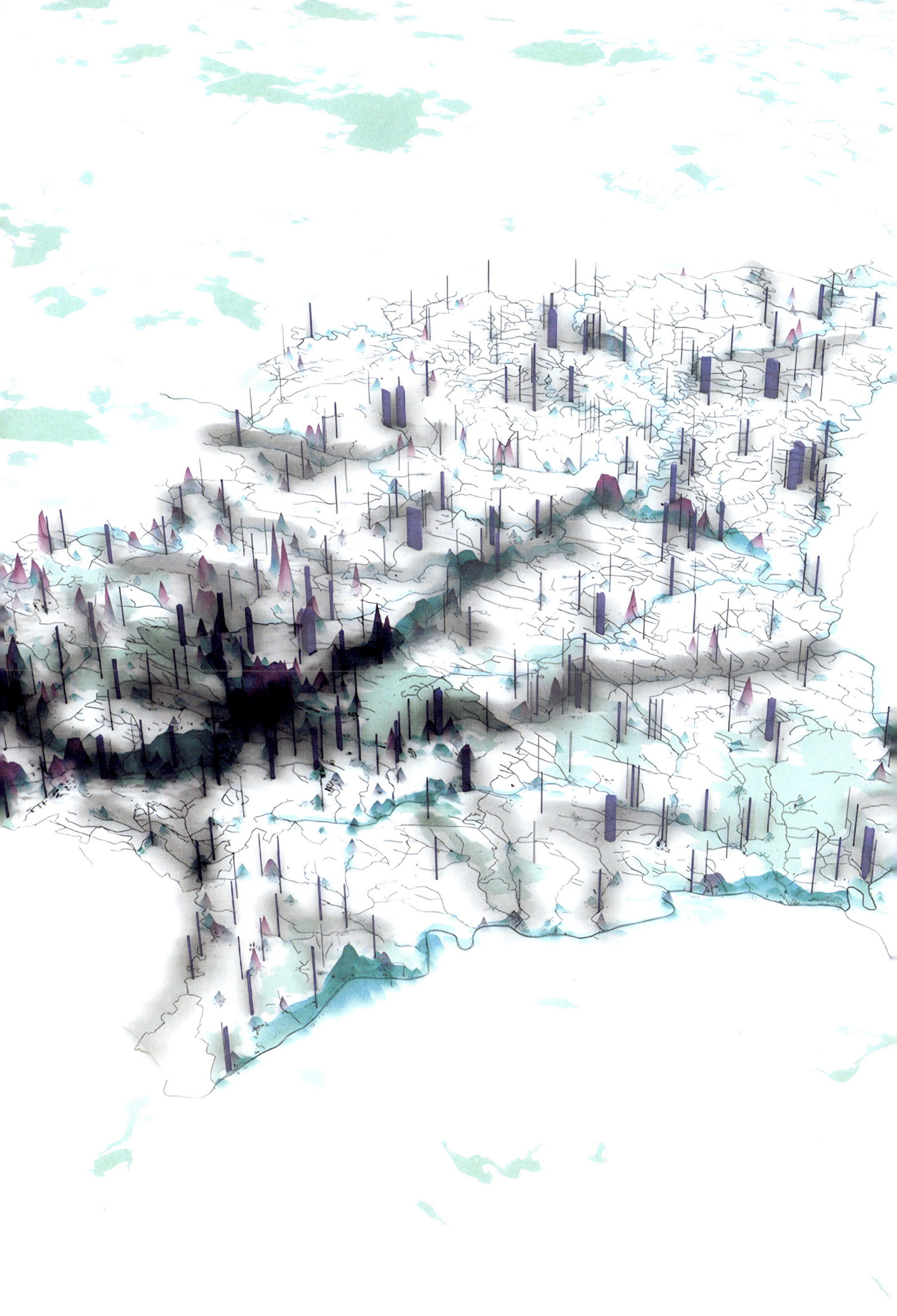

WWW.IAAC.NET

IAAC BITS n. 10
LEARNING CITIES
Advanced Architecture Magazine

Edited by
Areti Markopoulou

With contributions by
A.Markopoulou, M.Gausa, J. Vivaldi, B.Bratton, N.Leach, T.Vardouli, S.Chaillou, M.Steenson, A.Chronis, M.del Campo, S.Manninger, A.Sollazzo, A.Sojka, S.Zhang, D.Churchill, C.Bothma, J.Frazer, J.Sanchez, C.Farinea, S.Williams, R.Delso, J.Argota, M.Marengo, S.Lujang

Graphic Curation
Ramon Prat
Daniela Figueroa

Copy editing and proofreading
Angela Kay Bunning

Published by
Institute for Advanced Architecture of Catalonia , Barcelona
www.iaac.net

Indexing
ISSN: 2339-8647
ISBN: 978-1-63840-008-0
Printed in Arlequin, Barcelona

Publication date
November 2022

Distribution
Actar D, Inc. New York, Barcelona.
New York
440 Park Avenue South, 17th Floor
New York, NY 10016, USA
T +1 2129662207
salesnewyork@actar-d.com

Barcelona
Roca i Batlle 2-4
08023 Barcelona, Spain
T +34 933 282 183
eurosales@actar-d.com

Contact communications & publications office:
info@iaac.net

Institute for advanced architecture of Catalonia | BARCELONA